DIVIDED HEARTS

THE UNEXPECTED TURNS LIFE MAY TAKE

YAFFA TURGEMAN

Yaffa Turgeman- DIVIDED HEARTS

Copyright © 2025 by Yaffa Turgeman All Rights Reserved

Library of Congress control number-2024925394

All rights reserved © 2025 Yaffa Turgeman

Literary guidance: Navo Rozi

Literary and linguistic editing: Tamar Shita

Proofreading: Gili Tel Oren

Layout and cover design: Sarit Rosen

Printed in USA 2025

Danac code 800-2411227

ISBN 979-8-9887849-3-7

ONE
A SALUTE TO THE FLAG

WITH TEARS in his eyes and a loud, emotional voice, Oriel sang the American anthem with the large audience at the graduation ceremony for the officers' course at the "Oceana" Naval Base in Virginia.

Daniel and Lilah stood there in the hot sun, along with all the other parents, excited, happy, and smiling. They looked with admiration at their eldest son, the fresh officer, as he saluted the huge Stars and Stripes flag waving before them in blue, white, and red colors.

Despite the occasion and location, Daniel's thoughts drifted far away, to his own officers' course graduation ceremony at Base 1 in Israel, many years before. He, too, like Oriel, had stood trembling and emotionally, waiting to receive his officers' rank, and tears had choked his throat. He remembered trying to hold back but couldn't. Joy and excitement had overcome his efforts, and he'd let the tears flow. They'd streamed down his face, wetting and staining the crisp khaki shirt collar he wore. He'd glanced at the other soldiers standing in line with him, looking to see if they too had had tears in their eyes, but had quickly turned his face away to appear composed and steady, and had held himself tall and strong, looking straight ahead until the ceremony's end.

Just like his son, Oriel, Daniel had known from childhood that he'd wanted to be an officer in the Israel Defense Forces, and every plan he'd had before his enlistment included the phrase, "When I am an officer in the IDF."

When the longed-for moment had arrived to pin the coveted ranks on his shoulders, he was filled with joy. He'd felt as though he had conquered the entire world. A new breath of fresh air had flowed through him, and he'd been filled with the feeling that he had finally achieved the goal the boy within him had dreamed of accomplishing, the goal he had set for himself. The dream that had been an integral part of all his other dreams for the first twenty-four years of his life had come true. His parents had come to rejoice with pride, happiness, and satisfaction, teasing him about his expression, like that of a small child who said, "I did it, just as I promised myself, you all, and the whole world."

"Daniel," his father had said to him at the end of the ceremony, in a trembling and emotional voice, "You have set a precedent in our family. How proud we are of you, the first officer in the Lugasi family. Well done, rise and succeed, my son," and all the way back home they'd sung the song "You Will Not Conquer Me" by Yehoram Gaon, in a loud chorus in the car.

"Look, Officer Lugasi is here," his younger sister, Levanah, had leaped and cried out in her high voice, as they'd entered the house. "Come on, start commanding the cookies I made for you. Give him respect, Officer Lugasi!" She'd giggled and saluted him in a rigid stand. "And before you return to base, remember that you still empty the garbage every day, and when you come home for the weekend, pick up your mess off the floor so I have a floor to wash. Don't you think that now you're immune to my teasing, you hear? I love you, brother," she giggled again and hugged him tightly.

The welcome awaiting Daniel had been impressive—The Israel flag, blue and white, had stood in the doorway to the courtyard and fluttered in the wind, the front door had been decorated with blue and white balloons, and shiny blue and white ribbons had adorned the living room walls. The welcome had been extraordinary, and Levanah's welcome had been elevated to another level. She had already placed a bowl of cookies...in blue and white that had winked at him as he had entered, and the "Black Forest" cake, which he loved most, had stood in the center of the table, tempting him to dip a finger and steal a spoonful of creamy frosting, blue and white, of course.

The current impressive ceremony ended, and Oriel escorted his parents to the car. He hugged his mother warmly and said, "Okay, Dad and Mom, thank you so much for coming. Of course, we will celebrate when I get to Colorado next weekend."

He hugged both again, then stood there proudly and seriously in his new officer's hat, saluting them with a smile as Daniel drove the rented car. They waved goodbye to him, and Lilah sent another kiss through the window as they began the drive to the airport in Norfolk, Virginia, from where they would fly back home to Denver, Colorado. But unlike other trips, this was a journey they yearned for, to travel happily after four years of challenging studies and strenuous training that Oriel had undertaken at West Point Academy.

Daniel glanced briefly at Lilah and noticed that a tear had rolled down the corner of her eye. She pulled a tissue from her purse and quietly dabbed her nose, lowering her head.

"Still excited, Lilah?" he smiled, stealing a glance at her.

"It's okay, these are tears of joy."

"Be happy. We always knew this boy would go far, and now, the moment has arrived. Since he was a little boy, he talked endlessly about his desire to be an officer. Do you remember how much he loved to wear my officer's uniform that we brought with us from Israel? And the performances he used to put on after Friday dinner with the friends we invited for Shabbat? Shira was only five years old and was already collaborating in the role of the princess in distress, waiting for Officer Oriel himself to rescue her while he was 'commanding' his 'soldiers'. We were treated to a show and laughed until we cried—brave Officer Oriel conquering the castle and freeing the captive princess. And we all applauded and whistled encouragement."

"Oh, what memories you bring back," Lilah smiled through her tears. "Remember the prize we gave them for the play? The peach and cherry cake I made for dessert on that Shabbat Dinner. How could I forget? And how we laughed every time we saw your big officer's hat fall to one side and cover half his face, and he'd try again to put it on properly, with utter seriousness. I even took a picture of him; he was so cute.

"And then it finally happened," Lilah continued to reminisce. "I remember how I was startled by his cry when he opened the acceptance letter that arrived from West Point. You were at work, and he tried to call you. He tried three times and couldn't get through because his hands were shaking with excitement. Finally, I picked up the phone and called you, and he grabbed the phone from my hand because he wanted to tell you the big news himself. But you thought something had happened because you could hear the storm and thunder raging outside through the phone."

"Wait, yes," Daniel laughed, "that's right. It happened on the day there was a tornado in the town of Limon, east of Denver. The first moment he spoke to me, I was startled because I couldn't understand anything he was saying, and I asked him, 'What happened? What arrived? A letter from West Point?' And when I got home, the long-awaited letter was already crumpled from all the hands that had caressed and kissed it. Do you remember that he put the letter in a picture frame?"

"How could I forget? It wasn't a given that he would be accepted," said Lilah. "We were so worried when they told us that out of the 5,000 applications that West Point received each year, only 400 new students were accepted, and then there's the equality law and the integration, according to which even if you meet all the criteria, you are still not guaranteed to be accepted, because they must accept a certain percentage of students belonging to minorities and immigrant students, and of course a certain percentage of women, in the name of gender equality."

"Of course I remember," Daniel took off his sunglasses. The sky was beginning to cloud over, and the sun was no longer blinding him as before. "To be honest, that's what worried me the most. The rigorous screening process at West Point prevents many good students from being accepted, not to mention the fact that they required him to present a letter of recommendation from a senator, stating that he believes Oriel will contribute to the prestige and reputation of the academy."

"Luckily, Dan Miller from the Jewish Federation knows Senator Cooperman personally and put us in touch," said Lilah, "but as I said, West Point isn't just any university. It's also a military academy, and one of the highest-ranking in America."

There was little traffic on the road, which allowed them to move quickly. Lilah took a bag of food out of her bag, pulled out a health bar made of oats and raisins and dipped in honey, and removed the wrapper.

"Want an energy bar?" she offered with her mouth full.

"No, I don't feel like it," Daniel replied. "Wait until we get to the airport, we'll go to one of the restaurants there and eat properly. Those bars are full of sugar, you know I'm trying to watch what I eat." They drove in silence for a few more minutes, each lost in their own thoughts, only the sound of munching on the snack heard from time to time.

"Listen, Lilah," Daniel began again, "when it comes to West Point, I take my hat off to them. You can compare their level to the exceptionally high level of the Navy Seals, parachutes, or the air force pilots and marines in Israel, the most successful commandos, the bravest elite units of the IDF... nothing less. Oriel consistently holds himself to high standards and is dedicated to meeting them through his actions."

Lilah nodded absentmindedly and said nothing.

Daniel's thoughts wandered back to the parade ground at West

Point. With infinite pride, he recalled the image of Oriel standing there, a newly minted officer in his handsome uniform. He, too, had once felt that he had conquered the world, despite all the difficulties and obstacles that stood in his way.

Lilah, as if reading his thoughts, suddenly said, "But do you remember how many times he almost broke down? And how concerned we were to see him tired and exhausted every time he came home to visit? I remember you coming home from work in the evening and looking at him sleeping on the couch. Exhaustion had overcome him, and he couldn't wait for you to come home without getting a little more sleep. I refrained from waking him up because I knew how hard his training was and how much he needed that sleep, but I also couldn't wait for him to wake up, just to tell him that I had made the Black Forest cake that he had inherited his love for from you."

"I feel a little bad that we couldn't stay for the reception with all the other officers' parents," said Daniel, "after all his hard work. Well, at least we made it to the ceremony itself."

"It's not like we had a choice, Danny," Lilah reassured him gently. "We must be home tomorrow. Everyone has things they can't put off, and so does West Point. It's okay. We were at the main ceremony, and that's what matters."

Daniel refocused on driving. They were traveling on the straight highway, and he could once again reminisce about his officer commissioning ceremony. Standing next to the new officer, Chico, who had been red and sweating profusely, and how Feldman and Kesslasi had looked at each other because they had been afraid, he'd been about to faint next to them, and years later, they'd heard about the daring and courage he'd shown in a dangerous operation in Lebanon that he'd commanded, and, thank God, had been successful.

And how could he forget the moment when all the cadets had thrown their hats in the air, and Daniel had been worried that he wouldn't be able to find his hat, which was extra-large and had been specially made for him?

A smile appeared on Daniel's face as he recalled that after the ceremony, the cadets had stayed up all night singing songs into the morning with the hoarsest and funniest voices possible, and the commanders hadn't interfered because they'd understood how difficult it was for them to control their excitement and emotions, and who would have believed that they would still have the strength... After a whole night without sleep, they'd added eye drops into their eyes, went to the base kitchen at five in the morning, and made pancakes and fruit salad for the entire team that had tormented them for a year and a half. Wow, how surprised they had been.

Daniel smiled to himself wistfully. These were memories he cherished, experiences he shared with people who believed, like him, that they had to fight for their country, that it was a just war. Everyone's hard work to protect the Promised Land was part of keeping the promise—to live and thrive in the Land of Israel for generations to come.

And then it hit him. Where was he now in all this?

He was here, in America, 7,300 miles away from that parade ground where he'd stood and swore allegiance to his country. Where was he and where was the conscience that was born and raised with him in his homeland, the special something that connected all Israelis and Jews, the excitement felt by every Jew when he arrived at the Western Wall and touched the ancient stones that told the history of his ancestors, slipped a note between the cracks and whispered a prayer that his prayers would be answered.

Daniel felt as far away from that as heaven and earth, in the distant country to which he had moved a quarter of a century ago. Here, across the ocean, he felt that he had experienced many moments when the price he had paid for leaving was too high.

The road began to fill with cars as they approached the airport, and Daniel slowed down to allow the traffic coming from the right to merge into his lane. Lilah had already eaten her second granola bar, and her chewing made an annoying crunching sound. It was hard for her to resist chewing on something, especially when she was idle or stressed, and Daniel chose not to say anything.

Thoughts of the country he had left still flooded his mind. He felt that Oriel's graduation ceremony meant much more to him than the completion of an officer training course and the academic degree Oriel had earned at West Point. On the one hand, he was so proud of his son, but on the other hand, something inside him felt incomplete. At first, he hesitated to say anything, but then he decided to share his thoughts with Lilah. Perhaps it would be better to speak up and unburden himself than to keep it bottled up inside.

"Look, Lilah," he began, "we can't ignore the fact that Oriel and Shira don't feel as connected to the Land of Israel as you and I do, right?"

"That's true," Lilah replied while chewing, "but how can we expect them to feel as strong a connection to Israel as we do, when all the memories they have of it are just from visiting their grandparents on vacation?"

"Yes, of course... I know," replied Daniel, "but you must understand, it's not easy for me to just brush off ten years of service in the army, especially given the great responsibility I had. Don't forget that my experience and knowledge from what I did and contributed to the IDF are useful to me today in our business. I just think that here we are, twenty-five years have passed, our son is also enlisting and becoming an officer, but not in the Israel Defense Forces! He's an officer in the US Army, and I must accept that because he was born here and grew up here and went to high school here, and his childhood experiences are trips to the Rocky Mountains, not 'Gadna' trips like we did in Israel."

"That's true, Daniel, but we gave them a good childhood overall..." Lilah began to say.

"Yes, thank God, we gave them what every child needs," Daniel waved his hand, "but maybe we should have pushed Oriel to enlist in Israel, in the IDF? Don't you think so?"

"What's wrong with you, Danny?" Lilah was alarmed and raised her voice. "Are you ready for him to leave us? If he had enlisted in Israel, chances are he would have stayed in Israel after the army, and then you would have seen him maybe once a year, at best. It's likely that he would have met a female soldier in the army, and they would have decided to get married, and she wouldn't have been willing to leave the country. What would you do then? See your grandchildren once every three years or, at best, only once a year and be satisfied with that?"

Daniel was silent.

"And don't forget the whole issue of being a 'lone soldier,'" Lilah continued excitedly. "Do you know what it's like to go through all the training and difficulties and challenges alone, without parents, siblings, and childhood friends? With the language difficulties and differences in mentality, and guys who might look at him like he's a weirdo and start joking about his accent and the mistakes he makes in Hebrew? After all, it's impossible to ignore the fact that he speaks American English and that his Hebrew vocabulary is very limited, and there are many other reasons.

"So, no, thank you. I'd rather he graduates from West Point, and then he'll be here with us, and we'll see him, and in the future our grandchildren, all the time."

Lilah was upset. The thought of Oriel being so far away from her, on the other side of the world, angered her, stressed her out, and frightened her, and Daniel sensed the frustration and anxiety echoing in her voice and facial expression. She straightened the sun visor hanging above her on the right side of the car and put on her sunglasses.

The silence that now stood between them was disturbing and uncomfortable. Daniel clearly disagreed with her.

"Lilah, I understand what you're saying," he began again, "but these are two separate things. I mean that Oriel wanted to contribute his abilities as an officer, and if he had enlisted in Israel, the homeland would have gotten everything he could give. Don't you think we're being a little selfish about this?

"Look," he tried to calm her down, but also wanted to emphasize his point. "It's not easy for me. I'm an officer in the IDF, and I can't ignore the fact that the beautiful ceremony we saw today was not a ceremony to welcome Oriel as a soldier in our homeland, an officer in Israel. Oriel did not enlist in the IDF, did not serve as an officer in the IDF like me, and will not contribute his abilities to the IDF and our country like me. His uniform is not my uniform, and the bottom line is, Lilah Oriel enlisted in the US Army and not the Israeli Army. Honestly, it does bother me that today he did not salute the flag that I saluted and still salute, but rather the flag of a foreign country. True, this country is good to us, and we are prospering here, but it does not touch our hearts like Israel does. Understand, Lilah," he wanted to emphasize the point even more, "we live here, our lives are here, but just because we have built a family and a successful business in America, it does not mean that I have sold my heart to America. I don't know about you, but I will always have one foot here and one foot in our homeland. And I know what you're going to say," he continued, "these are things we should have thought about before we decided to leave Israel, right?"

Lilah's phone rang, interrupting him. On the other end of the line was a representative from some insurance company, and Lilah, in a tone that bordered on rudeness, asked her to remove her from the company's phone list immediately.

Lilah continued scrolling through her phone's camera and showed Daniel a beautiful photo of Oriel that she had taken at the graduation ceremony. It was clear that she wanted to change the subject.

"Wow, Danny, look at this picture, it's so clear and sharp. I think it's the best picture of Oriel from the ceremony, right? I was told that we could ask our Jewish community newspaper, Rocky Mountain Jewish News, to publish an article about Oriel successfully graduating from West Point and now serving as an officer in the US Army, and they would publish a short article and a photo of him from the ceremony. They are always happy to announce people from our community who have received special degrees from good academies."

"Yes, the photo is beautiful," he replied, and immediately turned his head away. He had mixed feelings. On the one hand, he wanted to look at the picture, but on the other hand, he also wanted to deny what his eyes were seeing and told himself that he wished the picture were a little different, for example, that Oriel was seen in it saluting the blue and white flag.

TWO
GENERAL KATZIRI

THE PHONE RANG with the intermittent ring that signaled a transatlantic call.

"Hello?" I answered quickly, hoping that everything was okay with my family back home. "Galit?" my young sister Pnina chirped in her high-pitched voice.

"Hi, Pnina, what's up? This is the second call this week. Is everything okay?" I began to worry.

"Everything's fine," Pnina laughed, "no need to worry. This time I need a big favor from you."

"From me?" I wondered. "How can I help you from the other side of the world?"

"That's exactly why," Pnina laughed, "Listen, sister, you know that my job at the bank is to bring in more customers—as I already told you, we've set ourselves the goal of becoming the largest bank in the country, and these days I'm setting up meetings with large organizations to sign their employees as our customers. We've also launched a huge advertising campaign and are offering terms and benefits to anyone who chooses to switch to our bank..."

"Okay, and... Did you call to try to convince me to become a customer?" I smiled at the phone.

"Galit, you know I work every day from sunrise to sunset to get the title of 'Employee of the Year' this year," Pnina continued in her squeaky voice, ignoring my comment. "If you help me, I'll be able to get all the citizens who are IDF employees to switch to our bank. That will change everything for me."

"So, how can I help you with that?" I asked.

Now, Pnina has piqued my curiosity even more. How could I, on the distant continent of America, help her bring new customers to the Israeli bank?

It was clear that I needed to sit down with a cup of coffee, because this was going to be a conversation lasting more than two minutes. I turned on the coffee machine and added water, inhaling deeply the aroma of freshly ground coffee beans and reminding myself that same day ground coffee must be one of life's pleasures. I took a jug of milk out of the refrigerator, sat down with my cup at the round kitchen table, and put the phone on the speaker.

"Today I went to a meeting with General Katziri," Pnina began. "He's the man in charge of all the civilians who are IDF employees in Israel. You may have heard of him; he's world famous for his invention, some kind of development that connects planes in the air to tanks... Never mind. I explained to him the new benefits the bank is offering to IDF civilian employees if they receive their salaries through us, and after I gave him a lecture for a whole hour, we talked a little in general. Among other things, he told me that he has a son who lives in Denver and studies computer science there. Can you believe it? I immediately mentioned to him that my sister has been living in Denver for many years and might even know his son. He was happy to hear that I have a connection to someone who lives close to his son on the other side of the world.

"Well, it's a small world," I replied with a smile.

But Katziri? I asked myself. I don't think I know anyone with that name. But why am I surprised? When you don't live in the country for so many years, you stop following or being updated on many things, and this is one of them.

"This guy's name is Matan," Pnina continued, as if reading my mind, "Matan Katziri. Do you know him?"

"No..." I replied hesitantly. "Are you sure that's his name?"

"Yes. Yes," she sighed impatiently. "Listen, the general told me that Matan is very lonely in Denver. He said he has almost no Israeli acquaintances or friends in Colorado and that it's hard and sad for him; he feels lonely, especially during the holidays. Luckily, he's busy with his studies and work, otherwise, he would have returned to Israel out of homesickness and loneliness. I felt sad for him," my sister added. "I could hear the frustration in his voice when he spoke. At that moment, all I saw in front of me was a worried father asking for help from anyone close to his son."

I listened to Pnina in shock. First, it's not true that there are no Israelis in Colorado, but there aren't as many as on the East Coast or the West Coast. Israelis come to Colorado mainly to study, for work contracts, or for family reunification. It's true that they are scattered throughout different areas of this city of a million residents, which may make it difficult to get to know them, but everyone tries to make connections, just like anywhere else in the world.

"It's strange," I shared my thoughts with Pnina. "How come we haven't heard of him here in Denver? I can check with our friend, Avi Toren. He's the dean of computer studies at the University of Denver. If Matan studies there, Avi knows him. Let me check, and I'll get back to you on that." My check with Avi revealed that he didn't know Matan Katziri and had never heard of him. This was a little strange to him, too, because he, like all of us, knew that Israelis abroad were drawn to each other like bees to a hive, to create some of the Israeli social life they were missing. In the days that followed, I asked other friends and acquaintances if they had heard of anyone named Matan Katziri.

But I couldn't find anyone by that name, and the sense of mystery only grew.

A week later, I called Pnina again, told her about my attempts to locate the guy, and asked what other details she could give me about him.

"Like I told you," Pnina chirped, "he told his parents that he started studying at the University of Denver and that everything is fine except that he hasn't really met any Israelis here. The general was excited when I told him that you live in Denver and asked if it's okay, if you could get in touch with Matan. Maybe through you, he'll be able to meet people his age. Maybe you could invite him over sometime, at least during the holidays, so he doesn't feel so cut off from the world."

To say my heart broke? You bet. That was the last thing I wanted to hear. After all, I was Galit, the one whose parties were the talk of the community, the one everyone wanted to attend the big events she produced at home or organized for the Israeli community in Denver. My house was the center of everything that happened in the Denver community, and everyone knew that I was the go-to person for anyone who was new here. I was the one who received transatlantic phone calls from every family that had been accepted here for work or study, and they had no less than a thousand questions before the move. So how come I couldn't find this guy named Matan whose father was the famous General Katziri? And how come his son said he felt so lonely because there were no Israelis here? Something didn't add up in this whole story, and I was determined to find Matan and solve the mystery surrounding the matter.

After five days of searching the public registry, the Jewish Federation, all the Jewish organizations in Denver, and all the synagogues and universities in Denver—I even considered checking hospitals—I decided to check with Pnina again.

"Pnina, get me another phone number for the guy." Keep in mind that this was 1990, when most people still didn't have cell phones or the internet.

"Um... maybe I gave you the wrong number?" my sister muttered. "Write down another number," she dictated to me. "And do me a favor, don't give up until you find him. Remember what a promotion I'll get at the bank if I manage to help General Katziri locate his son. I can already see the outstanding employee certificate on the wall, so come on, get to work," she enthused.

I hung up on her and dialed the new number she gave me. A few short rings and...

"Hello," a male voice answered.

"Hello," I said in English, "who am I speaking to?"

"Who are you looking for?" the male voice asked in hesitant English.

"I'd like to speak to Matan Katziri, please," I said.

There was a moment of silence at the other end of the line, and then...

"Who is this? Who are you?" The voice was quiet, somewhat panicked.

"Are you Matan?" I asked in a friendly tone in Hebrew.

"Who is this? And how did you get this number?" the guy asked again in a tense voice.

"Hello, Matan," I continued kindly, "my name is Galit. My sister Pnina knows your father, General Katziri, and..."

"Okay, what can I do for you?" he interrupted my explanation.

Although he still hadn't admitted it, I was already sure I was talking to Matan Katziri, and even though I could sense an unexplained dissatisfaction in his voice, I continued to explain how I had gotten his number and said I would be happy to help him find other Israelis in the city. "I wanted to make sure you were okay and get to know you a little. We would be happy to invite you to our home for Shabbat any weekend that suits you," I concluded.

"Oh, you're so nice, thank you very much, really, thank you," the guy said in a softer voice. He paused for a moment and then added, "Okay, I'd love to stay in touch."

I finally felt that the ice had broken. I told him that we were flying to Florida for Passover but were returning home to Denver to celebrate the traditional Mimouna holiday.

"I've invited all my friends from the Jewish community to an open house that evening," I said. "If you come, you'll get to meet lots of Israelis and connect with people you like. I know some people you should meet. Really, I'd love for you to come. What do you say?"

"Thanks for the invitation. I'm working and studying, so I'll see how it works out and let you know."

As our conversation came to an end, I exhaled in relief. I called my sister, told her I'd found Matan, and recounted everything we'd discussed. She was excited and said she would call General Katziri to tell him and encourage him that Matan was fine and that I had contacted him in Denver.

The next morning, I woke up to a busy and full day—in the morning, I was supposed to teach Hebrew at the Jewish school in the city and then meet with two students at the school for a private Hebrew lesson. In the afternoon, I had a meeting with the events committee of the Jewish community to prepare the newsletter announcing the Mimouna event to the community, and in the evening, we were invited to a friend's birthday party.

I was organizing important papers in my busy school folder when the phone rang in the kitchen. While I was still debating whether to answer or not, my husband, Eylon, answered the phone and handed me the receiver.

"Someone named Matan wants to talk to you." Matan? At eight in the morning? I was surprised.

"Hi, Matan, how are you?" I asked as I continued to organize my bag.

"Good morning, Galit," a concerned voice said on the other end of the line, "do you have a few minutes? I need to talk to you before the Mimouna party at your house."

I explained that I had to leave for work and suggested that I check when I would be free so we could meet.

"I promise to call you today and let you know," I said. "It's just that today is a busy day, from morning till night."

"Okay," replied Matan. "I'll wait patiently for our meeting, but I must ask you something. In the meantime, please don't tell anyone about me, okay?"

"Sure, of course..." I muttered.

I put down the phone, and a strange feeling crept over me. What could be so secret and urgent? But I didn't have time to dwell on it. I packed my heavy, cumbersome school bag and went outside. The cool April wind blew dry pine needles at me and shook the tops of the huge trees lining the street. I was glad that the forecast said it wouldn't rain today, but I also remembered the famous saying here, "April showers bring May flowers." I wrapped myself in my gray coat and walked toward the car.

By four o'clock, I was back home. My husband was still at work. I put my school bag aside and hung my coat in the coat closet, and then I saw the red light flashing on the answering machine, signaling me to check for new messages.

The first message was from an automated recording informing me that tomorrow, the weekly trash would not be collected because it was a federal holiday.

The second message was from my friend Dalit, to whom we had been invited that evening. Dalit had caught "pink eye," a virus that caused the eye to become swollen and red, so the birthday dinner was canceled. I started unpacking my huge work bag and sorting through important documents when I suddenly remembered my conversation with Matan that morning. I had a free evening, so why not invite Matan over? He wanted to talk to me about something, and now it was his chance.

I called him and told him that my evening was free.

Matan arrived at eight, and I greeted him with a light, warm motherly hug to show him how happy I was that he had come. It was important for me to convey confidence and trustworthiness.

As he stood at the entrance, I quickly scanned him. A young man who looked to me to be 23-24, no more, with fair skin and hair adorned with light blond streaks and carefully trimmed. His face was handsome, and his eyes were honey-colored, or perhaps almost green; it was hard to tell.

He wore a white plaid shirt, a gray cashmere sweater that barely showed the collar of his shirt, and black jeans.

He wore designer sneakers on his feet, and the silver watch he wore on his left wrist was incredibly delicate and reminded me more of a bracelet than a watch strap. A small silver earring sparkled in his right ear, and I noticed that he wore a smooth silver ring, reminiscent of a wedding ring.

I led him into the warm kitchen and showed him to the small dining area. I placed steaming cups of tea on the table, added a tray of hot, crispy mushroom burekas, and added my mother's fragrant Moroccan tea cookies, called "reyfat," with anise and sesame seeds.

"I wanted you to know that I appreciate you contacting me," Matan began. "You already make me feel like I can trust you, and honestly, I feel comfortable talking to you about the reason I came here."

"I'm glad you feel comfortable," I smiled. "I'll be happy to help if I can."

I felt how important it was for him to have a listening ear, time, and a place to get what needed to come out.

"Three years ago," Matan began, his voice a little shaky and hesitant, his hands clutching his cup of tea as if seeking more warmth, strength, and security from it, "during my leave from the army, I went to Eilat with some friends, and that's where I met Elliot." For a moment, I wanted to interrupt him and ask who Elliot was, but I sensed that he wanted to continue talking, so I remained silent.

"Elliot was just finishing his bachelor's degree and about to start his master's in law, and he celebrated his graduation with a trip to Egypt, Sinai, and Israel. He was born and raised here in Denver, and it was his first time visiting the Middle East. The chemistry between us was almost immediate, the kind of thing that happens to people once in a lifetime. I have no other way to explain it. I felt a magnetic attraction to him, electrifying, something I couldn't explain. At first, I didn't understand what was happening to me, because it had never happened to me before..."

Here, Matan paused for a moment and lowered his head. "I stayed with my friends in a run-down hostel, and Elliot stayed in a hotel for three days, after which I offered him to join us in the simple cabin we rented. He agreed and spent a few more fun days with us in Eilat.

"Elliot was friendly and easygoing, and the guys liked him. Every evening, we sat around with beers, a guitar, and jokes. We spoke in Hebrew, translated into broken English, and Elliot spoke in English, translated into funny Hebrew. Don't ask, it was a salad of words.

"We rolled around laughing and had a really good time. When the vacation in Eilat ended, everyone exchanged phone numbers and addresses with Elliot, and of course, I did too. Later, I learned that Elliot didn't stay in touch with anyone else from that group, but he wrote me a letter every week. At first, they were general letters about what he was doing on a daily basis, how his master's degree in law was going, about his dog that got sick and died, etc., etc., but every week the letters became more personal and emotional, and every week I, for my part, felt that I was writing to him in a more personal tone. After a few months of long and numerous letters, about one letter a week, I began to feel that I was getting excited and looking forward to Elliot's letters more than anything else. After three months of constant correspondence, I received a letter from him that ended with a sentence that I still remember by heart today, 'I can't wait any longer for the moment when we will meet again and be together. My Matan, I want to hug you, hold you close to me, because my heart is aching for you. Yours, Elliot.'"

Matan gasped for air, his face flushing.

"I couldn't believe what I was reading in that letter," he said quietly.

"I was stunned as I read the last few sentences repeatedly. I felt my whole body shaking. My insides were churning, and something inside me screamed, 'I wish I were there with you!' Then I knew and understood that this was everything I had been waiting for. Those words were the confirmation, the 'okay' I needed. A thousand thoughts raced through my head, and every day of thinking always ended with the same conclusion—I want to be with Elliot, to talk to him up close, not through letters and transatlantic communication. I want to tell him every evening about how my day was, share with him my doubts about university, what is important to me and what is not, go to the beach with him, hug him... I want him, Elliot. I want him so much. I miss him, I really miss him. Yes, that's the word, I miss him!"

Matan's voice cracked and trembled until he stopped talking. He took two tissues from the box on the table and blew his nose. Then he nervously adjusted his shirt collar, playing with one of the buttons. Another moment passed, he took a deep breath, and continued talking.

"Slowly and with much hesitation, I began to devise a plan completely different from the one I had after my discharge from the IDF. I told my parents that I was interested in studying computer science abroad, in Denver, and that I knew someone who had studied in that program. I promised them that I would only move to Colorado for the duration of my studies and swore that I would not leave the homeland permanently.

"After a thousand conversations and a million promises, my father agreed to let me investigate it. Of course, Elliot was secretly involved in all the details and remotely arranged my registration and sent me the appropriate forms."

"Did your parents help you settle in Colorado at first?" I asked gently.

"Yes..." he hesitated. "I couldn't have done it without their financial help. I love them and appreciate everything they've done for me, and they've done a lot. I knew they wouldn't like what I was about to do, and I also knew that my father would be the biggest stumbling block. My sister, Merav, was perhaps the only person who could understand me a little, but my mother? No way, and certainly not my father," Matan said decisively, shaking his head.

"If I hadn't been able to convince my mother that I was only going for the school year, she would have moved heaven and earth to keep me from going. And my father? It's hard for me to even talk about it. I don't even want to imagine how he would react when he found out that I am married, I live here with a partner who is not Jewish, and that I am active in the gay community here, under a different name and identity."

Oops, that's why I couldn't find you... a thought crossed my mind.

"Can you imagine what would happen if the Jewish community knew my real surname?" Matan continued. "The name Katziri is known not only in Israel, but all over the world. Just as you know the name Elon Musk, the developer of Tesla, or that doctor from South Africa, Dr. Morrison, who performed the first heart transplant, that's how famous my father is for the military invention he developed."

"So here in Denver, who are you?" I asked.

"I decided to keep the first letter of my first name and my last name," Matan said. "Here, I'm known as Manny Keren. No one knows the name Matan Katziri, and I work hard to keep it that way. Nothing that happens to me must reach Israel, especially not my father. Even in the gay community I'm part of, the name Katziri is well known." He smiled a little. "Once Elliot and I were sitting in a pub with a couple of friends, and one of them mentioned a senior general in the Israeli army who invented this thing that helps connect fighter jets to tanks—I don't really know any more than that—and of course, the name Katziri came up in the conversation. I sat there quietly, pretending to be busy, scratching my back to hide my embarrassed expression, and I felt frustrated—how could I identify with my famous name and speak?

"As far as father's concerned," he raised his voice slightly, "I'm betraying the Jewish religion, betraying my family, and guilty of abandoning the Land of Israel. I have become my father's worst nightmare. The son of a well-known and respected general in Israel and around the world is betraying all his values and everything he believes in, in the ugliest way possible. My father doesn't know I'm gay, and he won't forgive me until his last day if he knew that was the real reason I left the country. If only he knew how much I miss them and Israel.

"I am torn and broken into pieces. Here I have Elliot's love, but I don't feel like I have a loving and supportive family. I miss the close conversations with my sister, Merav. I miss the support I received from my father all my life. In every crisis and question, he told me another inspiring story from his past and his military experience, and I always came out of every conversation with him stronger and more encouraged. I miss the connection with my good friends from home because I lied to them too," Matan continued fluently. "They think I'm angry with them because none of them came to visit me in America, and that's why I cut off contact, but that's not true. I know how expensive it is to get here, not to mention the fact that I didn't invite any of them. How could I? It would eventually get back to my parents.

"I'm sorry I'm taking it all out on you," he smiled sadly, "but I miss speaking Hebrew so much. Since I'm here under a different identity, I don't speak Hebrew to anyone. Recently, I started ordering Hebrew newspapers from New York, so I'd have something to read. Elliot isn't interested in learning Hebrew now; he's focused on his career as a lawyer and wants to advance, so all our efforts and energy are directed in that direction."

"But Matan," I interrupted him for a moment, "you say there is great love between you. Do you talk to Elliot about all the things that bother you?"

He was silent, and for a moment I thought he hadn't really heard my question, but he had heard it loud and clear.

"Yes," he replied quietly, "Elliot knows how much I miss my family, how much I miss my friends. I miss the wonderful feeling in Israel on Friday afternoon, before the start of Shabbat, and how much I miss the feeling of the holidays we celebrated at my parents' house. I explain our holidays to him and try to share the experience with him, but it doesn't do anything for him, and that's fine with me..."

I'm not sure it's fine with you, I thought, *maybe you just prefer to repress it.*

"But if I could at least celebrate with friends, or go to events in the Jewish community to live out my Jewish identity a little..." His voice trailed off. "There's such emptiness inside me, something big is missing on this side of my identity, no matter how much I deny it in my daily life. I miss seemingly marginal, small things—the apple dipped in honey on Rosh Hashanah, my mother's Latkes on Hanukkah, the decorations on the huge Sukkah I helped my father build every year because half the country came to stay in General Katziri's Sukkah.

"I also miss being involved in the Jewish community. I always loved helping, volunteering, and now I stand on the sidelines and can't do anything, so that my identity won't be revealed. It makes me feel that I am limited to my will, restrained, bound by chains that I created for myself by my own choice. It's especially hard for me because I'm not true to myself, I live in two worlds, the world where I want to live with Elliot, and the world I had and no longer have, which I miss so much. I feel torn against my will..."

Matan could no longer hold back what came after those words. He covered his face with his hands, and his body shook as he cried silently.

I let him cry, knowing how important it was for him to unburden himself of the heavy load on his narrow shoulders. I moved my chair closer to him, held his hand tightly, and hugged him warmly.

Oh, what this guy was going through, and all alone, and my heart just went out to him in those moments.

He looked up and stared at me intently, "But Galit, I have a big request for you. Please don't ruin what I've built here."

I looked up at him questioningly.

"If you tell your sister Pnina that you met me, she'll immediately tell my family everything," he answered my unasked question.

"And I know they'll get here on the first flight they can find and try to convince me to go back with them to Israel. They'll remind me of all the things I'm 'missing out on' in life, my mother will cry that she won't have a daughter-in-law, and that she won't have grandchildren 'like she should' or 'like everyone else' in normal families. And she'll threaten me with 'what people will say' and ask if I don't love her and how I could do this to them, and my father will say he has a friend who can recommend an excellent psychologist who will be willing to 'treat' me, and so on and so forth, and after everything comes out, the Jewish community here in Denver will also recognize me and want to give me special treatment—after all, I am Katziri's son—and then I will have no privacy in my life. So please, Galit, understand if I don't come to your Mimouna celebration. True, I still have a month to think about all this, but since you called yesterday, I can't eat or sleep, and all I can think about is what to do..."

At this point, Matan was excited and shifted from side to side in his chair. His face was red as if he had just come out of a hot sauna, and every now and then, his voice trembled, and he wiped his face with sweat and excitement.

I handed him another tissue, held his right hand, and tried to calm him down gently. Without a doubt, his honest revelation moved me too.

I left him there for a moment and went to make more tea for both of us. When I returned with the hot teacups, I saw that he was sitting quietly, lost in thought.

I wanted to reassure him, to tell him that everything would be okay. The delicate soul sitting across from me seemed tormented by the painful struggle going on inside him, and it seemed to me that he couldn't bear the weight of the fears and upheavals that followed the choice he had made.

"Matan, first of all, I'm glad you're sharing this with me," I said and handed him the cup of tea. "I understand that you are going through a difficult time and that you feel very alone in this. But have you even tried to explore your options? The fact that your father is so concerned is important.

"As a mother myself, I can tell you that a parent's concern doesn't end when they go to sleep. It's a concern that they live and breathe every moment. I have two daughters, and I know that if I had to choose between endless worry and knowing what's going on with them, no matter what, I'd prefer to know. Parents' lack of knowledge about their children is tormenting and maddening. So yes, it will be difficult for your parents to accept who you are, but whatever their reaction, at least they will know that you are okay, that you are happy, and that you are doing well."

"Galit," Matan sighed and shook his head, "you don't know my father. He's a tough, conservative military man who sets the highest standards for himself. He would never forgive me if he knew how I live, and even more so, that I'm already married to the love of my life. As far as my father is concerned, the greatest betrayal of him is the betrayal of everything he believes in."

Matan calmed down, blew his nose again, and continued quietly, "Elliot and I have been married for a year now. We have built a warm and loving home. We both work and study, and on weekends we go out with friends to cute restaurants, and on Saturdays, depending on the weather, we like to pack sandwiches and drive to the mountains, breathe the clear air deeply, and soak up some of the peaceful atmosphere that disconnects us from the rest of the world for a few hours. We're happy here and we're happy together, I'm happier than I've ever been in my life…"

I sat alone in the living room for a long time after Matan thanked me again and left. I thought about the young man and the difficult decision he had made.

I thought about the difficulties a person encounters when they choose to "live divided," about the tormenting mental pressures experienced by a person living with a dual identity, and what that did to their self-esteem. What nerves of steel one must have.

How could one live in peace with the first, previous "I" and the second, new, current "I"? How much strength did this young and quiet man have? What mental strength must he muster, and what willpower did he have to wake up every day with the burning desire to experience his "feeling self," but also not to give up his "true self," to stand up with a divided soul and tell himself that today, too, he will be both Matan Katziri and Manny Keren at the same time?

THREE
SISTER'S REVENGE

"SOPHIA, FOR GOODNESS' sake, Sophia, please, open your mind and heart to your sister. You're as locked off as a pressure vessel. You're ruining my plans and throwing our dream into the gutter, open a channel of listening in your tiny ears for me," Alina grumbled, her voice whining.

Today, Alina decided to focus all her efforts, justifications, and charms to persuade her sister, Sophia, to continue with the original plan. She would cry, scream, wail, shed large crocodile tears, and stomp her tiny feet on the floor, even if it angered the neighbor downstairs. She needed Sophia's help to convince the millionaire, Eric, who was madly in love with Sophia, to invest in her clothing business. *If I can't win his heart, at least I want him to compensate me with money,* she thought. *Why not? It's crucial to extract as much money from him before he discovers our plan and throws us both into the abyss. They say you should share your bread, and I say you should also share your money,* she thought.

Alina was determined to adhere to her goal. What others said didn't matter—and she wouldn't let anyone tell her what to do or ask how Sophia would feel when she couldn't "return" Eric's investment.

Alina believed with all her heart that her plan would work perfectly, for her and for her sister, but now, at the crucial moment, she began to understand that Sophia had the courage of a timid rabbit, unwilling to be caught in her plot. Sophia staunchly refused even to consider the plan Alina had devised.

Alina paced the room like a restless goat, occasionally pointing an accusing finger at Sophia, who stood by the window, playing with the net curtains. Her sad gaze was fixed on the small playground next to their building, and she staunchly refused to heed Alina's plea.

"Sophia, please, you just must convince Eric to put the money down. Why are you turning on me suddenly? We had agreed on everything. And what will I tell the clothing company in New York? I've already signed a contract with them, 'Carnival' will sue me, it's no joke, do you understand? You're ruthlessly destroying everything we dreamed of in Israel, do you get it?!"

"No, Alina!" Sophia turned to her sister with a furious expression, "I warned you not to do anything on your own. I didn't force you to pay the last sum of money we brought with us as a deposit for 'Carnival Fashionwear.' I won't trick Eric. This guy is charming, kind, and gentle. We've only been together for two and a half months, and I'm not sure if I love him, and, moreover, he hasn't proposed to me. But for goodness' sake, get off the treacherous fantasy tree you're climbing. A one and a half million-dollar investment isn't a small sum, not even for a millionaire like Eric."

"Sophia!" Alina yelled angrily. Her eyes narrowed, and her face flushed crimson like a ripe tomato. Sophia stared at her with bewilderment. For a moment, she didn't recognize her sister's venomous, now distorted and red face, and recoiled in fear.

"You deceitful manipulator," Alina breathed furiously. "When I introduced you to him in Israel, you told me you would agree to marry him to get a green card. What happened to your memory? Did it shrink to a dried-up pea?"

Sophia, dumbfounded, didn't respond, and her sister continued, "Precisely, now, when we're finally in Colorado and living right under Eric's nose, and when everyone knows how much he's smitten with you, now you decide to be the Virgin Mary and want to be honest with him? Suddenly, love and honesty are important to you?" Alina grabbed a stained kitchen towel nearby and threw it angrily at Sophia's face.

"I'll nail your shoe; how much I hate you now," she seethed with rage, realizing that her aggressive persuasion tactics weren't working on her sister.

"Alina, try to understand me." Sophia covered her face with her hands and whispered in a quiet, despairing voice. "It's not easy. You expect me to pretend and lie to this nice man who is so nice to me. I can't do that. Please, leave me alone. I don't have the heart to marry him fraudulently, take his millions, and abandon him the moment I get my green card. It's prostitution."

"Look who's talking about prostitution," mocked Alina. "Too bad I didn't record you at the restaurant, then on the beach, when you knew he didn't understand Hebrew and spoke freely. I should have let you hear yourself building castles in the air, saying, 'Let's go to a green card and America, here we come, the gorgeous sisters, we'll start in Denver, have fun in Las Vegas, and reach our desired destination, Los Angeles. From there, just yachts, St. Tropez, and Monaco, nobody will stop us,' and how you danced, Sophia, remember?" Alina patted her small, red nose and nervously tugged at her curls. "Oh, how irritating you are, Sophia. You really are lucky I didn't record you then. Know that I'd play that recording for Eric without flinching."

"Enough, Alina. How much evil flows through your veins? How can you blackmail me? I'm not deceiving this nice guy, and I'm not going to ruin his life. Isn't it enough that he lost both his parents this year in a terrible accident? This man doesn't even have a brother or sister who can help him through the grief of the year of mourning. Doesn't it hurt you?"

Sophia was stunned by her sister's determination to continue the wicked plan. The more she got to know Eric, the more she felt he was a nice guy, a true gentleman, straightforward, and kind to her. Now she struggled to go along with their original plan, the one they concocted when they met Eric by chance at a Tel Aviv restaurant.

"By the way, Sophia, and you don't feel bad, you say? I shouldn't have believed you back home. And while we were at it, did you forget who paid for your flight ticket here? If not me, you wouldn't have been able to come here at all, and all your dreams of America would have exploded in the air. Do you remember how you begged me for the ticket because you were a dressmaker? Good things are quickly forgotten, aren't they, sister?"

"Yes, Alina," Sophia admitted, dryly, "I wanted to come to America, and I wanted to meet a rich man who would make me a queen. But now, having gotten to know Eric better and seeing how serious the guy is and how he wants to start a new chapter in his life after his accident, my heart aches for him."

"Come on, Sophie, open your eyes," Alina laughed. "You don't buy yachts with a broken heart, and you don't live in a palace. That only happens with smart plans. If you want, sit in a corner and wallow as much as you want, but stick to your promise and cooperate with me so the plan succeeds for both of us. And according to the plan, you're supposed to marry Eric, and I'll get some money from him to open a big business, to be close to all the rich people in the city. Then I, too, can find a stinky rich guy who'll make me a queen."

Sophia didn't respond. Her face was pale and expressionless.

"Eric is a millionaire," Alina screamed in a broken voice, clutching Sophia's delicate shoulders and shaking her. "A millionaire. One and a half million dollars won't budge him, even if the 'Carnival Clothes' business fails, he'll still have a lot of money, more money than he can count. Where will I find someone who'll give me one and a half million dollars to pay for the boutique franchise? And in downtown Denver, a place that equals Tel Aviv's central Square?

"And who will return my last two thousand dollars to me, which I have now given as a down payment to 'Carnival'?"

Alina grabbed her hair as if about to pull it out, and sat heavily on the sofa, shaking her head back and forth.

"Do you think that because you're prettier than me, you're allowed to manipulate me? I trust you and the feminine charm you know how to use on anyone you want. Did you hear what he told us last week at the restaurant? One hundred and seventy million dollars. That's his inheritance. That's worth the company his father left him with, and you're talking to me about the small sum of one and a half million dollars? It's nothing to him. Even if he doesn't get this money back, he's still a multi-millionaire. And someone who reveals such personal things to you is interested in more than just friendship; don't you get it?"

"Alina, you're a heartless person, you know? You're a thief the devil didn't create, and I'm not going down to your level. Enough..." Sophia completely broke down. Her body trembled, and she covered her face with her hands and cried into the patterned window covering of the small living room.

A phone rang in the apartment. Alina quickly grabbed the black cordless phone and answered. When she understood who was on the other line, her voice softened instantly, and a forced smile turned her voice into a sweet tone over the phone.

"Hi Jake, yes, of course, I'd love to discuss it later. Let's go over the boutique's opening... I'm still busy sorting and organizing the first collection and printing the invitations for the opening. Yes... Send me the names of your Colorado friends, and I'll gladly add them to the list. Yes... I'll certainly include her in the invitation too. And what kind of champagne did you serve at the opening of your store in Las Vegas?

"Oh, it sounds good, I'm writing it down. Yes, see, I understand there are rules in your company, but since we're in Colorado, I wanted the opening decoration to be appropriate. It's important to emphasize the Rocky Mountains and hang pictures of local animals and a ski jumper poster. And maybe rent some mountain men wrapped in animal furs to create an atmosphere that suits our location as a town in the Wild West. What do you think? Suitable? Wonderful, thank you. Certainly, we'll talk later. Thank you, Jake. With pleasure, bye."

Alina put the phone down, and her face hardened again. She was determined to change her sister's mind, whatever it took. If Sophia didn't agree to continue the plan they had devised back home, everything would fall apart—the money Alina had saved to come to America and the high sum she paid for Sophia's ticket, not to mention her last dollars she spent as a down payment for acquiring the right to represent the prestigious New York clothing company "Carnival" with its own store in Denver.

She turned to her sister again, this time in a normal tone.

"Do you remember you told me you hoped Eric would propose marriage to you immediately when we arrived, so you could start the naturalization process quickly? Do you want to tell me that what you planned yourself isn't fraud? I remind you that the handsome Israeli guy we met yesterday asked you if you were in a relationship, and you said you weren't. What happened? Did your sharp brain forget you were dating Eric?"

"I didn't forget," Sophia whispered in a desperate voice, "but I told you, I'm still not sure about my feelings for Eric, so I preferred to tell the Israeli guy I don't have a boyfriend. And why is this even your business?"

"And how is it my business, my deceitful sister?" Alina flared up again. "I brought you here mainly so you would strengthen your relationship with Eric, so both of us would benefit from it, not just you."

Alina paced restlessly back and forth like a lion in a cage, clenching her fists tightly and unclenching them alternately. Her curly blond hair fell over her face, and she pushed it back. In those moments, everything annoyed her, her faded hair that desperately needed a new color, her thumbnail, cracked and broken, unlike the other long nails adorning her small hands, everything.

Her head turned from right to left. *Gosh*, she thought, *what if Sophia really insists and refuses to ask Eric for the money? I already paid the down payment to show them how serious I am, and I was sure it would hurry her along. Ugh, how awful that Eric is into her, and not me!*

Elina remembered how happy Eric was when she told him they were visiting America, and even more so when they said they liked Denver and decided to stay. She was thrilled by all the "who's who" he introduced them to, especially clinging to all the wealthy men with bald heads and paunches, not to mention the restaurants Eric took them to, places they'd never seen before. Spectacular restaurants, she thought, as she couldn't find a better word. And his friends? Wow, one by one. This one was wearing Versace, and that one was in a Dior suit. Never mind that she was bored by the plays they were taken to see; she almost fell asleep, but it was part of the big show, right? She told herself, so be it. She had no problem playing the role of a theatre lover, showing that she was enthusiastic about the stuffy galleries, where she didn't understand a thing about art, and all the paintings looked like kindergarten drawings. She smiled to herself, thinking about all the idiots standing there, admiring what she thought was "trash" hanging on the walls. She knew how to pretend to be impressed by paintings she didn't understand. Just tell her what to do, and she'd play the part. Anything was possible to achieve the goal. She knew how to do plays well.

Alina fell silent and nervously checked her phone again, deleting uninteresting messages, then looked up at Sophia, who was still standing by the window, her face tight.

"Sophia, my sweet Sophia, listen to your sister," she tried again, her voice softer. "That's what you do to get ahead in life. I want to eat well and live in a luxurious castle like Eric's, where they serve me breakfast in bed, and every evening, I'll invite people to a party with waiters and cocktails, and every day I'll wear a dress that will make everyone's eyes pop out. All this will happen to me and you only if our plan succeeds..."

Sophia could no longer bear to listen. She covered her ears with both hands and shook her head from side to side in despair.

"Enough, Alina," she whispered in a muffled voice. "Ugh, it's tedious. Dreams are one thing, and reality is another."

She rubbed her temples with her fingers, the pressure in her head intensifying. She walked toward the kitchen and boiled water in the electric kettle to make herself another cup of coffee.

Alina wasn't about to give up. She quickly walked to the kitchen and forcefully banged her hand on the small plastic table. The table cracked, wobbled, and collapsed onto the floor.

"For goodness' sake, Sophia, you..."

Sophia's phone rang, making her stop, and startled both sisters.

"Shhh... Be quiet, it's Eric," Sophia whispered.

"Hi, Eric," her expression softened as she answered. "Alina is here... No... Nothing special. We're folding clothes and chatting... What? The restaurant we were at on Tuesday. Seasons 52? Yes, gladly. I'll ask her if she wants to join... Thanks, you didn't have to... Yes, okay. The driver will come at 6:30 to pick us up? We'll be ready... Me too, bye."

"Sophia, listen to me," Alina was now truly on edge. She blinked incessantly, excited as she spoke about her future clothing boutique. "Sophia, this is our chance. Tonight, be smart. During the meal, I will present the new business and show Eric photos of the beautiful clothes I ordered for the boutique, and that way, I will manage to get him involved.

"All you must do is be beautiful and nice and show him how excited you are about the idea of the business. When he sees you are truly into it, suggest that he invest the money I need for the franchise, and you'll see that he'll agree. And more than that," her voice rose and contorted as her face hardened, "I think that if he's busy with a new business, it will excite him, and he won't think about his grief. Don't you think so? Any psychologist will tell you that you need to find new things to do to excite unhappy or depressed people. It helps get them out of the state they are in. I remember when I told my therapist in Israel that I was constantly depressed, she told me that I needed to switch hobbies..." She spoke now quickly and almost without stopping to take a breath. "So, I want to start a new hobby, and instead of helping me, you are ruining my plans."

Sophia didn't say a word. She stood with her back to Alina and was busy preparing coffee.

"And I haven't even told you," Alina exclaimed, "Steve, the private investigator I hired, gave me more information yesterday. According to the new data he collected, the company Eric's father left him is worth much more than we thought. He didn't consider the land and buildings the company has in Hawaii, so the new calculation is over two hundred and twenty million dollars. And all of this belongs to Eric. Here, I'm preparing all the photos that Carnival sent me, and we'll show them to Eric at the restaurant today." Alina began rapidly flipping through dozens of photos scattered on the table.

Sophia slowly turned around, clasped her hands, and stared into her sister's eyes.

"Alina, I see you won't leave me. So, you know what? I'm not going to the restaurant today. I'm calling Eric to tell him I don't feel well. There's no other way to tell you that I don't want to be part of your plan." She raised her cup and took a sip of the hot coffee.

She tried to calm down. "Besides, you know we could easily be reported. We entered America as tourists, and our visa is only for three months. One word to the immigration authorities, and they'll send us back to Israel. So, leave Eric alone. This isn't going to be another Cinderella story. I'll marry Eric only if I truly want to build a lifelong future with him."

Alina raised her eyes and glared at her sister. She put the pile of photographs back on the table, stood up, and approached Sophia until she could see every muscle trembling in her sister's angry face.

"Sophia, I swear to you, if you don't help me convince Eric to invest in the boutique, you'll regret it for your entire life," she whispered cruelly. "If you thought you knew your sister, I have a surprise for you. Be sure that I'll ruin you long before you ruin me. Remember what I told you!"

Sophia, terrified by Alina's anger, pulled back her slight frame and left the small kitchen, headed toward the living room. Alina followed her, tripped over a laundry basket, kicked it angrily, snatched her black purse from the armchair, put her apartment keys inside, and stormed out, slamming the front door.

Sophia, trembling with fright, looked through the window at her sister rushing out, screaming as she tried to hail a taxi.

That evening, Sophia left the building in the cool air. A black limousine, Eric's, awaited her on the street. Joe, the loyal chauffeur who had served their family for many years, greeted her and started the long car. Sophia sat comfortably, looking out the window, her mind racing with thoughts about her sister's cunning plan. She wore the pink earrings she had bought the previous day at a small art market, an unbuttoned white sweater, and the pink, one-shoulder dress she'd bought at Target.

When she entered the restaurant, Eric was already waiting for her at the reserved table. He stood up, pulled out the chair for her, and she sat down.

"Sophia, what will you drink?" Eric asked with his usual charm.

"A martini, please," she replied, distracted.

"What's wrong, Sophia?" Eric asked after the waiter had gone to bring the drinks. "You seem tense. Is everything okay? Why isn't Alina here? I thought she loved the food at Seasons 52."

"I'm not sure, Eric," Sophia responded. "She said she's a little under the weather and maybe developing a sinus infection. It's okay; a day or two of rest will help her."

"I know you don't have a family doctor here in Denver yet," Eric said, holding her hand gently. "Do you want me to send my doctor to check on her?"

"Oh, no," Sophia exclaimed. "I don't think it's serious. I made her some honey tea before I left and took her temperature. She doesn't have a fever."

"But if it's a sinus infection, she'll need antibiotics. Maybe I should ask my secretary to send a doctor anyway?" Eric pleaded.

"No, Eric, I'm not worried. When I get home, I'll check on her and let you know, okay? Don't worry in the meantime. Let's look at the menu. I'm quite hungry," she smiled and lightly clasped his hand.

The drinks arrived, and Sophia took a large sip of her martini, trying to force a smile at Eric. As the waiter, Arnie, approached their table to take their order, Sophia looked around. The restaurant was full. It was a nice, well-decorated restaurant, the food was delicious and high quality, served on white plates with fine silver lines, as befits a prize-winning upscale restaurant.

"What do you feel like trying today, Sophie?" In the last week, Eric had started calling her by her nickname—Sophie—, and she loved the sound of the shorter name.

"Perhaps I'll try the veal chops with artichokes and asparagus in a lemon sauce," she said after quickly reviewing the menu.

"Congratulations on your excellent choice," said Arnie, turning to Eric. "And what will you have today, Mr. Robinson?"

Eric was a favorite customer at the restaurant, and there were even whispers in town that the company his parents owned supplied fine wines for the prestigious eatery. But when the inquisitive Alina tried to investigate, she encountered a solid wall, and perhaps that was for the best.

"I'll have the New York strip steak, Arnie," Eric replied with a smile, handing the waiter the menus.

Arnie nodded slightly and stepped back. Eric's full attention returned to Sophia.

"Sophie, today I instructed my company's lawyers to fly to Japan to sign a contract for a deal that should have been signed months ago. And I might have to fly there for a couple of days if my presence is needed. Would you like to join me for a few days in Japan?"

Sophia hesitated for a moment. A trip to Japan was one of her hidden dreams. But with Eric? At his expense?

"Oh, Eric, that's a wonderful and lovely offer," she smiled warmly at him, "but I'm not sure if I can. You know I already have four private Hebrew students to tutor, and that creates a weekly commitment. Besides, remember I told you I signed up for an English course? I don't want to miss the start of the course. It's important for me to learn proper English, and you know I've already paid for six months of classes."

"My dear," Eric smiled with his warm smile that captivated her heart, "don't worry about the money. I'll find you a private tutor. You can meet him at your apartment or wherever he teaches, and you'll have a personalized 'one-on-one' learning plan. This way, you'll progress quickly in your studies and won't feel frustrated in conversations with my friends."

"Eric, please, don't start worrying about everything for me. It's important for me to achieve things on my own and give myself the necessary time."

"That's one of the things I like about you," Eric laughed. "You have tremendous motivation to reach your goals in the most honest and correct way. That's what I also learned from my parents, and I really appreciate that quality."

Oh, he doesn't know anything about me, Sophia thought in panic. She lowered her gaze for a few moments and tried to disguise her expression, so as not to reveal her feelings. The thoughts of Alina and the plan they had cooked up together tormented her relentlessly. She composed herself, took a deep breath, and whispered, "Thank you, Eric. I'll take a few days to get organized for my studies and focus on the first chapter. When you return, I'll be in my second week and will flow better with the material."

"Fine," he leaned back in his chair. "But you promise me that if you need anything, you will contact my personal assistant, Emily? I gave her your phone number, and I'll instruct her to deal with everything you need, okay?"

"Thank you, I'm fine for now," she whispered gently and offered him her hand again. *How did I get swept up with my crazy sister?* she thought in frustration. *This guy is so genuine; he has the biggest heart I know, and you can see he truly cares about me. This could be a real Cinderella story for me. Perhaps I should get to know him better. We've been dating for almost three months, and he hasn't looked else-*

where. A guy of quality, and with a good character too. Where will I find such a wonderful guy?

Sophia scanned Eric's smooth face, which was somewhat flushed that evening, or perhaps it was the Merlot wine that had brought the color to his cheeks. High cheekbones and his black hair swept back in a stylish, glossy wave. Eric wore a crisp white button-down shirt. The secure Star of David necklace he'd worn from the day she met him glittered proudly on his neck.

Sophia decided to relax and enjoy the quiet evening. Eric ordered more Merlot and Martinis, and for dessert, they shared a delicious plate of peach-cream pistachio dessert and ended with a sweet Limoncello aperitif.

Alina wasn't home when Sophia returned to the apartment at ten o'clock at night. The living room was freezing, and Sophia checked the thermostat, which read zero degrees, and realized that, once again, Alina had turned off the heating to save on the electricity bill. *It would take a long time to warm up the small apartment*, she thought with despair. "Oh, Alina, what will be the end of you?" she whispered to herself.

She remembered the electric blanket they'd bought at Walmart just two days before, just in case, and this was a case of a genuine emergency. She took the blanket out of its clear plastic wrap, arranged it on the bed, and plugged it in. Then she put on warm flannel pajamas, got into bed, wrapped herself in the icy sheets, poking her nose out, and waited for the electric blanket to begin warming the cold bed. Within a few minutes, she began to feel the slow, pleasant warmth wrapping her body. She closed her eyes. The exhaustion from a long and tiring day of agonizing arguments with Alina overwhelmed her, and within a few moments, she fell fast asleep.

It was three-fifteen in the morning when Alina returned to the apartment, swaying, drunk, and disoriented. Her hair was tousled, strands falling carelessly over her eyes. The heavy makeup on her face had smeared onto her eyes and cheeks. The top two buttons of her shirt were undone, and the gray miniskirt she wore was stained with oil or food. She quietly took off her black high heels at the entrance and peeked into the bedroom. Sophia was fast asleep. Alina wrinkled her face in displeasure. The apartment was cold, and she rubbed her arms to warm herself a little. Then she went into the living room, checked the thermostat, which had already risen to 45 degrees Fahrenheit, wrapped herself again in the coat she'd taken off moments before, and lay down on the brown couch in the small living room, murmuring unintelligible words. The alcohol did its thing, and within a few minutes, she too fell asleep.

The morning was bright, warm sunshine melting away the remnants of snow from the storm that raged two days earlier. Sophia made herself a cup of coffee and looked at her watch. It was already nine-twenty in the morning; she needed to hurry, get ready, and go to the Hebrew class she had arranged with her new student this week, Hayden. She double-checked the address he had given her. It was near. It would take her no more than ten minutes to walk there. Thank goodness she had some private Hebrew students—at least it covered part of her rent.

She took another sip of coffee and nibbled on her cheese toast. Suddenly, the doorbell rang. She glanced into the living room; Alina was fast asleep, and she wasn't expecting anyone this morning.

Who could that be? she asked herself and opened the door.

Two officers in blue uniforms stood before her. The famous American eagle emblem was embroidered on the right side of the shirts they wore. Below the design were embroidered words in white, "The Republic of the United States of America, Immigration and Citizenship, Immigration Investigations and Enforcement Agency."

"Good morning, are you, Sophia Terranova?" asked one of the officers.

"Yes," replied Sophia.

The two officers pulled out their federal identification cards and showed them to her.

"We have an arrest warrant for you," said one of the officers, and showed her an official immigration document. "You must come with us for questioning at the immigration office in the city hall building."

"What? Wait, why?" asked Sophia.

"We'll explain everything during the questioning. You have the right to one phone call. You can call from our office," the officer was polite but firm. "For now, you need to come with us, and please bring any identification documents you have, such as your passport or other ID."

Sophia composed herself. She straightened her shoulders and quietly said, "Okay," and cast a glance toward the couch. Alina remained still. Sophia took her bag, checked that her passport was there, and quietly left the apartment. Two immigration officers escorted her to a black car waiting in the parking lot.

———

Five years had passed.

Sophia finished tending to baby Jacob and placed him in his crib. Her phone rang.

"Hello, Sophinka, how are you, sweetheart?" Lena, Sophia's mother, began their usual Tuesday morning call.

"Mama, how are you?"

"We're fine, Sophinka. Tell me how things are with you."

"Everything's alright, except Jacob has a cold. I'm worried because his nose is blocked, Mama. How did you deal with our runny noses when we were babies?"

"Oh, Sophia, what always worked for me was dipping a cotton swab in salt water and putting a drop in the nose. It makes the baby sneeze and helps get rid of the bothersome runny nose. Oh, Alina fought me so hard then, wouldn't let me clean her nose..." She sighed with remembrance.

"Okay, I'll try that trick today," said Sophia. "And speaking of her, how's my wayward sister?"

"I don't have anything good to tell you about her, but at least this week the doctor prescribed her new pills, and I hope that will help her feel less agitated and balance her out a bit. She's screaming and arguing with everyone, every day. Every normal day, I thank God."

"Mama, try talking to the social worker. Maybe Alina needs constant supervision," Sophia pleaded. "If she were capable of physically hurting me here in Denver, I'm afraid she might hurt you, too."

"Thank goodness she only hurt you, and thank God you healed all alright. What would we do without your Eric? I thank God every day and bless him in my heart.

"Thank goodness, at least you bring me joy. And Alina... oh, the foolish one. She is lucky she wasn't locked up in America and was just deported immediately to Israel," Lena sighed. "I agree with you and Eric that she needs serious treatment, but you know how bureaucracy works here. Everything takes so long. Now they have changed her diagnosis to bipolar disorder, and perhaps, I hope, the new pills will help her. It pains me that she'll have an institutional stay."

"But Mama, how painful is it that in the current circumstances I can't come to visit you, not while Alina is not under 24-hour supervision. It pains me that you haven't met Eric and the children yet, and Mia is four years old and has never met her grandmother."

"Sophinka, I miss you so much and want to see you all," Lena said, her voice choked with tears, "to meet your amazing Eric and the children, but what can we do that you live in America? You know I can't leave your father alone; he needs my help with everything. He can't do things himself, being in a wheelchair. My heart breaks."

"Okay, Mama, okay, don't cry. It's hard for me too," said Sophia, "but Eric won't agree to us coming to the country. He's so afraid Alina will try to hurt me again..."

She sighed. "I miss you so much, your food, and the whole extended family and my friends. I so want to show Mia our Israel, Mama..."

She sniffed, wiped a tear from her right eye, and composed herself. "Okay, I must go. I'll call you back after I pick Mia up from preschool, alright? Kisses, Mama, we miss you too..."

FOUR
HEBREW/ NOT HEBREW

IF YOU ASKED me if I would be interested in hosting a Passover Seder in a Colorado prison, I would ask you if I heard you correctly.

But believe it or not, it turns out that such a thing exists.

One sunny morning last January, I received a phone call from an old friend who was active in the B'nai B'rith organization in Colorado.

"Hey, Yaffa, how's it going?" My friend Richard chuckled into the phone.

"Hi, Richard, how are you?" I was surprised.

"I know, and I'm really sorry we haven't talked in a while," Richard replied, "but you know how it is. Time chases us, and we chase it."

"Yes, my friend," I agreed, "but we never win at this game of tag..."

We joked around for a few more minutes, and then Richard said, "Listen, my dear, I have a question. We at the B'nai B'rith organization have decided to approach you, because you are Colorado's culinary representative for Sephardic-Middle Eastern cuisine."

I thanked him for the compliment, and he continued. "We have a group of regular volunteers who travel to Canyon City every April. Have you heard of that city?"

"Oh, isn't that the city with several prisons?" I asked.

"Exactly," Richard replied. "And that's why every year during Passover week, we have a group of volunteers who travel there to hold a Seder for Jewish prisoners and then stay for an hour of questions and answers on topics related to the holiday and how different communities around the world celebrate it. A couple of our friends bought the amazing cookbook you published on Sephardic and Middle Eastern food, *Sephardic Balabusta Shares Tasteful Treasures*. We would like you to share your knowledge with the Jewish prisoners and contribute a little of the Mediterranean-Jewish traditions, customs, and special foods of the community. What do you say?"

The subject interested me, and I decided to accept the organization's request. I began a lengthy security screening process that lasted two months, during which I underwent various security checks, an official FBI background check, and more. The thorough screening was understandable because it involved a visit to a prison, something I was unfamiliar with but curious about.

And so, early one cool morning in April, we met in the parking lot of the historic stone building of the B'nai B'rith, located near the famous National Jewish Hospital, a hospital for the study of respiratory diseases whose beautiful stone building was also donated by B'nai B'rith, and helped load a blue minibus with food boxes, Haggadah books, and grape wine bottles. Then we got in and drove to the prison in Canyon City, Colorado.

Canyon City had three large prisons, one of which was considered one of the most secure prisons in America. It was particularly well-known for the famous "residents" who had been housed there over the years, such as the deranged killer McVeigh, who decided to blow up the federal government building in Oklahoma City thirty years ago, killing more than three hundred federal employees, and the killer from Sandy Hook Elementary, who shot 32 six- and seven-year-old children in cold blood at an elementary school.

Most of the city's residents work in prisons, serving the "guest community," which was complex, to say the least, and living alongside it, leading normal lives and their opposites—prison guards and prisoners, walls and bars versus freedom and parks, restricted lives versus rights, strict enforcement, and free choice.

The trip to Canyon City took almost three hours. On the way, I looked through the booklet that the group leader, Mr. Aronson, distributed to all the volunteers and memorized the rules printed in it. There was a lot to remember. The instructions regarding interaction with the prisoners were clear, strict, and uncompromising:

No bags were allowed in the prison, only ID cards; no talking to prisoners about their personal details or yours; no asking prisoners why they were there; you were not allowed to accept letters from prisoners to pass on to anyone; you were not allowed to exchange phone numbers from prisoners to pass on to anyone; and so on and so forth.

Another page of the booklet contained instructions on what we were supposed to do and the purpose of the visit:

You must answer any questions related to Passover; you must answer questions about kosher food; and so on.

"There are a lot of rules to remember, but such rules make sense when it comes to our special visit," I said to Steve, a member of the delegation who was sitting next to me.

"Yes," Steve replied, "after the visit, you will understand how important it is to the Jewish prisoners. They already experience many prohibitions and restrictions, so when they are recognized as Jews, given attention, and acknowledged their right to celebrate Passover, it lifts their spirits, and they are happy and grateful to us for making the effort to come to distant Canyon City.

"During this visit, we can also show prison administrators that we appreciate their attention to prisoners' rights and the fact that they allow the Jewish prisoners to experience Passover, eat kosher food, and feel some of the atmosphere of the Jewish holiday together with Jews from the community in Colorado."

The excitement grew as the crowded minibus arrived at the high iron gates of the prison. These were electric gates that opened onto a circular parking lot. The prison itself was a huge white building, and five tall towers rising in all directions immediately caught my attention. At the entrance to the high gates, huge pine trees grew, helping to fence in the white walls.

We stood in the circular parking lot and waited for instructions. A vehicle with several guards drove toward the minibus and parked next to us, and we were asked to allow the guards to conduct a security check inside the Minibus. We were then asked to continue on foot, while Joe, the smiling and dedicated driver who had been contributing his time to this important cause for many years, drove the minibus to another internal parking lot through additional iron gates, into the prison.

The sun, which had risen in the meantime, warmed us gently, and I was glad that we had set out early in the morning and not in the middle of the day, when the Colorado sun began to beat down mercilessly on anyone outside.

We stood in line at the electric iron gates and, one by one, underwent a manual physical inspection. Then we were asked to pass through a sophisticated metal detector for further inspection, where we stood in line again to help bring in the kosher food we had brought with us.

It was strictly forbidden to bring in anything that was not factory-made, so all the food was purchased, packaged in sealed containers straight from the factory, and we could not bring any food that had been prepared at home. All the products we brought with us passed through an electric belt and were scanned by a metal detector and a scanner like the one used for all objects at the airport. The guards themselves transferred our food boxes and then took them to another location for further thorough inspection.

Next, we passed through additional electric gates to another area of the prison building and underwent further inspection and screening. After that, the guards led us through huge, heavy electric iron doors into a small hall where tables were arranged in a semicircle, and covered with white paper tablecloths. Paper plates, cups, and white paper napkins, embossed with delicate yellow flowers that matched the design of the tablecloths, completed the festive look.

I glanced at the walls of the hall, which were bare of pictures, but the place itself was air-conditioned and pleasant, and still had a good atmosphere.

The head of the delegation, Mr. Aronson, instructed us to start unpacking the packages and boxes we had brought with us, and we all immediately set to work. Setting the tables was a joint effort by all the volunteers and guards, and everyone lent a hand to get the job done quickly and accurately, as we all listened to Mr. Aronson's instructions. I later learned that the man had been doing this sacred work for over thirty years.

The guards were the only ones allowed to touch anything made of glass. They explained to us that glass was not permitted in prisons because of the security risk, but there were exceptional cases, such as ours. Since the prepared gefilte fish came from the factory only in glass jars, it was agreed that the guards would empty the fish from the jars and immediately take them to another room to dispose of them. The kind guards placed two pieces of fish on each plate and added two tablespoons of sweet charoset, also from a glass jar.

We were allowed to open all the other cardboard boxes we had brought and the packages of matzo, and we placed a few pieces of matzo next to each plate. For safety reasons, the guards instructed us not to open the glass bottles of grape juice we had brought with us for the four cups, but they poured the juice themselves into paper cups and placed them on the tables. Immediately afterward, they collected the empty glass bottles and took them to another room.

I opened one of the cardboard boxes and began handing the bottles one by one to the guard standing near me.

"Thank you," said the nice guard. In Hebrew!

I almost fell over. Luckily, I managed to grab the juice bottle in my hand tightly and save it from breaking.

"Do you speak Hebrew?" I asked in English, completely stunned.

"I understand and speak it," the man replied in melodious Hebrew. He looked about sixty years old, a handsome, tall man with smiling eyes, gray and white hair, and a mustache of a similar color.

"How is that possible? Are you Israeli?" I asked with a puzzled smile.

"Yes, I'm originally Israeli. But I've been living here for many years," he replied in Hebrew with an American accent. "I came to the United States when I was young, on a post-army trip, and in Las Vegas, I met the woman who became my wife. She grew up here, in Canyon City, and after we got married, she wanted us to live near her parents. We've been here ever since; we raised four children here, and I'm about to retire from work and go into retirement."

Wow, I thought I had seen and heard everything, and here—another surprise, who would have believed it? In my wildest dreams, I never thought I would meet an American Israeli guy here in prison who was also one of the veteran guards here.

For a moment, I was speechless, but I quickly recovered and felt that I wanted to take advantage of this special opportunity and hear more from him. However, I remembered that we were only there for two hours and that I was there to help organize the Passover Seder for the Jewish prisoners. So, under intense pressure and while arranging the food on the tables, I took advantage of the few minutes I had to talk to David, the nice Israeli prison guard.

David told me that the prison commander had chosen him to supervise the Passover Seder in the prison because he himself was Jewish, familiar with the Passover Seder tradition, and spoke Hebrew. Not that it made any difference to the prisoners. They were all American Jews, after all, and what were the chances that any of them spoke Hebrew? Or maybe, like the average American Jew, they knew how to say "Shalom," "good," and "thank you," and perhaps the names of Israeli dishes such as "hummus" and "falafel."

"Do you have family in Israel?" I asked.

"Yes, my parents have passed away, and my two brothers are also gone, but I still have three sisters in Israel. They all live in Safed, with their families, of course."

"Do you visit them?"

"Uh..." David smiled sheepishly. "I haven't visited in a few years. You know how it is. When my parents were alive, we traveled quite a bit—it was important to me that my children get to know them and remember them—but now that my parents and half of my family are in heaven, we travel less. You could say almost not at all," he added quietly, lowering his eyes for a moment.

"Have your children ever joined one of the delegations that offer a free trip to get to know Israel?" I asked.

David looked at me in surprise over a plate of fish. "No. What is that? I'm not familiar with such an option."

Now I was surprised too, but for the opposite reason. "Jewish boys and girls under the age of 26 can visit Israel for free," I explained. "There are several Jewish organizations, one of which is called 'Taglit' or 'Shoresh,' that accept donations to fund trips for young American Jews to Israel.

"The idea behind these initiatives is that no Jewish youth living in the Diaspora should be prevented from visiting Israel solely because of financial constraints. For this reason, Jewish-American billionaires fund various worthy programs.

"My daughters also joined one of these delegations and enjoyed it, even though they had visited the country many times," I concluded.

"Sounds interesting," said David.

David thanked me again for the information, and we continued working in silence. But my curiosity got the better of me, and I asked to know more about the life of the Israeli prison guard in the American prison, far from his former life, so I started the conversation again.

"When was the last time you traveled to Israel? Does your wife travel with you?" I asked gently.

"Oh... when did I go to Israel? A long time ago..." David placed an empty glass bottle in the designated box. "My wife didn't come with me. She's not Jewish, and she's not interested in these visits. She's the head nurse at the neighboring prison and works a lot. You know, Canyon City is a prison town, so everyone here works in the prisons. And thank God," he smiled gently, "there are a lot of inmates and enough work for everyone."

"And your family in Israel," I asked, "do they come to visit here?"

"Actually, not many," David's face clouded over a little, "but I understand them completely. It's expensive to come here, and they also lose workdays... Everyone in our family works and raises children; my sisters are full-time grandmothers, helping with their grandchildren. Fortunately, in this age of FaceTime, Facebook, and Zoom, I get to see everyone on screen. My sisters' grandchildren love to talk to me in broken English and slang Hebrew, which I don't understand at all."

I smiled understandingly. I was aware of the language challenge.

"It's difficult, isn't it?" He laughed, "The slang Hebrew is difficult. The last time I was in Israel, I went to the market with one of my sisters and asked the vendor, 'Are the oranges fresh?' He replied, 'Crazy,' and I stood there wondering what he meant. Did he mean that I was crazy? My sister laughed and said, 'No, David, he means the oranges are as fresh as they can be.'

"I also heard two people arguing in a café, and one said to the other, 'I'm telling you, it's the end of the road.' What does it mean when they say, 'the end of the road'? I thought. What road? What did he mean?"

"Excellent question," I laughed. "I also heard that expression and didn't understand it until my sister explained its meaning to me."

"And the young waiter at the restaurant, when I asked him before ordering the veal if it was tasty, he replied, 'It's delicious on a whole other level.' What does it mean when someone says, 'on a whole other level'? On what level? Why on a level? Compared to another level?

"I don't understand all these new expressions that have become part of everyday language in Israel. When I lived there, we spoke differently."

"Believe me, I'm with you on that," I laughed. "I'm sure you were also confused when you heard everyone calling their friends 'brother' 'Bro, what's up?' 'Yeah, bro,' 'no bro'... You'd think all Israelis were brothers," I added with a half-smile.

"Yes, you're right, I heard that too and didn't really understand what it meant," said David. "Or that everything that happens is an 'event'. People no longer describe something as a story that happened or a wedding, a bar mitzvah... Everything has become an 'event'." I nodded in agreement, and he continued, "I noticed that every time I came to Israel, I encountered new words that are a mixture of Hebrew, English, and who knows what else, or strange expressions that are added and whose meaning I don't always understand.

"And I stand there completely confused, wondering if I'm really in Israel or some other strange place. I feel that today's Hebrew is so different from the language I grew up with. To tell you the truth, I no longer feel comfortable speaking it, which may be why I don't want to return and visit the country."

Although we were having a lighthearted and cheerful conversation, I could see that David was speaking from the depths of his heart and in a sad tone, as if he could finally tell someone who really understood him and was going through something similar, a kind of "we share the same issue," the things that had been bothering him so much.

"And I'm starting to feel embarrassed and like a stranger in the place that was my home and where my childhood memories are engraved, which is my homeland," he added somewhat reluctantly. "I also understand that the problem is with me, not with the Israelis in Israel. I distanced myself from them, not them from me."

"Naturally, there are changes, as everywhere else," I said gently, trying to calm the storm I saw stirring within him because of our meeting.

"A lot has happened in Israel in the years we've been away, and some of it has naturally affected the language as well."

"That's clear, I understand what you're saying," he smiled again, "I accept change and progress and all that, but when it comes to language, to communication, I want to hold on to what little I have, to what remains of my identity as an Israeli. And an important part of that is the Hebrew language. Even though I don't live in Israel, I try to preserve it as much as I can. It's my language, it's the language in which I spoke my first words, but my Hebrew and the Hebrew spoken in Israel today are very different from each other."

At that moment, his phone buzzed.

"The prisoners are about to enter," he said, and headed for the doors.

I was excited and nervous at the same time. As I tried to remain calm, there was a loud screech of metal, and the electric metal doors in the room opened. A group of twenty-seven male prisoners entered the small hall. They looked around with slight embarrassment and then sat down in chairs facing the tables we had set for them. All the prisoners wore gray overalls with tags attached to them with their first names and two other symbols whose meaning I did not understand. Their faces wore serious expressions accompanied by excitement, and some of them showed tension and a little nervousness, constantly touching the utensils on the table. Most of them looked to me to be in their thirties, except for two who looked to be at least fifty.

Mr. Aronson was the first to speak. He greeted the prisoners and told them that B'nai B'rith was the organizer of the event. From time to time, he raised his hand and waved to one of the prisoners. Later, I realized that some of the prisoners knew him from previous years.

Then he introduced us, the volunteers from the Jewish community in Denver, and we began to read the blessings. The frosty atmosphere began to warm up, and smiles appeared on the faces of the participants.

The prisoners were also invited to read from the Haggadah, and I was surprised to see that all of them, without exception, volunteered to help read a short chapter in English. Thus, on the strangest and most surreal Seder night I had ever attended, ten volunteers sat in front of Jewish prisoners and read the Passover Haggadah, with our Mr. Aronson signaling the next reader to begin, and in between, we also raised glasses of grape juice. With each reading and each glass, I felt that the prisoners were slowly becoming more relaxed and cooperative.

From time to time, guards entered the hall with new paper cups filled with more grape juice, and the prisoners enjoyed the delicious fish and even asked for another serving of the New York charoset.

I glanced at David, the Israeli guard, who was sitting at the table opposite me. He was quiet most of the time and did not participate in the reading of the Haggadah, until we began to sing "Dayenu." I could see that suddenly, this song we were singing sparked something in him. His expression was serious and somewhat dull, like that of a person who had momentarily disconnected from his surroundings and was in a completely different place, far away from us, both physically and spiritually.

It seemed that the song brought back memories of the years he had lived in Israel, his childhood years in his parents' home, with the Seder in Hebrew, when all his brothers and sisters sat next to him at the holiday table and sang the familiar "Dayenu."

Then he began to sing with us, at first quietly, almost shyly, but his voice grew louder, until halfway through the song he began to tap gently on the table with his empty glass, a slight smile spreading across his face. When our eyes met, he raised his glass and clinked it in my direction in a "L'chaim" (cheers) gesture, then turned to the prisoner sitting to his right and clinked glasses with him. The Jewish prisoner smiled, and his face lit up for a moment. A shiver ran through me as I watched this scene—a Jewish prison guard and a Jewish prisoner, each dressed in his official uniform, each in his position, raising a glass in a toast to the holiday of freedom! My heart pounded. I was excited when the thought occurred to me, was there anything stronger than shared roots?

When we finished reading the entire Haggadah, the prisoners were given the opportunity to ask questions about the history of Passover, the Seder itself, and the traditional foods we had brought with us. Now it was my turn to talk about and explain Sephardic customs in different communities around the world. I showed them the latest book I wrote on Sephardic/Mizrachi food from various communities around the world, and it was nice to hear some of the prisoners share with us the Spanish foods they had tried in the past. The conversation about food eased the tension even more. It was good and pleasant and brought many smiles to the prisoners' faces. I could see that some of them were reminiscing about family gatherings and holidays with traditional holiday tables.

"Food is a bridge," I told them and showed them the back cover of my cookbook, which read: "Food is a bridge. When I invite guests from different backgrounds, with different languages and traditions, to a meal I have cooked, the food encourages conversation, creates warmth around the dining table, and helps to form new connections."

Indeed, even in prison, at this Passover Seder table, I saw how the sentence I wrote on the back of my book created warmth and a feeling of something shared among all those gathered.

Finally, Mr. Aronson signaled us to come over and shake hands with all the prisoners and allowed us to talk to them a little, within the limits of the restrictions and prohibitions, of course.

For a moment, it seemed to me that one of the prisoners looked very much like someone I knew in the Jewish-American community in Denver, and perhaps there was a family connection, maybe a brother, but I immediately decided to put that thought aside—all within the restrictions.

The Jewish prisoners behaved impeccably. I could see that they greatly appreciated the attention we gave them. They appreciated the effort we made in coming from afar to help them feel the Passover holiday.

A little bit of home, a little less harshness and formality than they experienced in their daily lives in prison. They were quiet and nice, and for a moment, I thought that if I didn't know that they were prisoners who had committed crimes that led them to prison, I would think they were normal people with feelings and desires who wanted to feel at home and receive attention like everyone else.

The two hours allotted to us passed quickly, perhaps too quickly. We said goodbye to the prisoners with warm handshakes, and they thanked us again for our efforts and goodwill.

I shook David's hand goodbye.

"I would hug you if it were allowed, but you know you can't hug here," he smiled, his eyes sparkling.

"That's okay," I replied, "it's all part of the prison restrictions. I was very happy to meet you," I added.

Now we had to wait until all the prisoners had left the hall. Then the kind guards helped us pack up the rest of the items we had brought with us, and only then were we allowed to leave the hall through the electric metal doors. After passing through the metal detector and X-ray machine one last time, we were allowed to walk outside toward the minibus that had brought us there.

This time, I sat next to Mr. Aronson, who was happy to tell me about the B'nai B'rith organization and its mission, and it was heartwarming to hear about all the different initiatives.

On the way, Mr. Aronson pointed to the huge plane standing at the entrance to the Academy of Aviation and Aeronautics, located at the entrance to Colorado Springs.

"Did you know that the Academy of Aviation hosts Israeli pilots?" he asked.

"No, I didn't know that. What brings Israeli pilots here?" I asked with interest.

"You know that Israeli pilots are famous all over the world." Mr. Aronson smiled proudly. "The flight academy invites Israeli pilots every year to come and stay here, and they come here and train with pilots from the US Air Force."

We continued driving in silence. I looked at the view from the window, and my thoughts returned to David, who had lived in

Canyon City for decades, and his struggle with the difficulties of his native language, the ever-changing Hebrew language. Since he lived on the other side of the world, it was difficult for him to keep up with the pace of change. And the fact was, there was a lot of truth in what David, the prison guard, said. When I travel to Israel, I too experience all the changes taking place there, including changes in language, different ways of behaving, priorities, and almost every area of life. I know that we, who live far away, were more aware of these changes and experienced them more intensely, which was why we were surprised by them. But why? Why didn't we like them, or manage to get used to them? Perhaps because we were disappointed that the Hebrew language we remembered was no longer our language. Maybe it was because of the strong desire we, humans had to preserve things we were fond of, because our vocabulary was shrinking due to lack of daily use of the Hebrew language, or because of things that brought back sweet memories of things we no longer had, such as pictures of our Israeli family's past, the Israel we grew up and lived in before we decided to move to the world of divided hearts. Change was an inevitable part of life. Technological advances, looking at other countries and wanting to copy what seemed more correct, more attractive, more colorful, more acceptable, and more popular to us—all of these were acceptable changes, but we lost something along the way when we adopted new and innovative things, something of our authenticity, something of our roots, and sadly, something of our history.

FIVE
FLIGHT OR TRIP

THE OFFICE of Yaron Air Conditioning resembled an urgent care station after a tornado. People came and went, the phones ringing incessantly, and Jenny, the secretary, tired of listening to customers' repeated pleas and requests, was about to tear her hair out in frustration. She had to repeat the same answer to all the anxious customers —there was no available time slot to schedule their air conditioner installation this week. At times, just when it seemed that silence had returned and Jenny breathed a sigh of relief, the phones immediately came back to life.

The stream of ringing did not disappoint, either in its distinctive shrillness or in its annoying persistence.

"What a busy day," Yaron grumbled when he finally got home that evening, but immediately thought that he shouldn't complain for a moment.

The hot, endless summer was very good for his business, so thank God for every day. He leaned against the wall at the entrance, took off his heavy work shoes, and with a sigh of relief hung his sweat-soaked baseball cap on the hat rack and ran his hand over his forehead, red from the cap. Then he walked in his socks to the kitchen to fill a glass of water. Noa, his ten-year-old daughter, saw him from the living room and jumped up excitedly to greet him.

"Hi, Daddy, how are you? Today, during recess, Adidush told me that they are going to visit their grandparents in Israel this summer. Are we going there too this year?"

"Maybe, my princess," Yaron replied, stroking his daughter's curly head. "I hope so. I'm trying to find good-priced plane tickets. We'll see."

Noa smiled and skipped back to her business, and Yaron continued toward the refrigerator. Orit, his wife, who was in the kitchen, busy preparing dinner, looked at him for a moment, her serious expression betraying her dissatisfaction. "I'm not sure, Noa, don't get too excited," she shook her head and turned her gaze decisively to her daughter, who was sprawled on the black leather sofa in front of the TV. "We probably won't be going to Israel this year. I want us to have fun this summer. You want a fun vacation too, right? There are still many places here we haven't visited: Disney World, Yellowstone, Delicate Arch in Moab, Utah, Rocky Mountain National Park..."

Yaron's face fell when he heard Orit's response.

"Orit, don't tell Noa we're not going to Israel," he said quietly. "We haven't decided yet, right? And I do want to go to Israel this year. We haven't been there in two years, and you remember that on our two previous visits we didn't end up meeting Einat and the Atias family, and we didn't go to visit Allegra Buskila, Yigal's mother, the kidney transplant recipient who came to Denver for the transplant, and we didn't get to..."

"Oh no, Yaron. No, no, no," Orit wiped her hands on a yellow kitchen towel and hung it on her shoulder. "I don't agree with what you're saying. With all due respect to the Buskila family and Yigal, and I don't know who else, it's time we went on a vacation that is enjoyable. I want a real vacation, one that will give me room to breathe, one that will recharge my batteries. I want to see beautiful scenery, learn about a new place we've never visited before, discover another corner of the big world, and enjoy food that will be prepared and served to me. I want a fun annual vacation, one that we will remember and smile about every time we mention it.

"We deserve it too, and this year we'll give it to ourselves. No more long, tiring trips that are all about visiting people's homes just so we don't hurt anyone's feelings in the extended family or among friends, close or distant. Enough, I'm done with it."

"Are you starting again, Orit?" Yaron raised his voice and looked at her reproachfully, even though Orit pointed to the living room and to Noa, who was sitting there and put her finger to her lips to signal him to lower his voice. "Damn you. Since we moved to Colorado, for ten years now, every summer we argue about this. It's time you understood—you don't decide this on your own, and you can't decide for everyone in our house. We haven't been in Israel for two years, the kids want us to go see the family, so why are you choosing a trip here, in America, instead of a trip to Israel to be with the family?"

"Come on, Yaron!" Orit was furious. "Look at all our friends: Eitan's wife Dina booked a Caribbean cruise for the whole family, Dalia already bought tickets for her whole group of seven people for a vacation at Disney, and wait, I almost forgot Reuben, he rented a camper, and they're taking the whole family to Yellowstone. They'll stay in a cabin, ride horses, and eat barbecue at the ranch that's hosting them for a fee. David and Tami are planning to take the whole family to see the longest suspension bridge in the world on Mount Evans, which is here in Colorado. And what about us? Tell me, what are we doing this summer?"

"Visiting family..." Yaron began to say, but Orit interrupted him in a mocking tone, rolling her eyes in contempt.

"Visiting family? Let me remind you what happens when we visit family in Israel. Besides the fact that it's hot and humid and disgusting, all we do is go from house to house to another house, and in case we forget another house, and when we're not visiting another house, I must help your mother prepare all the meals for the whole family. So, no. Thank you very much."

"Is that how you feel about traveling to Israel? How much do you need to help my mother? I can't believe it." Yaron sat down heavily in a chair in the kitchen and rested his elbows on the round table. "What is wrong with you? You'd think someone was punishing you when they remind you that it's time to visit our families."

Orit nervously threw the towel on the counter. The fact that Yaron had told her the truth she didn't want to hear annoyed her, but she wasn't willing to let his accusations go unchallenged, instead of supporting her.

"Sure, Yaron. Shall I remind you why you enjoy traveling to Israel? Let me tell you how you spend your time when we're there: You call your friends and arrange to meet them for beer, and if it's not your friends and beer, you happily accept every invitation to tables full of fatty foods that help you happily grow that belly—sometimes at your mother's and sometimes at your brothers' houses; the whole time we're there, you're a 'guest'. You don't bother running to the market every time your mother needs something in the kitchen. When I go on vacation, I don't want to go shopping or spend time frying food or washing dishes, while you eat happily, and after the meal, you go out with your father for a walk in the neighborhood while cracking Sunflower seeds. And if, God forbid, I ask you where you're going, the answer is always, 'Just a walk around the neighborhood, to walk off the food!'"

Orit fell silent. Uncontrollable tears flooded her eyes from the frustration and disgust she felt every time she remembered the routine of the boring visit that awaited her in Israel.

"Come on, Orit," Yaron chuckled angrily, "is that what bothers you? That I meet up with my friends? That I eat at my brothers' houses? That my mother prepares big meals and needs help? What can we do? We're staying at my parents' house, and all my brothers and the grandchildren come to visit us there. They come because they miss us, because we live thousands of miles away from them. Besides, you know I help with a lot of things, so why are you complaining?"

"Yes?" Orit watched and didn't give up, "Remind me exactly how you help when we go to Israel—you go to the butcher, for example, to get your mother the meat she likes so she can make you meatballs. Does anyone ask me what kind of meat I like? No. Or when she wants to make you the jam you like, I run to the market to find the cheapest peaches available. No, Yaron. Enough with that. I want a pampering vacation. We work hard all year, and I want to enjoy it. Why does it always have to be a trip to Israel? Why does all our money have to go to visit family?"

"Orit," Yaron tapped the kitchen door angrily. "It's not my mother's fault that we decided to leave Israel and live in America," he almost shouted. "Okay, we can choose not to go to Israel this summer. But remember, she's an elderly woman, and if something happens to her and we're not there, I'll have to live with that for the rest of my life, not you!"

"Here we go, the drama king has started," Orit chuckled, "Is that the scene this time? That she's not feeling well. Last time, you told me we had to go to Israel to celebrate your brother-in-law's Torah scroll because his surgery was successful. You said we had to be there for the event, and on the trip before that, you said we had to go because you and your brothers were organizing a family meeting to decide whether to move your parents to a house without stairs, and that such a meeting could not be held over the phone. And I will never forget the trip before the 'family meeting trip,' which was, of course, completely unnecessary, because, come on, did we really have to be part of the decision about where your family would buy the grave plot for your parents? It's not like you changed the cemetery, so why did we have to be there to help the brothers choose?

"I'm sorry, Yaron," Orit took a deep breath for a moment and continued speaking from the bottom of her heart and in all seriousness, "Your mother is feeling great, and I'm not going to Israel this year. After the kids go to sleep, you and I will sit down at the computer and look at places to travel. Maybe we should also talk to Reuben, because the trip they're taking this year sounds like a great family outing. Maybe we can still book a wooden cabin at that ranch in the Rocky Mountains where he booked a place for his family?"

"Leave me alone, Orit," Yaron said, standing up angrily. "I'm not going to sit here and look at trips. We don't have to do what all our friends are doing. They have their own considerations, and they allow themselves things that we don't. They work in high-tech, and maybe their salaries are higher than ours. It's none of my business, I don't check up on them, and I don't need to know what they give up affording such grandiose vacations. Maybe they can afford both an annual trip in America and a flight to Israel in the same year. Good for them. I look at what we can and can't afford.

"I look at the fact that it's not enough that we don't live in Israel, and our parents miss us and their grandchildren so much, so even their little pleasure of enjoying every moment we're there and doing those little things together, like preparing food—the few experiences our parents still have with us—you want to deprive them of. I know how much they miss it, longing for moments together with their children and now with their grandchildren..." He started to leave the kitchen toward the living room, then stopped next to her. "You know what? I'm sick of it too! I'm sick of having to go through this nightmare with you every summer. It's our broken record every year. What are you complaining about?" His voice rose again. "About traveling to Israel? The place that is our second home?

"Who told you to move to the other side of the world? You chose to live here, and you didn't ask yourself how much pain we were causing our parents. Didn't you think there would be consequences? You wanted to live in the big world, learn another language, but when the time comes...

"Deciding to go and treat your parents who miss you every day of the year, you don't even want to give them this little pleasure. You're sickeningly selfish, Orit, you're so self-centered. There, I said it."

Yaron continued into the living room and sat down angrily on the flowered armchair. He held the glass of water he had poured himself earlier and took large sips from it. His right foot tapped restlessly on the floor tiles.

Orit didn't give up. She followed him with the vegetables she had taken out of the refrigerator for dinner and pointed at him reproachfully with her free hand.

"Yaron, listen to me, I'm telling you unequivocally, we moved to America, so let's travel in America, and next year we'll think about it again.

"We work hard, and I even agreed to work on weekends so we could have a little extra income. We're trying hard to save money, and I didn't even tell you that sometimes I give things up to save a little more. I want to finally enjoy what I've saved with so much effort," she took a deep breath. "All our savings can't go just on trips to Israel. I'm tired of being the one who pays to see the family. What do they think over there? That money grows on trees in America. If they miss us so much and want to see us so badly, why doesn't anyone bother to come to us? Is it hard? Is it far?

"Expensive? It's hard for us too; it's far and expensive, the flights are long and tiring, and the hassle of flying back and forth is the same every time. I'm not even talking about the delays and the fact that we've been stuck and waited for eight or nine hours at one airport.

"So please, anyone who wants to see us should make the effort, save up for a plane ticket, fly all the way here, and experience a little of what we go through. You know what? Maybe we'll agree that they'll come to us once every two years, and we'll travel once every two years? That way, we'll have time and money to travel here in America, like all our friends. If we're already spending all that money on flights, why not combine it with a real vacation, a trip to beautiful, interesting places, or a vacation with our friends here? When was the last time we went away with friends? Who even remembers..."

Yaron was silent. Orit's comments saddened him greatly, but there was also something that made sense in what she said.

There was a long silence. Orit noticed that Noa was no longer in the living room and remembered that the last time she and Yaron had argued about something trivial, like whether to give their dog Diamond a bath, Noa had left the living room immediately.

Oh, Noa, my sensitive Noa, a tormenting thought crossed her mind, *I always get carried away in arguments and don't notice how hard she takes it.*

"Orit," Yaron's voice shook her out of her thoughts, "did you hear what I said? My mother is sick, really, and her latest tests weren't good at all. We must go to Israel this year. You don't want something to happen to her, and we don't get to see her, do we?"

Orit suppressed a sarcastic reply, thinking that all possible excuses had already been made. The only reason left was the one that ended every argument with an intensity that was hard to resist, and it was not long in coming. But she wasn't going to let emotional manipulation win.

"Yaron, don't be so dramatic and don't try to play on my emotions," she smiled the little smile that Yaron usually loved, but now it really annoyed him. "Your mother is just getting older. Do you think that every time she doesn't feel well, we, who are on the other side of the world, rush ourselves and our young children and immediately fly over to 'see her before it's too late'? It doesn't work that way, sweetheart, and it won't work. There are too many things to organize before every flight, not to mention spending all our savings, and if we haven't saved enough, buying plane tickets on our credit card or borrowing from good friends, which is hard for me. I'm not willing to be in such an awkward situation in front of Dalia or Ruben again."

"Orit, come on," Yaron almost begged, "I wasn't talking about traveling every time someone in Israel feels sick. I was talking about this summer. We can go on vacation in America whenever we want, but traveling to Israel is a necessity at least once every two years, if not every year. I'm asking you, think about the kids. They don't see their grandparents sometimes for years; they're growing up and changing, and it's hard for our parents to keep up. And the longer the time between visits, the greater the disconnect between our family and us. Look at our children, Noa is already ten, Gili is seven, and

Lili is four. You know how much a child grows and changes in two years? It's a huge difference. Do you want our parents to see them once every six or seven years? Think about the children, too, those little ones who are the most important thing in the world to us. You can change your house or your car, but you can't change your children, so don't do them any more harm than we've already done by not letting them grow up in Israel."

Orit looked at him without batting an eyelid, her face as cold as ice. He felt that his pleas were falling on deaf ears.

"Orit," he continued softly, "if we don't try to let them see their grandparents and cousins as much as possible, they'll lose all connection with them. Our parents will become people our children barely know, like grandparents only in pictures, and so will our siblings and their children. They'll hug each other once every few years, and that's it. They won't share any childhood experiences, growing up experiences, preparing for college... All the memories you and I have, for example, think about it, Noa won't have the same special memories I have of my grandfather Moshe, or the sweet memories I have of my grandmother Rachel. I remember how much I waited for the holiday to come because I knew I would get my usual treat from her, new sneakers, and the new shoebox was always full of candy that she stuffed between the shoes. As a child, it warmed my heart. Things like that show a child how much they are loved, how important they are to their grandparents. I prevented those memories for my children when we decided to move to America and have them grow here..."

"But they'll have other memories..." Orit began to say, but Yaron interrupted her.

"Look at the children of your friend Smadar. They haven't seen their grandparents in seven years. The oldest is finishing high school this year, the middle one was two years old the last time he saw them, and the youngest has never met them. The children vaguely remember their family in Israel and don't know them except by looking at family pictures. A strangeness has developed between them, and it doesn't bother the children at all. But on the other hand, if you tell them to give up a trip to Yellowstone or Disney, the whole street will hear them screaming at home, God forbid.

"Do you understand the situation our friends are in, giving priority to other things instead of visiting Israel to stay in touch with their families, especially their parents? Do you realize that they sacrificed this important relationship? Because of selfishness, because they thought like you, because they didn't value close family ties for their children."

"Why should I only think about the children?" Orit's anger flared up again, as if Yaron had stepped on a very sore spot.

"What about me, Yaron? Me, Orit, why shouldn't I enjoy a real vacation? Where is it written that I must spend every year the little I've saved to pay for another expensive trip to Israel just to be at home with our families? I'm broken; I'm fed up. I deserve more than this."

Tears streamed down her cheeks again. She wiped them away nervously and then stared at him intently.

"You know what, Yaron? I've made up my mind," she said in a trembling voice. "I'm not going to Israel this year. You want to go? Go by yourself. If you want to take the kids, go ahead. But I'm staying here, and that's my final decision. I'm not going. You can tell your mother and your brothers and your friends that my work wouldn't give me time off or make up any story you want."

Yaron was stunned by Orit's extreme reaction. Admittedly, she did occasionally turn up her nose when it was time to fly to Israel for another visit, and it was true that she wasn't happy about having to stay with her mother-in-law, but was that really a reason to react so strongly?

For a moment, he wondered if things would have been different if they had stayed with her parents in Israel, but it was a futile thought.

Orit's father had died ten years ago, and her mother had moved into a nursing home for Alzheimer's patients and had already failed to recognize Orit and her brother on their last visit.

Yaron was speechless and just stared at his phone. Without realizing it, he went to Facebook and saw that his best friend, Reuben, had posted something that day. Instead of liking or commenting, he scrolled down and decided to send him a message.

"Hey, Reuben, what's up?"

"Hey, Yaron, I'm cooling off a bit from this heat, want to grab an iced coffee?"

"Sure, I'll be right there," Yaron replied on the spur of the moment.

It suited him perfectly to get away from home, to get some fresh air and escape the tense atmosphere. He knew that this argument could escalate into other burning issues that were best left untouched and not even thought about. He remembered what happened the last time they argued about a trip to Israel.

They didn't speak to each other for two whole days, and in the end, they went anyway, and Orit suffered throughout the entire visit. The last thing he wanted to see in his mind's eye was Orit's reaction when his mother told her that her back hurt and asked her to clear the large table after the huge meal they had prepared for the entire extended family...

Without another word, he stood up, shoved his phone into the back pocket of his faded jeans, put on his work shoes, grabbed his keys from the table in the entryway, and left the house, slamming the door behind him.

"Wait, Yaron," Orit hurried after him. "Where are you going? Dinner is almost ready."

"Eat without me, don't wait for me," he replied without turning to her. "I'm popping over to Reuben's."

Orit's face fell. She went back into the house and stood with her back to the door for a few moments, hoping he would change his mind and come back, but the door remained closed, and the silence in the house weighed on her more than ever.

SIX

NITZA IS TORN

THE SAD CASE of Nitza "shook me up," so when Revital told me that Nitza had also volunteered to help me prepare desserts for Revital's daughter's bat mitzvah, I was happy. I hoped to hear good news from Nitza.

I met Nitza on my previous visit to St. Louis, when I came to prepare a dessert buffet for my dear friend Revital's housewarming party in St. Louis. She was a small, thin woman with dark, curly hair and a thin face with a permanent sadness, even when she tried to smile.

I got up early in the morning to prepare all the ingredients for the big baking day, so that when Revital's friends arrived to help, everything would be ready and organized.

I was happy and excited to help Revital with the preparations. I had met her after she moved with her family from Israel to Colorado, following a five-year contract as a software engineer with an information systems company, and at the end of the five-year agreement, she received a promotion that involved a move to St. Louis, Missouri. I was happy for them about the coveted promotion, but saying goodbye to her made me sad. It took me months to recover from parting with such a good and genuine friend, who had become our family on the other side of the world. In Colorado, and like any place out of the homeland, the friends you made became your family, 7,300 miles away from your biological family, and if you hadn't made any social connections, you were alone. There was no one who would ring your doorbell, and there was no one to sit with you at the holiday table. In exile, friends and family were a matter of choice.

I quickly got organized, and a few minutes later, I was standing in the kitchen going over all the recipes she had chosen, calculating and preparing the ingredients for the day of baking. Revital, her husband, and the children had already left for work and school, and the well-equipped, modern kitchen was all mine.

The doorbell rang, announcing the girls' arrival. I opened the door, hugged Daphne and Nitza happily, and led them into the warm kitchen.

"I'm so happy to see you, Nitza," I said warmly.

"I'm happy to help. It's the least I can do to thank Revital for all the help she and her friends have given me during this difficult time," said Nitza. "Luckily, the lady I work for on Mondays canceled, so I could come," she added.

"Okay, girls," I called out, "I've got aprons for you. I'm sorry one is long, and the other is a half apron, but that's all Revital could find after she dug through every closet she could."

"Oh, it's no big deal," laughed Daphne as she tied the long apron around her waist. "Come on, let's have a fun day baking in honor of Amit. Yaffa, what desserts are you planning to make?"

"Daphne, I think I'm the only one who calls Amit Amitush, but I've gotten used to it since the day she was born." I smiled.

"Revital loves my babka with chocolate and hazelnuts," I replied as I wiped down the countertop on the kitchen island.

"We're also making date rolls, pistachio and rose pudding, tiramisu, limoncello cake, and five Moroccan jams. The highlight, which Amit asked for especially, will be my chocolate soufflé with layers of mascarpone and fresh raspberries."

"Wow, Yaffa, the desserts sound great. Maybe it will help me gain some weight," Nitza smiled and added quietly, "I've lost even more weight lately."

I approached her and hugged her warmly. "We'll make you gain weight, and we'll bring you back to Israel with your children. Amen."

"Amen, amen," added Daphne, and she also hugged Nitza gently.

"Okay, girls, let's start with the date rolls," I suggested.

I divided a huge bowl between us, and we began preparations. I really hoped that things would work out for the best in Nitza's sad story.

When I met her last time, there were a lot of guests at Revital's house, and the time and place didn't allow us to talk privately for more than a few minutes. In my phone conversations with Revital, I had received updates about her, but I still felt like I was missing a lot. I hoped that on our baking day together, I would hear a little more and prayed for good news in this sad story.

Now, while mixing and kneading the dough, I turned to Nitza.

"Nitza, tell us, what's going on now? What has changed, and how are the children? And what about Mark? We don't really know him at all. I just remember you saying you met him in Israel, right?"

"Did he live in Israel, or did he just come over occasionally for work?" asked Daphna.

"Oh..." Nitza wiped her hands on the blue apron she was wearing, took a sip from the clear glass of water standing next to her, and then looked at us. "I see you're a little confused about the story, so let me clarify it for you. Unfortunately, my situation hasn't changed much, and my heart is broken. I'm living in a nightmare, a daily nightmare."

"I'm sorry to hear that, Nitza," I replied warmly. "I was hoping to hear good news. You must be strong," I added. "For your children. One day, they will understand that you didn't abandon them. Don't stop doing what you can do. Don't give up, for the children."

Nitza nodded and wiped the tears that quickly filled her eyes.

Then she began to speak, and we listened and remained silent, allowing her to share her pain with us.

"Mark, my husband, wanted us to have children right after we got married. In five years of marriage, I gave birth to four children. It was incredibly difficult, but until the fourth birth, Mark was gentle, kind, and supportive, a real gentleman."

"How did you meet?" Daphne asked.

"Mark came to Israel on a work contract with a large company whose headquarters are in St. Louis. He and another engineer came to Israel for a year of work."

Her face became serious, and she paused for a moment, as if weighing her words.

"We met at a pub in Tel Aviv that I liked to go to with my friends," she continued. "Mark was sitting alone at a corner table and kept smiling at me. He looked cute, so I asked the waiter to invite him to join us. Mark agreed and immediately joined our table. He wasn't just charming, he was handsome. I realized he wasn't Jewish, but I didn't make a big deal out of it. I was dazzled by his beauty." She shook her head slightly and smiled sadly, as if to say to herself that now, in retrospect, it was actually difficult for her that he wasn't Jewish. "He was Paul Newman's doppelganger. His green eyes seemed to say, 'Hey, I'm interested,' and his blond forelock... If you had seen him, you would have wondered why the movie world hadn't snapped him up.

"In short, I couldn't take my eyes off him. We talked all evening, and I felt drawn to him like a magnet that refuses to stay away from metal. I didn't even notice that my friend who came with me got bored and left the pub. It didn't bother me, I didn't notice time passed, and by the end of the evening, we were holding hands. I felt and began to believe that there really is a seventh heaven because I was in it."

"Wow, Nitza, that much?"

"Did you ask him a little about his background? If he's in a relationship? Married?" Daphne and I asked as we cleaned the sticky flour off our hands.

"I didn't ask. I was in shock. He was a handsome American, and when he asked me to meet again, I agreed immediately. Two days later, he invited me to dinner at the Montana restaurant in Tel Aviv. Can you believe it? I had never been to such an expensive restaurant, and my heart melted when I saw what a gentleman he was; he picked me up from my house, opened the car door for me, moved my chair at the restaurant, made sure I ordered first, and only then did he order...

"Listen, girls, I wasn't used to that. At the restaurant, he held my hand and caressed it the whole time, the wine flowed freely, and I flowed with the wine to the seventh heaven, which I now realize was a heaven of illusions."

She took another sip of water, and I took the opportunity to suggest to Daphne, who was struggling with the sticky dough on her fingers, that she should add a little flour.

Nitza smiled a little, scooped some flour from the bowl, and continued her story. "A week later, he invited me to the apartment he rented on Dizengoff Street, a very expensive location to rent, with a friend from work and introduced me to him—Sean, another heartbreaker. I asked Mark if Sean was in a relationship, and Mark replied that he didn't interfere in his friend's private life.

"How didn't that seem strange to me even then? After all, they were roommates; how could he know nothing about his roommate's life outside of work?

"Today I realized that I was simply blinded, and when something bothered me, I immediately pushed it aside. I fell head over heels in love, and I'm ashamed to say—even over my own head. I gave him my heart, my soul, and my body. He drove me crazy in bed, and if I'm honest, girls, I didn't even know a quarter of the things he could do in bed.

"After two months of a crazy relationship, going out and eating at fancy restaurants, I told my family about him. My father immediately said, 'But Nitza, he's not Jewish.' My parents are religious and live in a small moshav near Dimona, and the whole thing with Mark really didn't seem right to them. I didn't give up. I showed my family pictures of Mark, told them we were in love, and that I believed I had found the one and only man I had ever wanted. I announced that I was choosing him as my partner for life, come what may! And listen to how amazing it is. On the day I brought Mark to meet my family, it rained cats and dogs the whole way, as if God was signaling something I refused to accept.

"My mother loved his beauty. She took me to the kitchen and said, 'This guy is handsome, Nitza, it's a shame he's not Jewish.' Everyone accepted him politely, but after that visit, my family began trying to convince me to change my mind.

"I cried, screamed, raged, and told them that at my age, I was thirty-four, they couldn't decide for me. And indeed, after six months of a turbulent relationship, Mark took me back to the amazing Montana restaurant, hired a violinist to play for us at our table, and hired a flower seller who came and gave me a bouquet of red roses. Inside was a note with gold lettering: 'Will you marry me?'

"I pinched myself and felt like I was in a real Hollywood movie. Of course, I said yes without hesitation." She took another sip of water and breathed in the aroma of the first date roll baking in the oven. I felt it was a perfect time for a coffee break and some first tastes.

"So how did you get married if he's not Jewish?" Daphne asked a few minutes later. She held the coffee cup I had made for her in both hands.

"Did you go to Cyprus?"

"Oh, no," replied Nitza. "He asked me to find out if we could find a judge to marry us. I didn't know that judges could perform marriages, so I started looking into it. Someone recommended a judge who offered marriage ceremonies without the need for a rabbi, something like a civil marriage, and the judge's secretary arranged for two witnesses to be present when we signed the contract. We got married in the judge's office, and of course, my family boycotted the ceremony.

"I moved in with him in the apartment he rented with Sean and lived in paradise," Nitza continued her story.

"Mark earned very good money, and we allowed ourselves to eat at good restaurants. During the day, I spent time at the beach and with friends, and every day was more fun than the day before. Mark was at work most of the time. Sometimes he would be away for two or three days, usually telling me he was flying to England when it came to work. In retrospect, I know the truth, but back then, I loved him so much and believed every word he said as if it were the absolute truth. No one in the world could have convinced me otherwise.

"When we visited the moshav, my mother served him malawach with hard-boiled eggs and harissa. He loved Yemenite food, but he made no effort to get my family to like him. Once, when I mentioned the possibility of conversion, he got angry and snapped, 'You want me to convert just to make your parents feel comfortable. What if I don't feel in my heart, deep down, that I want to be Jewish?' And that was the end of the conversation about conversion. I understood from his anger and outburst that it wasn't worth mentioning again.

"I went with the flow. Mark told me he'd be happy if we started thinking about children, and that made me happy. One morning, I threw up at home and immediately made an appointment to get checked out. I threw up again in the doctor's waiting room, and after the exam, the doctor told me I was pregnant. How could I not have seen the change in myself? My breasts started to swell, and I felt exhausted. Before, I was a night owl, and suddenly I found myself falling asleep at seven in the evening.

"When I told Mark I was pregnant, he suggested we celebrate again at Montana and invited Sean to join us. Two days later, Mark told me that the company's project in Tel Aviv was ending and that within two months, they would have to return to the company's head-quarters in St. Louis, Missouri, and that same week, we started planning for it at the American embassy in Israel so that I could get to St. Louis with the proper paperwork.

"I was delighted. I thought people try for years to get a green card, and it doesn't work out, and I'm as lucky as can be. Wow. Within a month, I received a resident visa through the American embassy, and that was it, I got my green card and was moving to America. And Mark? He couldn't have been happier."

Nitza sighed and fell silent for a moment. Daphne and I continued to work diligently on the babkas. I noticed that Nitza hadn't touched her dough, but I didn't say a word. Her story was more important than any cake.

"The four children were born in St. Louis," Nitza began again, quietly. "That's exactly what he wanted. I was constantly tired and fat from the pregnancies, and I developed gestational diabetes, but Mark made sure I was treated by excellent doctors. Despite the difficulties, Mark never suggested we take a break between pregnancies, but that didn't arouse any suspicion or feeling of lack of consideration on his part. After Shirley, our fourth child, was born, he asked me to have my tubes tied. He said that four children were enough for us, and I happily agreed.

"When I returned after the surgery, I felt that the atmosphere at home was different. Sean visited us more often, buying gifts for the children, playing with our sons Uri and Danny, and spoiling Michali. I quickly noticed that Mark invited Sean more frequently to stay for dinner at our house. We were financially secure, and Mark's high salary allowed us to order food from good restaurants. Mark would order the food, and Sean would bring it with him when he came over for dinner. It became almost a routine, and still, no red flags went up in my mind.

"In those days, I used to sleep in baby Shirley's room, on a small sofa bed, both to breastfeed her and to allow Mark to sleep peacefully. He worked long hours every day, and I wanted to be considerate.

"One night, I even remember the time, 3:15 in the morning, there was a snowstorm raging outside. I finished breastfeeding Shirley and wrapped her in a flannel blanket. Suddenly, I heard unusual noises coming from our bedroom. I thought Mark was talking on the phone with his office in Australia or England, according to the local time, and it didn't seem unusual because it happened sometimes. I peeked in from a distance, but I didn't see any lights on in the room, and I also heard occasional whispering and the rustling of blankets.

"These noises didn't sound like part of the snowstorm and the winds raging outside. I remember that for a split second, I thought we had a burglar in the house, but how come the alarm didn't go off?

"I put Shirley in her bed and tiptoed toward our bedroom to tell Mark that I was hearing strange noises. I couldn't believe what I saw —my beloved husband, Mark, and Sean, his best friend and roommate in Israel, completely naked, in the throes of sex on my bed, sex in the full sense of the word, understand that however you want!

"Imagine the situation," Nitza cried bitterly, tears streaming down her face and falling into the bowl of flour. "I'm after a difficult birth, with swollen, scratched, and sore breasts from breastfeeding, stitches and bleeding, and swollen hemorrhoids. Shirley is crying, and I'm dazed from lack of sleep. I witness this scene and ask myself what kind of bad dream I'm having.

"I felt my heart beating fast, weakness overcame me, and I covered my mouth so I wouldn't scream. I don't remember how I got back to the baby's room. I lay down on the small bed with my eyes open and stared into space all night, trying to process what I had seen. I don't know where I found the strength to get up in the morning and make food for the children." Nitza sighed through her tears.

"When Mark came into the kitchen and looked at me, I looked into the eyes that once seemed to me the most beautiful in the world and now were cold and narrowed, radiating hostility and evil. Suddenly, Sean also entered the kitchen, clean-shaven and with wet hair after a shower. I looked at both and said quietly, 'I saw you in bed.' Mark and Sean looked at each other. Mark narrowed his eyes even more, came closer to me, looked deep into my eyes, and in a deep, harsh voice said, 'And there's nothing in the world you can do about it.' That news was the opening shot of the nightmare and torment that has been cutting into my flesh every day since..."

I stopped cutting the rolls, which had cooled in the meantime, and looked at Nitza. Extremely thin, a walking skeleton would be a more accurate description, a pale face devoid of joy, sunken eyes surrounded by dark circles that testified to chronic fatigue, her hair faded, dry, and unkempt, that had seen better days, and the smell of heavy smoke wafted from her.

"Three years have passed since that morning," Nitza continued her story, her voice now dry and hollow. "The children have grown up, the judge gave me a restraining order, and I only see the children for an hour every two weeks, under the full supervision of a social worker."

"What?" Daphne burst out in anger and frustration. "How did it get to this point?" I, too, fell silent, unable to find the right words.

Nitza took a sip of water. Her hands were shaking. She touched the pack of cigarettes next to her, and I could see she wanted to smoke, but she had to go outside to do that. Her hand returned to the glass of water.

"Mark went to court, where he managed to convince the judge that I was unfit to raise children, that I was mentally ill, and that at night I talked to myself and sounded really weird, that I was a violent mother, that the children went to kindergarten in torn clothes and with dirty fingernails. He photographed a shirt belonging to Uri, my eldest son, with a stain that wouldn't come out, and photographed Danny after playing in the mud to show how neglected he was. He testified falsely that I beat the children and starved them, and because I forgot to take little Shirley to the doctor, he said that I deliberately didn't want a doctor to see the children and find out that they were suffering."

"But Nitza," I protested, "it's not that simple. Every claim must be proven, you need facts and witnesses for every accusation..."

"Yes, that's right," Nitza sighed, "and he took care of that too. Very well. One day, when I picked up Uri from kindergarten, he slipped in the snow and broke his hand. The judge asked Uri what happened, and Uri replied, 'Mom was talking on the phone, and I was following her, and I fell.' The judge wrote: 'Complete disregard for the safety of young children.'

"When I combed little Michal's hair, and she cried, Mark photographed us and told the judge that I was abusing my daughter. Michal told the judge, 'Mom hurt my head,' and the judge accepted the claim and wrote: 'Abuse of a child.'

"And when Danny came back from school and fell off his bike, and he had bruises on his back, Mark photographed it and claimed in court that Danny didn't get enough training on his new bike.

"And again, the judge accepted his claim and wrote: 'Neglect of safety and complete lack of understanding of the issue of safety on the part of the mother.' And I naively thought that a judge should examine everything thoroughly and not make such a cruel ruling so easily. Who would have thought that even in front of a judge, you must pray for good luck. And these are just a few examples," said Nitza in frustration. "Mark photographed and documented other incidents and even called two close friends of his to the witness stand, who testified that, based on what they saw at home, I am unfit to raise children.

"He told the children that I didn't love them and that I intended to poison them, and that is when I noticed that my son Uri was afraid to come near me. He told his teacher that he was afraid of me, and she reported it to the social worker who supervises his class. All the reports reached the court and led the judge to rule that it was in the children's best interests not to live with me."

Daphne and I exchanged shocked glances. Could this be true?

"At first, I hid everything from my family in Israel," Nitza lowered her gaze and spoke in a low voice. "I was ashamed to admit that I had made such a fatal mistake. They were shocked when I told them. My parents are in pain and broken, and I want to go back to

Israel, but how can I go back to Israel without my children? Why should my children grow up without their mother?" Her voice suddenly broke. "My children are my life. They are not just Mark's children, they are mine too; they are the flesh of my flesh and part of my soul. My parents and siblings told me that if I manage to return to Israel with the children, they will help me with an apartment and food and surround us with love. My family wants to support me, even though I didn't listen to their advice and married Mark. They are willing to forget everything, the anger, the disappointment... The main thing is that I return to Israel with the children. But in the meantime, Mark has issued court orders preventing the children from leaving the United States. My children are growing up in the home of a couple of crooks who planned everything from day one. The crooks got my little angels, my four pure souls. God, give me back my children..."

Nitza burst into heart-wrenching, uncontrollable tears again. Her body shook, and with trembling hands, she took a small box of pills out of the bag she was holding. I rushed to fill a glass with water and hand it to her. Nitza swallowed one pill from the pack, sniffed, and said in a voice choked with tears, "Look at me, I live on tranquilizers. The doctor has given up on me because I tell her the pills don't help me."

She pulled a few more small plastic boxes out of her bag and showed us the different markings on each box.

"These are antidepressants, these are for immediate relief, and these are the sleeping pills I take to fall asleep at night, and these are for my thyroid, which has been damaged by the stress and anxiety I live with every day."

She looked up at the ceiling of the kitchen and prayed in a weak, trembling voice, "Help me get back to Israel, God. How I miss my country. I was so happy there, God. Take me back to my mother's house, take me back to my family, to my four children, so I can raise them there. So, I can take them to the chicken coop, teach them how to feed the chickens and hold the chicks that are born, and my mother will give them seeds to feed the chickens, and I'll let them pet Tilda the cow, and I'll teach them to listen to the foxes that come from the fields every night and try to get into the coop to eat the chickens, and I'll read them stories in Hebrew and let them play with the dough for the Sabbath challah, and I'll let them feed the ducks dry bread-crumbs, and I'll ask our neighbor Zachariah to teach them to ride his horses, and they will help him feed them, and Uri will learn to rake dry hay for the horses, and as I know him, he will tell me that there is not enough food for Tilda and the chickens in the coop, and every morning I will wake them up to come with me to the coop, and together we'll count and collect the eggs the chickens laid during the night. Help me, God, to take my children on a fun picnic on the beach with all my nephews, and my brother Dor will help them build a sandcastle, and my sister Shira will bring her children and we will collect seashells together and Dor will teach Uri how to fish, and my father will teach Danny how to play 'Gogo' with apricot pits like he taught me. Wow, when I was a girl, I was the neighborhood champion at that game..."

"Nitza, stop for a moment, breathe deeply," I hugged her warmly, even though my breath caught in my throat for a moment. The simple and innocent life that Nitza longed for shook me to my core. The way she talked about her childhood memories showed her longing for the simple, happy rural childhood she wanted so much to give her children.

"How are you getting by in the meantime? Financially?" I asked quietly, trying to bring her and me back to the "here and now."

Nitza was silent, took a deep breath, and sighed.

"Barely," she said. "Even though I've been here for years, my English isn't very good, so I couldn't find a job, certainly not one with people. So, I clean houses. The court ruled that I can't get much from Mark because the children don't live with me, so he only pays me a thousand dollars a month.

"The rent for the studio alone is $1,800, and I live on the rest. So, I sit alone in the small apartment I rented and think about the good life I could have had with my children in my country. But my children don't even understand Hebrew, can you believe it?"

"You can talk to them in Hebrew when they come to visit you, can't you?" asked Daphne. "What about reading books in Hebrew? There's a small library in every Jewish kindergarten or synagogue. They'll be happy to lend you books."

"My friends lent me some children's books in Hebrew, but Mark sent them back with the social worker," said Nitza with a sad expression.

"He told the children that learning another language would only confuse them and that they didn't need to know Hebrew anyway, that it was too difficult for them, and that Jews were a sect of ugly people with big noses..."

"What?" exclaimed Daphne. "That's a terrible thing to say to a child whose mother is Jewish! Not to mention that according to their religion, your children are Jewish themselves."

"How did you find out that Mark said such a terrible thing to the children?" I asked, horrified.

"One day, Uri looked at my nose and asked me in all seriousness why I didn't have a big nose. When I asked him why he was asking such a question, he replied that he had heard his father and his friends laughing about how Jews have big, ugly noses. How could anyone expose a Jewish child, or any child for that matter, to such terrible conversations? It breaks my heart..."

Nitza covered her face with her trembling hands and shook her head from side to side. I quickly gathered myself, washed my hands in the sink, and suggested we take another coffee break. Then I put my hands on Nitza's head in a loving embrace and thanked God that no one else had witnessed the drama that had unfolded in the kitchen. I looked at Daphne and felt a little guilty that instead of cheering Nitza up, we had brought her back to all the bitter feelings and difficult emotions she was experiencing these days.

We were silent for a long time. We gave Nitza all the time and space she needed. She gradually calmed down and stopped crying.

Daphne filled another cup with cold water, tore off some paper towels, and gave them to Nitza to wipe her face.

Nitza's phone buzzed in her bag, saving us from the slight awkwardness that had settled in the kitchen. She was startled, shook herself, took it out, and hurried to the living room. I understood that she wanted to talk in private. When she returned a minute later, she excitedly announced that it was a call from her doctor's office, who had agreed to see her today to discuss the pills and the additional help she had requested.

"Will you forgive me if I leave now?" she asked us. "I must go home to shower and change before my appointment with my doctor."

"Of course, Nitza," Daphne and I said together. "Don't worry. Go take care of yourself, and we'll continue here."

We accompanied her to the door and watched her get into her small car and drive away.

"Wow," said Daphne. "What a story. It's heartbreaking, isn't it?"

"Yes," I agreed, "It really is. And she needs iron willpower to keep going. In a crisis like that," I added. "I'm glad we let her talk and listened to her. Revital told me that the whole community in St. Louis is trying to help her in any way they can."

We went back into the kitchen and continued baking until five o'clock, when Revital and the children came home. We went out to help them carry all the huge shopping bags into the house, and while we were doing so, I told Revital about my conversation with Nitza.

"The saddest part of this whole story," Revital responded, "is that those two crooks planned it all in advance."

"What?" I put the bags on the floor and looked at Revital in shock. "What do you mean?"

"Nitza didn't tell you?" Revital wondered. "Mark and Sean have been together for twenty years. Their work contract in Israel was only valid for one year, and the clock was ticking. They had a plan— to 'hunt' a girl who would help them achieve their goal. They wanted children born in America, so that the mother couldn't take them if she wanted to leave. It wasn't really a love story between Mark and

Nitza. She was just a tool for him and Sean to carry out their plan. They lied to her the whole way. As soon as Nitza became pregnant, they began planning their return to America before she gave birth, because they knew that legally they could claim that the children would remain with them if the mother left. The four children are American citizens."

I was stunned. A lot of pieces of the story were now falling into place, except for one thing.

"But still, Revital, how can you be sure that it was all planned?"

"You wouldn't believe how small the world is," Revital smiled. "The cleaning lady at the company where the two crooks work has been there for seventeen years. If anyone can pass gossip from one office to another, it's her."

I nodded without saying a word.

"That's how she knows that Mark and Sean have been in a relationship for many years," smiled Revital.

"When she heard that Mark had returned from Israel married to an Israeli woman, she was surprised. Of course, there was a lot of whispering among the clerks and other employees there, but in America, people don't ask too many questions. As you know, unlike in Israel, privacy is sacred here. No one interferes in the life of another. But one day, the cleaning lady heard the secretaries talking about how Mark's wife had been kicked out of the house by court order, and that the children had stayed with Mark, and Sean had moved back in with Mark, just like in previous years. Then she realized what a plot the two of them had planned, and she felt very sorry for Nitza.

"One Sunday, I took the children shopping at the mall, and when we were done, they asked for pizza. Behind us at the pizzeria sat none other than the cleaning lady with two of her friends, also cleaners at the company, as I understand.

"So, imagine my surprise when I suddenly heard the names Nitza, Mark, and Sean coming from the table behind me, spoken by three gossiping women in English and Spanish. I had my back to them, so I moved my chair closer to hear better, and that's how I heard all the details of Mark and Sean's plot. I was horrified to hear the horrific story.

"But..." continued Revital as she put dairy products into the huge refrigerator, "I have some good news in this whole terrible story. It turns out that Mike Batito, the Jewish millionaire who owns all the shopping malls in St. Louis, heard about Nitza's sad story and asked Erica Cohen, the Missouri governor's slick lawyer who never loses a case, to take on Nitza's case.

"He'll cover all the legal fees. Erica agreed to take the case to help Nitza return to her family in Israel with her children."

I bent down to pick up the empty shopping bags and hoped with all my heart that Erica Cohen would help Nitza.

In the end, all Nitza wanted was to find a loving partner and start a family that could give her children the happy childhood she had growing up in Israel.

But the path she chose to achieve her goal led her to pain and suffering. Only in the end did she realize that everything she really wanted was right there, in her homeland, but she chose not to see it.

SEVEN
CHAMIN

TELL ME, who invented this heavenly delicacy called "Moroccan Chamin" (also called Defina or Schena), and how was it related to raising children? (and if you are already getting excited, all the recipes mentioned here are from my book—*Sephardic Balabusta Shares Tasteful Treasures* on Amazon or Bookpod in Israel)

I grew up in a Moroccan Jewish home where soul food was served, succulent delicacies seasoned with artistry worthy of the name, in the best tradition of Moroccan cuisine.

First courses have always been arranged in a "military formation" of colorful salads, jostling each other so as not to fall off the laden table—the playful winks sent my way by the red matbucha bowl (slow cooked tomato salad), from which sprouted garlic cloves swimming in a sea of cooked tomatoes, lined with olive oil, or the carrot salad that never disappoints my guests with its sweet and spicy flavor, and the beet salad seasoned with vinegar and aromatic cumin, and how could I forget the assortment of salads with pickled, smoked, or red-sauce-drizzled eggplant? My mouth is already watering. But it was always my mother's Moroccan cholent/Chamin that captured my heart, and I waited for it from Saturday to Saturday.

Many years have passed since then. Our daughters, Inbar and Aviv, grew up in America and adopted many different foods from the region, especially Mexican food from Colorado's big neighbor to the south, but they also adopted many dishes from the Middle East. We, too, have been exposed more to other foods and flavors, such as healthy Thai food and spicy Indian food, because how can you say no to a dish of vegetables in coconut milk and curry?

With all that, we never gave up on the taste of Moroccan Chamin. The brown dish filled every room in our house with the intoxicating, sweet aroma of food baked at a low temperature for a long time. I have never had greater pleasure than treating my family, friends, and acquaintances to authentic Chamin whenever they asked for it.

———

It was Wednesday afternoon. I was immersed in checking the weekly Hebrew tests when the phone rang. First, I was reluctant to answer, but when the ringing continued, I turned my head and answered. How could I not? It was my Inbar.

"Hi, Mom, how are you?"

"Hi, sweetie, everything's fine. How are you?"

"Everything's normal." I could hear her smiling. "I'm here in the cafeteria having lunch with my friends, and as usual, they're all complaining about the traditional 'fresh 15' (the greasy, fattening food served in the cafeteria, which causes students to gain fifteen pounds in their first year of school). They want real, home-cooked food. I told them about our dish called 'Saturday's meal that's cooked for twenty-four hours,' and since then, they've been bugging me to let them try it. So, I invited them over to eat your cholent. What do you say? Are you sure I'm not putting a huge burden on you?"

"Of course it's fine," I replied immediately and happily. "That's wonderful. When would you like to come?"

I must admit, making cholent always reminded me of long flights to Israel. The excitement of deciding to go, booking tickets, driving to the airport, waiting and waiting, boarding the plane and flying, and then remembering and saying to ourselves, "Wow, we forgot how long and complicated the trip is."

That was what happened to me with cholent. I decided to make it, thinking excitedly about the taste and aroma of my favorite dish. Then I buy the ingredients, chop, peel, wash everything, and imagine the taste the whole time. I make that sweet meat log that I love so much, and for those who don't know and have never tried them, this is a meat log with more spices and lots of nuts, and tastes and smells that are hard to resist. It cooks in the cholent pot, and in the morning... Oh, how delicious, and it melts in your mouth. And so, throughout the night, the contents of the pot slowly cook and send aromas throughout the house, waking me up more than once.

I get up at least twice in the middle of the night to check that there is enough water in the large pot, and in the morning, when I am tired from my nighttime checks, I remember that I am also hosting guests for lunch and wonder how I forgot that you don't sleep half the night when you are preparing this kind of food. Not to mention that you can't open a window in the kitchen or dining room to air out the house, because if it's cold outside or snowing, it will let cold air in. We're in Colorado, remember?

Early Saturday morning, I walked into the kitchen. I took in the smells of chicken and meat that had spread everywhere after cooking for ten hours. Add to that the garlic heads I had tucked into the pot, which had turned into a sweet garlic jam, and the cloth bag containing wheat berries seasoned with dried chili peppers, oil, and spices, which were now soft, plump, and well-baked. I took the pot out of the oven, placed it on the counter, and opened it carefully. A wave of aroma wrapped my nose. I carefully turned over the sweet and spicy meat log bag, revealing the chickpeas peeking out from underneath, to help the other side of the meat log cook well, and moved aside a few large bones.

Then I pulled a brown egg and a half-cooked potato from the bottom of the pot. My special treat on Shabbat, when we have cholent, I sat down at the table, cut the potato into small squares, and mashed the hard-boiled egg on top. It had a deep, dark-honey color that only baked food could give it, and that you couldn't get in any other dish except Moroccan cholent. I sprinkled salt and pepper on everything and enjoyed my little plate of heaven all by myself.

Inbar and her friends arrived at noon on Saturday, and suddenly the house was filled with the voices and laughter I had missed so much. Since our daughter grew up and moved into the dorms at Colorado State University, the house had been quieter, and there had even been times when I felt it was too quiet. I missed the mess, the gatherings, and the laughter that filled the house when Inbar's friends came to visit, and which now, of course, filled her room at the university.

I looked at Rafi, who was standing next to me in the kitchen, busy uncorking a bottle of fine red wine. He smiled in response to my glance. We were both thinking the same thing—how wonderful it was that Inbar was coming home and filling the house with her presence.

When we sat down at the table, I served each of her friends a large plate filled with all the components of the Chamin/cholent, and I enjoyed watching them wipe the brown, honey-like sauce I had scooped from the bottom of the pot with slices of challah bread.

Two of the girls had never heard of this special dish, and two others had heard of it but never tasted it. It was interesting to see how the cholent filled them with positive energy, a love for new foods, excitement, and joy, all before they even knew the history of this amazing dish.

Jackie and Julia were both of Ashkenazi descent, but they were unfamiliar with cholent, which is the Ashkenazi community's version of the Moroccan Chamin. At their homes, cholent was never prepared. Eileen and Katie were not part of the Jewish community and had never heard of "Shabbat food" cooked for twenty-four hours.

"This is so delicious, I can't stop eating it," said Jackie, her mouth full of the sweet and spicy meat log.

"How do you make something so delicious, Miss Yaffa?"

"Mom, you have the recipe in your cookbook, right?" asked Inbar.

"It looks really complicated to make this tamin," said Eileen, nibbling appetizingly on the bone marrow.

"Not tamin," laughed Inbar. "Eileen, listen, it's Ch-m-i-n," she corrected her, and everyone giggled.

"Chamin or tamin, give us chamin, chamin or rock and roll, give it to us, no questions asked..."

The girls started singing as they clapped their hands on the table in unison, each singing in a different tone and moving in their chairs in rhythmic dance movements. The energy of the young people was contagious, and Rafi and I joined in, clapping our spoons and forks to the beat. We sang and laughed until tears streamed from our eyes.

"Look what good food does to people," Rafi laughed.

"Sorry, Mom, you know my friends," teased Inbar, "they're all crazy."

"Don't worry," I replied with a smile, "you know I'm used to your laughs and giggles."

"But really, please, Miss Yaffa, what is the history of this delicious dish?" asked Kate, scooping up a spoonful of spicy wheatberries.

"Oh, yes," said Julia with her mouth full, "I also want to know who invented this delicious dish. Is it typical only of Morocco?"

"This recipe is the same one my mother, who is from the Jewish community of Moroccan descent, used to make at our house," I explained. "Every community makes cholent in a different way, but what they all have in common is the long cooking time."

"So, what's the idea behind cooking on Shabbat? I thought that people who observe Shabbat aren't supposed to cook on Shabbat, right?" asked Eileen, crushing one of the baked garlic cloves, which had turned into sweet garlic jam, and spreading it on a warm, soft potato.

"You're right," I replied, "but Jews from different communities found a solution to that, too. They found that if you start cooking on Friday before Shabbat begins, you can leave the dish on the stove until Shabbat ends and still observe Shabbat. That's why the cooking is so slow and long. Hence the common sense, 'I continued, pouring myself some more red wine,' to cook over a very low heat so that the food doesn't burn, and the results are what you're eating here today."

"Smart," Kate said, biting into a juicy chicken leg. "Hey, Eileen, try the chicken," she added, "it's so tender, a real delicacy!"

"Girls, you can see I made a lot, and you mustn't leave any leftovers," I laughed when I saw that the pot was still half full.

"Hey, Miss Pretty, me, me, and me too, we'll take the leftovers," the four girls raised their hands immediately.

The playful group finished the meal with a fresh fruit salad.

At four o'clock, the girls thanked me with warm hugs and a personal promise from each of them that soon I would receive photos of a similar dish they would prepare in the small kitchen of their university apartment in Boulder.

I took a deep breath and hugged Inbar warmly.

"How about you stay until tonight?" I asked, looking into her green eyes.

Inbar shook her head. "No, Mom, I can't. I must go back to studying. I have an important test on Monday morning."

"Inbar," I tried to insist, "let your friends go without you, and we'll drive you back to the university in the evening."

But Inbar wouldn't agree. She gave me another kiss and said warmly, "Mom, I'll be back in two weeks, don't be sad."

She put on her short denim jacket and headed toward her friends, who were already waiting in the car with the engine running. I waved goodbye, blew her kisses, and closed the door behind her. In the dining room, Rafi was still sitting at the table, sipping his cup of tea.

"It's nice that Inbar brought them," he said when I sat down next to him.

"Yes," I replied with a sigh, "it's just a shame she couldn't stay a few more hours."

Suddenly, I felt as if a feeling of emptiness and heavy sadness was spreading inside me.

The day, which had been happy and fun, disappeared and was forgotten, leaving its place to something else, something sad and already filled with longing.

Rafi took another sip of his tea, then got up and began clearing the table. I looked at the chairs that were now empty, poured myself some more tea, and added a few fresh mint leaves to my large cup, and suddenly, without warning, my eyes filled with tears, and I burst into uncontrollable sobs.

Rafi heard the crying and ran quickly from the kitchen to the dining room. "Yaffa, what's wrong? What happened?"

I covered my face with both hands, my body shaking, and let the tears wash over me. It hurt that Inbar was gone, and I couldn't stop crying even if I wanted to.

Rafi sat down next to me and held my hands gently.

"Why did she have to go, why?" I cried into the cloth napkin he handed me. "We don't see her very often, and all I wanted was for her to stay a little longer, just for a little while. Our big house was full of people, voices, and laughter, and it made me feel so good," I continued to sob.

"Yaffa, calm down," Rafi asked in a soft voice. "You can't ask Inbar to stay here with us when she can't. She has commitments; she has to prepare for her exams. You want her to do well in college, don't you?"

"Yes, yes, Rafi, of course I know all that, and I completely understand. I just wanted to feel her a little longer. I miss her so much. When she's not here, and then when she comes, I want her for a little longer. What, I can't ask that?"

Rafi leaned back in his chair, and we were both silent for a few long minutes. Then he said, "I want to remind you of something you may not have considered. Many years ago, we also left our parents.

When we decided to leave Israel and our family and move to the other side of the world, we didn't consult with them or ask their opinion. Remember? We just told them that on March 27, 1990, we were moving to America."

I listened to him as I wiped my face and blew my nose. Slowly, the crying subsided. Rafi refilled my cup of tea from the copper kettle and continued to hold my hand. "Here, drink some more. You had an exciting day and laughed a lot with Inbar and her friends. Let's not end this good day on a sad note."

The words "sad note" wrapped me in my thoughts, and the tears began to flow again silently.

"We always knew that the day would come when the girls would leave home," Rafi continued in his calm voice. "I remember how hard it was for you when Inbar chose to study far from home. We must keep reminding ourselves that it's her choice and respect her decision, just like our parents accepted our decision to leave and didn't try to change our minds. They didn't want to make us sad or to burden us with guilt or insecurity. They didn't object to our leaving because they understood that everyone has dreams, and when we wanted to fulfill our dream of going out and seeing the world, learning about other ways of life, and establishing ourselves financially in the land of unlimited opportunities, they didn't cry in front of us when we told them we were leaving.

"They didn't try to play on our conscience to make us feel bad and change our minds, and they didn't refuse when we asked to leave boxes in their attic, even though I'm sure their hearts were breaking as they helped us pack. And on the last day before our flight to Colorado, they didn't break down in heart-wrenching tears. They waited until we left, holding back all their sad and difficult feelings."

"My mother sprinkled some salt on us," I muttered with a half-smile. "Luckily, it's a custom she brought with her from Morocco."

"And my mother, instead of saying 'bye and have a good trip,' prayed and smiled and blessed us until we disappeared into the road," added Rafi, "but then they went home, and I'm sure she sat quietly in the kitchen and shed tears and asked herself when she would see us again."

"Right," I sniffed. "She must have been so sad…"

"And think about how your mother and my mother felt when we had children on the other side of the world. They weren't here to see them grow up, they didn't live here to spoil their granddaughters and make them hot soup when they were sick, or enjoy Friday night dinners together, and those are just two examples."

I shook my head. I knew all this, but most of the time I just preferred to repress it and ignore it. Rafi continued, "Did you think about how much we hurt our parents when we left and cut ourselves off from them and their world? Because that's exactly what we did. We cut ourselves off from them, from our siblings, from our immediate and extended family, from our friends, and from everything we had, and that was a part of us. Sure, there were those who were excited for us and happy, but if you ask me, our parents were deeply saddened. So now, Yaffa, you feel exactly what they felt when we left. The pain of a child leaving, almost complete abandonment. And everything we did after that was 'throwing them a bone', and I mean that bluntly, because that's exactly what it was. We 'threw them a bone' in the form of a visit to Israel once every three or four years, once every two years, and in the best case, once a year. And unfortunately, the 'best case' only happened in the year when someone died.

"So yes, we are now experiencing what our parents experienced, in a slightly different context. It's true that Inbar left to study at university, but even if she comes home after she finishes her degree, one day she'll leave for ten other reasons, and we must accept that and let her spread her wings and fly. Remember Arik Einstein's song 'Fly, Little Bird'?"

I nodded again, and tears welled up in my eyes. He was so right. "All I'm saying, my beautiful girl, is that sometimes you don't know how strong you are until the moment comes when being strong is the only choice you have. And our mothers, simple but warm and wise and with the right instincts, understood this before we did and let us choose how and where we would live our lives, whether it suited them or not. So now, my dear, it's your turn. Now you're the one who must be strong and let the girl live her life the way she chooses and where she chooses, even if it's hard for you and even if you miss her. In the end, you must support her because it's the only choice you have," Rafi concluded.

EIGHT
WEDDING

WITH A WEAK AND TREMBLING HAND, I hung up the phone and placed it on the island between the kitchen and the living room. Tears streamed down my face, and my eyes stung from prolonged crying. I felt I had to sit down. As if in a fog, I walked slowly, dazed, toward the yellow armchair in the living room. When I reached it, I was suddenly overcome by weakness throughout my body and reached out to steady myself. I took two deep breaths to help me catch my breath and sat down. *I'm alone*, I thought, *I'm alone at home at one of the hardest moments of my life.*

I covered my face with my hands and burst into heart-wrenching tears, like someone who had received the worst news imaginable and was mourning a precious loss, and shook my head from side to side, unable to believe that this was happening to me.

Many minutes passed as I sat alone, sobbing, trying to process the news my daughter had given me. The salty tears wet the thin shirt I was wearing and dripped onto the armchair. I tried to get up to reach the box of tissues that was always kept on the kitchen island. I placed my hands on the smooth wooden armrest of the chair, but I couldn't get up. My body betrayed me; I had no strength, and my hands fell back onto the chair. The weakness overcame my whole body until I could no longer move, a feeling of solid stone passed through my hands, and my fingers refused to move. I felt as if two metal pincers were holding my hips tightly, preventing me from moving right or left. Hysterical crying overtook me like a tormented child unable to control himself.

The armchair I was sitting in was right next to the west window, which faced our neighbors, the Farrell family. Through my tears, I saw Miss Beverly's head busy in the kitchen, and the smell of the chicken roasting in mustard that Miss Beverly usually made for lunch. I paused for a moment and hoped she hadn't heard the shouting and my crying on the phone with Shira. Damn, our window really was too close to her house.

In the background, I could hear Alvin, the neighbor downstairs, walking down the building's entranceway and talking on his phone, trying to explain to someone how to get to him. I tried again to get up to close the window and pull the curtain aside.

I was embarrassed. I didn't want any of the neighbors to see me in my moment of weakness, but my efforts to get up ended with me collapsing on the cold living room floor, as a stream of my tears flowed freely. I couldn't control myself. The trembling that ran through me wouldn't stop. I wrapped my arms around myself to warm up a little and tried to stretch my neck upward because I felt the need to breathe deeply again, but I still felt a lump in my throat. I lifted my face up to open and expand my windpipe and shouted at the ceiling, "Why? Why?!"

I remembered that only once in my life had I cried so hysterically, and that was when they called from Israel on that cursed weekend and told me that my dear brother and best friend had died suddenly. The news of his death broke me to pieces, and I remembered that something inside me died at that moment. It was a pain I had never experienced before, a pain I didn't even know existed, like a stone stuck in my throat, a burning regret in a burning pain that refused to go away. That was how I felt now, after my conversation with Shira.

The tissue box, far away from me, frustrated me even more. I was wet from tears and snot, and feeling disgusted with myself, I desperately wiped my face on my shirt. I had no strength left for anything, and who cared about a wet and sticky snot during the pain and sorrow I felt at that moment.

The lump in my throat grew, and I felt the stone stuck there pressing hard on my windpipe.

Oh no, I thought in terror, *I'm scared. It's getting harder to breathe.*

The pain cut through me like the sharpest knife in the world. I was in pain because of the pressure in my throat, and I was in pain because it was hard to breathe, and I was in pain trying to digest the bitter news, but I wanted to breathe deeply so I could cry more, so I could break down, let out my frustration, refuse to accept reality, deny the news I had received, and I continued to cry with an intensity that even I couldn't understand.

Why am I so cold? I suddenly thought, *I'm terribly cold.* A chill wave covered me and penetrated the slits that the knife had carved into my body, deep cuts through flesh and bone. I was in pain as if there were no tomorrow, and I could no longer remember anything. Everything in front of me turned white, and I couldn't see anything anymore.

I fainted.

A strong, rough, warm, and soothing hand touched me and caressed my face. The touch of a familiar hand. I regained consciousness and recognized my husband's hand, Eli.

"Everything is fine, Sarah, everything will be fine. Thank God, Sarah, you're okay. I was about to call an ambulance."

I shook my head. "You're here, Eli, thank God, there's no need," I whispered.

"Well, thank God, Sarah. God will protect you. Breathe deeply, don't worry, you'll be fine."

"Yes," I whispered.

"Sarah, what happened?" Eli asked gently. "Did you feel unwell?

Was anyone here while I was out? Did someone upset you? You know you shouldn't get upset… with the medication you're taking."

Eli's deep voice calmed me, as always. *I'm not alone*, I thought, and began to remove the wet paper towels Eli had placed on my face. I grabbed one paper towel and crumpled it tightly in my hand.

Eli stood up for a moment, staring at the window that faced the Farrells' house. He scanned the neighbors' windows, especially Miss Beverly's, which were directly across from our living room window.

With red, puffy eyes, I looked at him and said nothing, then scanned the room. I was home, and my sense of security slowly returned. I saw that I was lying on the big yellow couch. I touched my face, which was damp, and noticed that my hair was wet from the water. I brushed my hair away from my face and touched the shirt I was wearing. It was damp with tears and water and stuck to my body like sweat. On the living room table was an almost-empty bottle of water, and I realized that Eli had sprayed water on me to wake me up.

On the coffee table in the living room was a large paper towel soaked in water, and next to it was my bottle of Estée Lauder. That was it, now I understood why I smelled perfume. Eli brought the bottle of perfume close to my nose again and looked at me with a serious and worried expression.

"Saralina, smell it some more, it'll do you good. Come on," he tried to lift me up, "try to sit up if you can. I want you to drink some more water. Come on, try to sit up, my Saralina. God bless you. What happened? Tell me."

I moved my body with some effort and sat down half-reclined on the yellow sofa. Eli sat down next to me and gently brushed off all the wet hair from my face. Oh, how I needed those warm, familiar caresses at that moment, and he still didn't know…

"Come on, drink some water," Eli urged me encouragingly. "Maybe you're just dehydrated?"

I looked at him, my eyes still stinging from crying. I knew that in a moment I would tell him the thing he didn't want to imagine in his worst and saddest dreams, and I remembered the famous phrase we say to each other every time we are confronted with another consequence of the fateful decision we made thirty-four years ago—to leave Israel, "Every decision has its advantages and its price."

I lowered my eyes. "No, Eli, I didn't dry up. Shira called from New York," I added in a whisper, my eyes still downcast and fixed on the gray carpet covering the living room floor. I took a deep breath, preparing myself for the painful storm that was about to come.

Eli's expression changed suddenly, his face contorting with concern. "Our Shira? Oh no! What happened?"

"Shira's fine," I whispered, shaking my head. "She's fine." My throat felt dry, and just the thought of sharing the news with Eli made me tremble again. I brushed a strand of wet hair from my face.

"So, what happened, Sarah? Does it have something to do with Shira? Come on, tell me," Eli urged me impatiently.

"Shira," I said in a choked voice, and my heart began to pound again. *Oh no, God, help me hold on,* I prayed.

"Our Shira wants to get married," I whispered in a pained, strained voice that I could barely get out. I took a deep breath, just like they taught me at the hospital the last time I had a nervous breakdown. They prescribed me medication for depression and anxiety. My chest rose and tightened as I took two more deep breaths, then I gathered my courage.

"Shira called to tell us that her boyfriend Kevin proposed to her," I whispered sadly.

Eli grimaced as if it were no big deal and said mockingly, "That's it? That's why you're crying like that?! So, what if he proposed? Shira will never agree; she knows exactly how we feel about it. There's nothing to talk about. Kevin isn't Jewish, and our daughter won't marry a non-Jew. Never."

I looked at him and said nothing. A few seconds passed, and the expression on his face took on a questioning look. It was clear that he was waiting for my confirmation that this was indeed Shira's response to the marriage proposal. When he saw that I wasn't responding, his fears crept into his voice, and his expression changed to that of someone watching a nightmare. His face became serious, his eyes narrowed, and his lips trembled.

"Shira said yes. No, it can't be. It was just a causal relationship, right? Our Shira is intelligent and educated and has so much more to offer a suitable Jewish husband."

Eli raised his hands and looked at me again questioningly, waiting for my confirmation.

"She said yes," I whispered in a choked voice.

"We spoke just a short while ago, and I reminded Shira of our opinion on the assimilation of Jews in America," Eli continued, ignoring my answer, as he opened the bottle of cologne again and brought it close to my face.

Memories flashed through my mind of the many conversations we had had at home on the subject, between ourselves or with friends whose children or other children we knew had married non-Jewish spouses. It had always been important to me that Shira be present during these conversations, for fear that she might one day have a non-Jewish boyfriend. I used to give her examples from Temple Emanuel, the Reform synagogue where I had been teaching for 33 years, which had a school for Hebrew and Judaism, and I described to her the complex, complicated lives of families in which one spouse was not Jewish. I always emphasized to her that the highest divorce rate in the Jewish community in Colorado was due to intermarriage between Jews and non-Jews. At least half of the students in my class came from assimilated families, and they told me about the frustrations they experienced and the choices they made every day at school, especially during the holidays, whether Jewish or Christian. These students felt divided and confessed to me that they didn't really know where they belonged. They heard their parents arguing every Sunday about whether to take their child to Temple Emmanuel to study Hebrew and Judaism because their Jewish mother wanted them to absorb some of her Jewish history or go with their Christian father to hear the weekly sermon at the church where he grew up.

I told her about the crises, difficulties, and arguments that arose with a partner who understood nothing about Judaism, and that he was not interested in introducing his children to the roots of his partner. After all, as soon as the first child was born, the problems would begin, and I emphasized to her that if it were a boy, the parents would have to decide whether to have him circumcised. It was possible that the non-Jewish partner would choose to say that he didn't care about any circumcision ceremony, and why on earth would they circumcise a tiny baby, and how cruel it was to hurt a baby who was only eight days old... Why should he care about circumcision? He was not Jewish, right?

It was important to me that Shira understood the consequences of intermarriage, even though, admittedly, at first, you didn't see the difficulties because you were blinded by love and excitement about a new phase in your life. I reminded her again that there was nothing more blind than love, and I spoke from the bottom of my heart when I tried to explain to her that we saw so many mixed couples who ended up becoming enemies and haters because they came from such different backgrounds. Knowing all the difficulties and suffering, I hoped that my daughter would never experience them, and now it had happened, just as I feared.

"Eli," I began again quietly, "at first, I spoke to her calmly, I really wanted to explain to her that it wasn't simple. Then I asked her to refuse Kevin, but when she insisted on telling me that she was already wearing his ring, I started crying. I didn't have the strength to hear what she was saying to me. I hung up on her and cried and cried until I couldn't hold it in anymore and collapsed."

Eli sat next to me on the couch, slumped over as if his world had been destroyed in an instant. He didn't look at me anymore, and I could see that he was trying to process what I had told him. He muttered to himself, "But why? I don't believe what you're telling me, Sarah. Are you sure she already told him that she agreed?"

I nodded and lowered my head, tears streaming down my face. I wanted to blow my nose and pointed to the box of tissues in the kitchen.

"Can you get me some tissues?" I whispered.

Eli stood up and looked at me. I saw that his eyes were filled with tears. I knew that this would hit him hard. Eli came from a religious family. He was twelve when he immigrated to Israel from Morocco with his family—his parents and nine siblings, of whom only the eldest daughter was married. It wasn't easy for them, but Eli's mother was a kind woman who gave her children everything she could. My family was more conservative than his, but I always found a way to bridge the differences. With a little compromise, effort, and smiles, we got along well throughout our forty years of marriage.

Eli returned with the box of tissues, and as he pulled out three tissues, he whispered, "Sarah, tell me exactly how your conversation with Shira went. Tell me everything from the beginning. What exactly did Shira say to you?"

I took a deep breath, blew my nose, and took another tissue to wipe my face. I moved the hair that was stuck to my face again and took another deep breath as I pulled Eli's hands away.

"Kevin took her out to dinner yesterday at that vegan restaurant, you know, the one she always talks about, 'Three Chairs'. He bought her a dress she had pointed out in the window of a famous Italian boutique, and after she opened the gift and was thrilled with the dress, they went to dinner. Kevin told her that in honor of this special evening, he wanted them to order dessert, even though they never ordered dessert, and when it arrived, he took the ring out of his pocket, got down on one knee, and told her he loved her, that she was everything to him, and proposed to her. And she immediately said yes..."

My crying started again, as intense as before. "Do you understand?" I sobbed, "She immediately said yes, right there, in the restaurant. And he put the ring on her finger, and they kissed, and that was it. She didn't call us yesterday because it was already late at night, and she decided to wait until morning with the 'happy' news..."

Eli got up and started pacing back and forth in the living room. He put both hands on his forehead, and when he spoke, his voice was already high, angry, and trembling with frustration, almost stuttering.

"Sarah, why didn't you call me right away? I'm her father! Why was I not present for this important conversation? Doesn't Shira think I should be part of such a significant conversation?"

After the initial shock, anger began to rise within him. "No, it can't be, I won't allow her to trample on our identity," Eli raged, stamping his foot on the gray carpet.

He paced around the room, muttering angrily, occasionally placing his hands on his sweaty forehead. My heart broke when I saw how hard it was for him. My tears started flowing again, and I covered my face with my hands. Eli stopped walking, came over to me, sat down next to me, and handed me another soft tissue.

"Come on, Sarah. Come on, get up. Wash your face, calm down, and then we'll call Shira. We'll talk to her, and if necessary, we'll drive to New York. What's going on here? Don't we have a right to express our opinion on such an important matter? She's talking about her future, and we don't have a say in the matter? She's all we have, and we want her to have a good future and be happy. We raised her and nurtured her. She had a Jewish and Israeli childhood that many children can only dream of... Where did we go wrong? I don't understand—what did I do wrong?"

Eli stared at me with wide eyes, seeking confirmation of his words. With burning, red eyes, I looked back at him, and silence fell between us for a moment. But I immediately pulled myself together and said, "No, Eli, we didn't do anything wrong. If there's one thing, I'm sure of, it's that we did everything we could under the circumstances. We may have decided to live in exile, but I believe we gave Shira everything a Jewish home can give. Always remember the big holidays we celebrated at home. Remember how much we paid for private Jewish summer camps so that she would be surrounded by a Jewish atmosphere even in the summer. Shira grew up in an Israeli home, not just a Jewish one, and from the beginning, we insisted on speaking only Hebrew with her at home. Ninety percent of her friends are Israeli and Jewish. As a teenager, she even worked at a school teaching Hebrew and Judaism. I don't blame us for her lack of exposure to Judaism. Shira has a more Israeli and Jewish background than any other Israeli born in Colorado." I finished speaking and felt a heaviness and helplessness take over. I tried to get up from the couch but felt weak all over and remained seated.

"Eli," I whispered with the last of my strength, "Shira said she's already made up her mind. She loves him. He makes her feel like a queen."

"A queen?" Eli's voice rose again in anger and frustration. "What kind of queen? Until they start fighting? And what names will he call her when the arguments start? How will he refer to her then? Do you think she'll still be his queen, or will he start calling her names—stubborn as a mule, inconsiderate, a narcissist who only thinks about her own needs... And what will happen when they argue about whether to set the table for Passover or Easter? Or whether to buy mezuzahs for every door in the new house they just moved into, or to put the decorative ceramic cross he received as a wedding gift from his best friend in the kitchen?

"And when their first child is born..." Eli continued angrily, "he'll want to bless him in the water ceremony that all Christians do in church and he'll want his priest to perform the traditional baptism of the baby boy or girl in water blessed by the priest, thereby officially declared a Christian, or when he starts arguing with her at the house of friends who invited them over for a barbecue to eat roast pork, he'll tell her not to insult his friends and ask her to taste a little of the pork out of politeness."

Now I wasn't crying anymore, just tears continued to flow silently from my eyes.

Eli stood facing the window with his back to me and continued talking as if to himself. "And what will he tell her when she fasts on Yom Kippur?" he asked the question without waiting for an answer. "He'll eat his meals as usual and drink his coffee, because Yom

Kippur doesn't interest him at all. He hasn't done anything wrong to anyone, so why should he suffer and fast? And when she dresses up in white to go hear the shofar at the synagogue at the end of Yom Kippur, he'll sit and watch a movie because that's more interesting to him, and what's so interesting about going to hear a horn blown from a deer, and those strange Jews, who blow a horn that belonged to a poor deer who could have been proud of his beautiful horns and instead they cut them off and try even harder to make strange sounds with something that wasn't meant for that at all. Come on, let them go buy a trumpet if they want to blow something so badly. Who knows what thoughts he'll have about our holidays?"

"Eli…" I tried to stop the frustrating monologue.

"What about the traditions of my mother and father and yours?" He turned and looked at me. "Nice, Kevin will surely mock all the things he doesn't understand and doesn't know about the history of the Jewish people. No matter how hard we tried to pass on our family roots to Shira, who's to say he won't take control of her and convert her? How far would she be willing to compromise with him for the sake of peace in the home?

"And what will happen when they have children? I still remember the story you told me, Sarah, about the boy in your class who told you that his mother pays him ten dollars every Sunday, otherwise he refuses to go to Hebrew and Jewish school, and that's how he blackmails her. Or the student who told you how much fun he has because he gets presents both at Hanukkah and at Christmas, because he has a Jewish mother and a Christian father. Can you imagine us going to their house on Christmas morning so the children can open the presents that are under the tree they helped their father put up in honor of the birth of Jesus? And what will Shira tell us then? That there's nothing we can do, that the children know their father is Christian, and she can't stop him from celebrating his holidays too? Can you imagine such a situation? Can you imagine?"

Eli spoke passionately and loudly, and I was already afraid that the neighbors could hear him, because he was almost shouting. I remembered that Miss Beverly, our neighbor, had once called the police because her neighbor, Mr. William, was arguing on the phone with some annoying customer service representative who wouldn't respond to his request for a refund for damaged merchandise. The whole building heard Mr. William's shouting, and to be honest, we also thought something terrible had happened. The police officers who arrived within minutes almost broke down the door to the apartment. Mr. William let them search the entire house to make sure no one was hurt. It was very frightening.

"Shh... Eli," I signaled him to lower his voice.

"Wait, Sarah, I want to see if she left me a message at least," he pulled his phone out of his pants pocket and checked, but no. There were no messages from Shira.

Eli sat down heavily on the yellow armchair next to me and stared into space. For the first time in years—in fact, I couldn't remember when I had last seen him cry so much—his tears flowed freely. I thought that in all our forty years of marriage, the only time I had seen Eli cry was when his mother died. Oh, how he cried then. Every time we mentioned his mother, I saw tears, and the blue eyes that I loved so much in my strong, big man were now gray and red.

"Sarah, how could this happen?" he asked, his voice now quiet, little more than a whisper. "I ask myself what we did wrong. Shira grew up in a Jewish, Israeli home. We may not live in Israel, but our home has always been Israeli in every sense. Shira worked as an assistant at the Jewish school where you teach, went to Jewish summer camp, traveled with Jewish-American teenagers, climbed Masada, placed a note in the Western Wall, and visited the Knesset in Jerusalem. It can't be that all of that didn't mean anything to her. I don't understand," he whispered painfully. "It's my fault, that's it, it's my fault. I didn't instill enough Judaism and love for the Land of Israel in her; I don't know. I guess I didn't do enough..."

He raised his hands again, half in despair and half in prayer, then got up and paced back and forth across the room, unable to believe it, shaking his head from side to side.

Memories of Shira's childhood flooded my mind and images from previous years flashed before my eyes—Shira helping me set the huge Passover table—holidays were always a big affair in our house, which meant 25-45 guests—and we even bothered to move the furniture out of the sunroom to make room for such a large Passover Seder; and Shira writing down the names of all the guests—she always asked to be the one to write down the names of the guests, each next to their chair. And when she decided to become a vegan, she started making matzo ball soup herself, and hers always turned out the best; she read from the Haggadah in Hebrew, and all the guests complimented her on how clearly she read Hebrew, even though she was born in Colorado; I remembered how moved I was and how I cried when she went with students from the Hebrew school to Camp Schweder in the Rocky Mountains, and when she came back full of experiences, she showed us a picture of a Holy Ark inside a tree! Who would have believed that at Camp Schwender's nature camp in the Rocky Mountains, they carved a space inside one of the trees and put a Torah scroll inside it so that the students would have a Holy Ark for Shabbat. And how we missed her when she flew to Israel with Taglit-Birthright and told me how much fun she had, even though it wasn't her first trip to Israel, since we traveled every two or three years to visit family and friends.

The ringing of the phone in the kitchen on the island snapped me out of my thoughts for a moment. I got up quickly, faster than I thought I could at that moment, and answered.

"Shira?" I whispered into the phone and pressed the speaker button so that Eli could hear our conversation.

"Mom," she sounded remarkably calm. "I'm calling to see if you're okay. Have you calmed down?"

Eli took the phone from my hand and spoke into it in an agitated voice. "No, Shira, she's not calm, and neither am I. What do you think you're doing? What disaster are you bringing upon us? We raised you to be Jewish and to love our roots, and you decide to marry a non-Jew? Why do we deserve this? Why?"

Eli's voice was loud, and I could feel his frustration. He didn't wait for Shira to answer and continued, "How can you betray us and the whole family in Israel? You know your grandfather in Morocco was a rabbi and..."

"Dad, listen to me too. Kevin is a good guy. He understands me and respects me, and we love each other very much..."

"We're trying to prevent you from making mistakes," Eli interrupted her. "A smart and intelligent girl like you can't be about to make such a serious mistake, and we're just going to stand by and watch. Forget about love and respect; all that will go out the window the moment you start arguing. What will you do when he wants to go to church every Sunday? And wants you to kiss his priest's hand? And when he goes shopping and tells you that his favorite thing is pork ribs? What will you do then? Will you be disgusted every day by the smell of pork filling your house? And you're a vegan..."

"But Dad, you remember my last boyfriend, you know how he treated me and why I left him," Shira said angrily.

"He had no respect for me, and don't forget—he was Jewish..."

The painful conversation with Shira lasted over an hour. She and Eli argued and fought until they were exhausted. Finally, when Eli hung up the phone, he sat down on the couch, slumped over, and withdrew. We were both left speechless.

I lay down on the couch next to him, my mind racing. Shira was making a mistake, I told myself, Shira was putting herself in a certain situation knowing full well that this was a complex and difficult situation, and if I tried to think ahead, one of the following would happen —Either she would come to terms with her new reality, build a family with Kevin, and it would be a mixed Christian-Jewish family, or she would not be willing to allow anything Christian into her life, which would cause problems in their relationship to the point of separation. It was also possible, I tried to encourage myself that Kevin would compromise, agree to run a completely Jewish home, and give up everything related to his Christian life.

Whatever happened, I decided in my heart, I would not give up my daughter. No matter what happened, I would not punish myself further by cutting off contact with my daughter.

———

Three years had passed since that conversation.

One spring day, I made plans with my friend Carmen, whom I hadn't seen in several months, to go for a walk in the park. The warm afternoon sun had already begun to set behind the Rocky Mountains, casting orange and red streaks across the long ridge line to the west.

Carmen was there at the appointed time, which was what you call American standard time.

Carmen bent down to tie an annoying shoelace on her blue sneakers, and we started walking.

"So, what's new, Sarah?" Carmen asked.

"We're fine," I replied. "I got back from New York on Monday. I stayed with Miri, my childhood friend, whom I told you about. She lives a ten-minute walk from Shira's apartment, which is convenient."

We started walking around the large park, which was crowded with people, but we were absorbed in our walk and tried not to bump into the other walkers.

"How's Shira? How was your visit?"

"A visit full of Jewish content," I smiled. "And Shira says hi. She wanted to know if you're still running marathons."

Carmen stopped walking and looked at me with puzzled eyes. "What do you mean by 'fully Jewish'? Is there something I don't know?"

"I'm just saying that maybe our prayers were answered," I laughed. "Do you remember when we talked about how one thing was clear to us when she married Kevin? We told ourselves that we only had one daughter, and that it was our decision to move to America, so nothing and no one in the world would ever be a reason for us to sever ties with our daughter or sour our relationship with her in any way.

"And as you know, we overcame every difficulty that came our way, yet every day we prayed that Shira would not give up her Judaism, her roots, and the identity she wants to pass on to her next generation."

"Right, now tell me everything in detail," said Carmen as we began our second lap.

"Shira told me that she feels very alone with everything that's going on in Israel these days. The worst part was that she started receiving unpleasant messages from friends she liked, especially her two friends, Ophelia and Margaret. They helped her a lot at her wedding to Kevin, but they didn't support her when the arguments between her and Kevin started, like when Shira didn't want to join him for the traditional Christmas mass at the church he and his parents went to, or when Kevin wanted her to organize an Easter party with costumes for all their friends, and other times when he asked her to celebrate Christian holidays with him and she refused.

"The climax came when Israel went to war in Gaza after the terrible terrorist attack on October 7, and Shira was surprised to receive messages condemning Israel. She realized that her best friends were big haters of Israel and cut off contact with them. Later, she met a Jewish girl named Cheryl on Instagram, and they decided to start a group of Jewish friends so they could create a 'Jewish community' and organize Shabbat dinners and other joint events. When I told her that I was coming on Thursday, she asked if I would be willing to cook some Sephardic dishes that she missed for the new group."

"Of course," laughed Carmen, "who wouldn't want to eat your food?"

"So, I stood in her tiny kitchen for a few hours on Friday and prepared vegan delicacies, and for the first time in Shira's life, she set a colorful and appetizing Shabbat table for her new friends. My heart just melted to see something I'd been hoping for years. With a heart full of admiration and joy, I even forgot how my feet hurt from standing in the kitchen for five hours. And I'll tell you more, I would have stood there for another five hours to make them another Shabbat dinner, just to see her celebrate the start of Shabbat."

"Wow," said Carmen, "I'm happy for you. Especially for your beautiful Shira."

"Thank you," I said, hugging her affectionately. "And what makes me happiest," I added, "is that these were her decisions. She concluded on her own that connecting to her roots has a strong meaning and is important to her. I suppose she probably had some doubts, even if only very slight ones, about her choice to marry a non-Jewish person. But she really loved Kevin, and like many other couples in love, she hoped that love would overcome all obstacles, including different religions. But she did not, and ended up divorcing him after all. Now I pray and hope that her future choices, in every area of her life, will make her happy and at peace with herself."

NINE
A MISSPELLED GREETING CARD

DEAR RIKI

Mali and Yosi

"Here," I announced, "the greeting card is ready. Just sign the check that we included as our wedding gift and put it in this envelope," I added, placing the greeting card on the kitchen table. "And now, I'm going to pick out clothes."

I skipped up the light wooden stairs, humming cheerfully. I wanted to give myself enough time to choose a dress, earrings, a necklace, and matching shoes for Riki and Michael's wedding tonight. How lovely to put on your finery, I smiled at myself in the mirror.

I opened the window in the room and let the afternoon sun stream in, to get the maximum daylight as I chose and matched clothes and jewelry.

A grating creak of wood, reminding me that Yosi still hadn't oiled the hinges of the closet, sounded as I opened the closet door. I pushed aside the heavy winter dresses and browsed among the dresses categorized as "events," wondering what "message" I wanted to convey

113

through the dress I would adorn myself with. In my mind's eye, I already saw all the people who would come to the wedding tonight, including the colorful and diverse Israeli community in Colorado, and of course, their critical eyes. I took out a few pretty dresses from the closet, placed them on the white bedspread, and began my "remembrance parade selection" from the past year.

I was absorbed in my task for many minutes, choosing, smiling, rejecting, and justifying, and as I examined each dress and thought about the events that each dress reminded me of from the past year, I heard Yosi calling me from the first floor of the house.

"Mali, come down for a moment," he requested, and I could hear laughter in his voice. Casually, he shouted, "What a laugh, what fun, wow, you haven't made me laugh like this in ages, Mali. You have so many spelling mistakes. Now, where are you, your goofball? hahaha..."

"What's the matter? I'm choosing a dress for the party," I retorted from the second floor.

"Forget the dress for now. More importantly, you need to see how you wrote the greeting card for Riki. Plenty of spelling errors in Hebrew, plenty... What happened, Mali? Is it dementia at sixty?"

From my position in the bedroom, I thought I wasn't hearing correctly, but then Yosi called again, "Mali, come here, come here for a moment, you have to see this. Your spelling reminds me of a new immigrant from a remote Tibetan village who came to Israel yesterday on an old donkey from the Himalayan peaks."

"Yosi? What are you talking about?" I asked from the staircase while I measured the red dress I finally chose.

"Wow, Mali, I'm not a Hebrew teacher, but I know a little bit about writing. This card is completely messed up. I'm shocked by you. Now, come, you have a lot of work to do here..." and his booming laughter continued to roll in waves.

Oh-oh, I thought. Honestly, I'd been stammering for a long time when it came to my Hebrew spelling.

"Okay, I'm coming to check," I replied. I quickly put on the dress and went downstairs.

"What's wrong with you?" Yosi chuckled affectionately as he zipped up my dress and then caressed my exposed shoulders and squeezed my cheek. "You can't give a greeting card with so many spelling errors. Do you want people to laugh at us?"

"Okay, Yosi. Let's see what you're talking about," I replied reluctantly. I sent him to get ready and sat down at the round table in the kitchen. Warm sunlight streamed through the white blinds, coloring the kitchen and living room in golden-orange hues. I looked at the greeting card I had written, read it again, five times, and was speechless. Indeed, it looked quite terrible. I went to Yosi's office and took out an English-Hebrew dictionary, brushed off the dust that had accumulated on it (and it just showed me how long I hadn't bothered to check my Hebrew spelling), and checked the first few words I had written on the greeting card. It was crazy, unbelievable, and perhaps "bizarre" better defines what I felt at that moment. I couldn't believe the number of errors I found in the first paragraph. Sadness and shame overwhelmed me. What happened to me? Seriously, it was terrible.

How embarrassing and shameful, I thought, that was how I intended to give the greeting card? Full of errors? How did this happen to me? I, who used to correct everyone's spelling mistakes, had reached a point where I needed to verify and use a dictionary when spelling each word according to the correct Hebrew grammar. Honestly, I was ashamed of myself. It was a moment of self-criticism, a stinging blow that shot shafts of shame into my most sensitive parts. Suddenly, I was no longer the Mali with self-confidence bordering on arrogance when it came to writing in Hebrew. After all, when we lived in Israel, I gave private Hebrew lessons while Yosi was studying at the Technion, and we needed additional income because Yosi worked as a gas station attendant for two days on the days he did not study, and did not receive a large salary. To my delight, there was a great demand for my private lessons, both because I did not charge exorbitant prices and because it was fun to learn with me.

"Let's begin," I said to myself, reluctantly, and reread the card again. I couldn't believe I forgot how to spell basic Hebrew words. I wanted to bury my face in the ground and hope that no secret agent filmed me writing this illiterate greeting card.

"Yosi, how did this happen to me?" I asked him when he returned to the kitchen, wearing tailored gray pants and a white linen shirt. He looked so good. "Unbelievable that I forgot my Hebrew language so completely. Shame and disgrace. I've really heard from people who have lived here for many years that suddenly it's hard for them to express themselves in Hebrew, but I always thought that was far away from me, and not relevant at all. It was always 'their problem,' not mine. And now I can't believe this is happening to me, too. I never thought there was even a shred of truth to the idea that Israelis living abroad start to forget the Hebrew language and begin forgetting how to spell Hebrew words correctly."

"Mrs. Mali," Yosi smiled, "why are you so surprised? You live only in English—you work in English, you teach only in English, you correct exams only in English, you shop only in English, you read everything only in English—from pretty gossip in magazines to recipes, accounts, and books, you chat on the phone only in English, you sing songs with your neighbors in English, you watch local news in English, and even scold the president you dislike in English, and let's not forget—you gossip with your American friends in English. So how will you remember your Hebrew, sweetheart?"

"But still, what happened to my first language?" I replied to him with pain. "Yes, we've lived in Colorado for decades, and life demands that we live in the common language here, and what can you do if the common language here is not Hebrew? It's English, I can yell at myself as much as I want and instruct myself to write in Hebrew and read only in Hebrew, but that doesn't solve the problem. It's almost impossible. After all, there are no Hebrew books here! Not in the local library, nor in the popular bookstore Barnes & Noble, nor in that legendary old store Tattered Cover, nor in the Jewish synagogue libraries here in Denver. So, if you haven't brought books from Israel, which take up half your already limited luggage weight, you won't have any Hebrew books, and how many times can you reread the same book just to 'practice the language'? And if you don't put an ad on Facebook that you're willing to be the 'vacuum cleaner of the small Israeli community' here, you won't be able to 'suck up' Hebrew books or exchange them with other Israelis.

"Of course, you can order Hebrew books on Amazon or other sites, but then you'll pay for shipping, before you realize that the selection of Hebrew books available on the sites doesn't always contain the type of books you want to read. So what? Do I have to change my book preferences just to buy books that Amazon offers? What happened to freedom of choice and personal taste?"

Yosi was silent, and I continued with vigor, "Perhaps I'm actually starting to become senile, and that's the reason for the spelling mistakes? Who knows? But I'm only sixty, is that it? Are the good times over? What do you say? Should I make an appointment with Dr. Berman and tell him I've forgotten my Hebrew?"

"Mali, calm down," Yosi said, noticing that I was drifting into the depths of frustration. "Just sit still and try to write the greeting card again," he added, quietly leaving the kitchen to give me the time and space to cope with my frustration. But I didn't calm down, and thoughts raced through my head. What was happening to me? It couldn't be that I, Mali Cohen, who was so proud of my writing, I, who was nicknamed "Bookworm" because my face was always stuck inside a book—I, who wrote Yosi's entire final project thesis for the Technion at the end of his degree (and how he flaunted the 95 he got with blatant arrogance, and danced on the table in class)—I no longer remembered how to spell simple words in Hebrew?

All I needed was for Yosi to tell everyone about this today at the party, a tormenting thought crossed my mind. And I knew him. I knew he'd tell. It would just give him material for jokes, another reason for him to amuse the guys...

This thought gave rise to the next one—could it be that Yosi was playing me? Maybe the devil wasn't so terrible, and some of the words were spelled correctly? In any case, I must check them very thoroughly, because if he was right, and I didn't correct all the mistakes, imagine all the persistent critics who were just looking for where else they can criticize something. And what would Riki think of me? She'd certainly ask herself what I was smoking when I wrote this greeting card, and right now, I wanted to strengthen my bond with her, and this wedding party was my opportunity to show her what a great friend I was.

So, I couldn't afford to make even a single mistake, and that started with the groom's name. Now, what was his name? Ah, Mica-hael. No, I was wrong, Michaeel. No, that was not good either. Wait, how did I spell his name before?

MICHAEL. Finally, I spelled his name correctly. I was not some idiot who didn't understand anything, but I was a serious goof-up, or how did they teach me on my last trip to Israel? You had to say—a goof-up to the max.

So come on, let's get to work, open a dictionary, Mrs. Mali, or as of today, "Mrs. Malili" because I truly deserved to lash myself a bit about this. Here I began, with extreme attention:

"Dear Riki"

Mali, was the Hebrew language important to you? Then, with blood, sweat, and tears, restore your first language to yourself. It was no one's fault that you rejected the Hebrew language and prioritized the English language. You left Israel of your own free will... but don't leave your original language too.

And you chose to live in Colorado, and one of the things that happened when you don't use a language was... a surprise, you lose/forget the language. And don't forget, it was your choice.

"Food"

Hey, Mali, what did you think? Even your grocery list wasn't written in Hebrew. You went to the supermarket with a weekly grocery list in English, and when you ordered food at a restaurant, you ordered in English. So don't complain to anyone about forgetting your Hebrew. It was your choice, too.

"Crazy Escapes"

Didn't you see who was running away here? Did you know you have such courage? You ran away from your mother tongue. No longer did you feel the sweetness of the language you grew up with and loved and were proud of. You chose to go into a world of another language, in this case, English. And here, too, you could only blame yourself. This was your choice, too.

If you wanted to experience living in a divided world, you succeeded! And the medal you received? It was for first place in forgetting your first language. How was it?

Language loss was just one of the losses you've experienced following your decision to leave your country. It was hard to maintain a language when you didn't use it. Your native language has become a secondary, forgotten, hidden somewhere deep inside you, crying to come out, to express itself, to rekindle its light and beauty. Now that you were losing it bit by bit, and this, too, was your choice

"Moved by Emotion"

After four decades of not speaking Hebrew, you found yourself moved and stirred, and you did not even pay attention to it. Remember that in life, everything has a price, and here was the price of choosing a language other than your native tongue. But this, too, was your choice.

"When We Estimated the Magnitude of Change"

There were times in life when it was difficult to estimate the magnitude of the change, its intensity, and its consequences. When you choose to live in another language as part of your new world, you consciously or unconsciously push your native language to the side and adopt another. You, who chose and forced yourself to live in a world of less clear self-expression, participation in conversations accompanied by insecurity, hesitant comprehension, all because of the lack of a full vocabulary like your first language, and a fuzzy understanding of others. While your English improved more than the

English you had when you were in Israel, forty years later, you are a "native English speaker," and that, too, was your choice.

"And We Criticize You a Lot"

What, Mali? Were you a little self-critical? How could that be? After all, you chose to live in a divided world! I have news for you; many things in life were a matter of choice, including the choice you made decades ago. No one chose for you; this was your choice, too.

"And We Criticize You with Great Severity"

Remember that every choice has a degree of selfishness? Or mostly selfishness, because let's remind ourselves that over forty years ago, your goal was to reap the first fruits of dollars in daily life in America. You wanted to start a business and become a millionaire who harvested the first fruits from the trees in your garden, even during the fall season, according to your theory, because dollars grew on trees over there. Right? So what? Were you disappointed by the barren harvest of the first fruits of dollars? No big deal. This, too, was part of your choice.

"And Know That Michael Will Support You"

You will need a lot of strength and patience, Mali, to help yourself overcome all the mistakes you are admitting to now, because of your decision to leave your country and your language, and your inability to accept that some things are lost when you live in a divided world. But hey, this, too, was your choice.

"Navigating a Warm and Hostile Home"

Since you decided you wanted to move to live on the other side of the world, Mali, you've navigated yourself in a direction different from your previous life. You navigated toward dreams that don't necessarily come true, just as you navigated yourself to lose vocabulary and partially forget correct writing and self-expression. Don't you think it's utter foolishness to change your life, location, and language without expecting to lose a significant portion of the things that were in your previous life?

For a long time, I sat at the small table in the kitchen. The calm evening light filtering through the blinds illuminated the table, and I immersed myself in correcting spelling errors with the aid of a dictionary and "Google Translate." Yosi finally stopped giggling at my spelling errors and decided to be kind. He made me coffee with chocolate—the "hug" I get from him when he understands I need one. And so, I sat quietly, one hand wrapped around the mug in a kind of self-encouragement and focused on rewriting the greeting card. I went over every letter and word, and when I realized that more editing was ahead, I returned to Yosi's office, brought a few pages of rough drafts—I confess that I didn't have the courage to write directly on the new greeting card—and with the help of Google Translate and the dictionary I began to erase, correct, and revise and improve the style. Only after rewriting the card at least ten times and being satisfied with the result did I allow myself to smile and let out a sigh of relief.

What could I tell you? While I was pleased that there was such a wonderful product as "Google Translate" that translates and shows me how to write correctly in Hebrew, there is only one thing it cannot help me with. Google Translate cannot help me overcome the feeling of disappointment I had that I had forgotten my Hebrew and the experience of failure in trying to preserve it, feelings that I could have avoided if I had chosen differently. But in choosing to live in a divided heart world, I caused myself to forget how to spell correctly in Hebrew, the language of my mother, my first language, into which I was born and with which I grew up.

TEN
SKI LEG

I ENTERED the warm pizzeria and immediately absorbed the enticing aroma of freshly baked, crispy pizza emerging from the stone oven. I sat down on one of the orange plastic chairs, shook off the snowflakes, removed my gloves, and rubbed my cold hands to warm them up. While deliberating which hot drink to order, I heard a voice behind me.

"Excuse me, could you move your chair a little?" a young man asked me in English.

"Yes, of course," I replied, shifting my chair to allow him to pass.

The speaker was a tall, smiling man in his early thirties, with dark curly hair and large blue eyes. He settled at the table next to me, placing his still-wet-from-snow skis aside on the floor and removing his thick, black flannel ski cap and yellow ski goggles from his forehead.

His movements, the young man's, were somewhat peculiar, or rather, constrained, but I couldn't yet pinpoint anything specific.

"Thank you," he said in English with a foreign accent. "The skis need to be close to the wall, so I don't block the way for people," he added, pushing his ski equipment against the wall.

"How are the slopes today?" I inquired.

The man took a paper napkin from the metallic napkin dispenser on the table, wiped his sun-reddened face, and sat down heavily.

"Not bad," he replied, "even though there wasn't much snow on the slopes. For some reason, they didn't run the snowmaking machine. I told the main office several times how hard it is to give lessons to beginners when there isn't enough snow."

He opened the menu and began to browse through it.

If I hadn't been sure up until this point that he was speaking Hebrew, I now replied directly, with a smile, "You speak Hebrew, right?"

"Wow, hello there, friend," the man's eyes lit up. "Hebrew in Keystone? Impressive. It's not every day you meet Israelis in Keystone." He smiled enthusiastically and placed the menu on the table. As he stood to shake my hand, he leaned on his right leg, using the back of the chair for support, and then I saw it... The Israeli ski instructor had a prosthetic leg.

"I'm Etan, hi," he warmly shook my hand.

"Nice to meet you, I'm Marom," I replied, trying to hide the embarrassment that washed over me as I tried not to look at his pros-thetic leg.

"First time in Keystone?" Etan asked, pulling something from the large pocket of his apple-shaped vest.

"No," I smiled. "We come to Keystone every couple of months. My daughter and her husband have a vacation apartment here. They're crazy about skiing, and sometimes my wife and I join them for a weekend, being with them and their children. My daughter and her husband are skiing today," I explained, "and my wife is watching over the three little ones at home. To do my daily walk, I told them I'd come by foot and meet them near the gondola."

"How lovely," said Etan. "Skiing is a great sport, and it's popular here with kids, too. Most of my students are children aged four and up. They're... such sweet little ones. I enjoy teaching children. When I see the excitement in their eyes, it reminds me of how thrilled I was when I learned to ski, and I feel that excitement with them."

Etan sat down and began to take off the heavy ski boot attached to his prosthetic leg, which weighed him down. With remarkable skill, he released the two metal clips that fastened the special ski boot to the edge of his knee, which produced creaking and clicking sounds. He also removed the black Velcro straps that wrapped around the padding on his amputated knee and served as additional security for attaching the ski boot to his prosthetic leg, and then carefully and expertly placed the heavy ski boot under the chair and sat down to read the menu again.

I looked at him with admiration. In my wildest dreams, I hadn't thought that people with prosthetic legs could ski.

Etan gave me a warm look. "Hey," he smiled, "don't be too impressed by me. I'm used to people's looks. A ski instructor with a prosthetic leg isn't something you see every day."

I was slightly embarrassed for a moment about having started, but quickly recovered. "Could I join your table?" I asked, and to my delight, Etan replied affirmatively.

After we settled in, I asked when and under what circumstances Etan came to Keystone. "I've been teaching skiing here for one and a half years," he began his story, "I moved here from Austria, where I lived in Arlberg, a beautiful and fantastic ski resort. My uncle has a hotel there, right below the ski resort gondola. That's where my skiing obsession began."

"Oh, you haven't lived out of Israel for a long time..."

"About seven years," Etan brushed his curls with his hand. "I left Israel a year and a half after I was injured."

"Because of the injury? May I ask how you were injured?" I hesitantly asked.

"I was injured during my military service," he replied, which is exactly what I had been thinking.

"And how did that happen?"

"I was part of a patrol force that was ambushed near the southern border. I don't remember much, only that we drove along the border fence to carry out our daily patrol. It's a mountainous area, not easy to traverse, and is considered a quiet area for our patrols. At the end of the patrol, on the way back to base, we encountered an ambush by terrorists who managed to get close to the border fence. They fired an anti-tank missile at us."

Etan fell silent, appearing to be lost in thought, returning to that moment that had changed his life.

"The explosion was deafening," he recounted quietly, "I felt the patrol vehicle disintegrating around me, and everything inside was thrown in all directions. Do you know the way they describe how even the air is shattered? A kind of earthquake accompanied by a tremendous roar, that's what we felt at that moment.

"I woke up in the hospital two days later. The doctors tried to save my left leg, which was quite shattered, but ultimately had to amputate it. Time passed, and even after weeks of recovery, I couldn't stand on my right leg. I thought I would never walk again, but then I began a series of rigorous therapies and physical therapy exercises that helped strengthen the remaining leg. It took a few more months until I was able to stand on it. But forget it, I don't want to go into too much detail," said Etan.

I could see that the memories were painful for him, and I didn't press him with questions.

"I prefer to tell you about the guys from my unit, my true brothers in arms. They came to visit me in the hospital every time they got leave or weekend passes and boosted my morale. Their support was unwavering, people with warm hearts, caring 'brothers' in the true sense, not just brothers from the battalion. They spent hours sitting by my bedside, brought guitars, and sang songs I love..." he added.

"Are you still in touch?" I asked. "Do the guys know you're a ski instructor today?"

"Yes," he laughed, "they certainly do. Everyone knows. Even the doctors who treated me know," he added, and his eyes shone briefly as he mentioned the medical staff, "I'm still in touch with the doctors and nurses on the rehabilitation ward at the hospital."

The cheerful waitress came to our table, and Etan gave her a small hug without getting up from his chair. "Hi, Cindy, what's up?"

"Hey Etan, finished your lessons for today?" she smiled sweetly, and I sensed her tone was slightly more friendly than usual.

"Yes, the slopes aren't the most well-groomed today. I have seven lessons scheduled for tomorrow. That reminds me, Cindy," he smiled, and his blue eyes smiled too, "Tomorrow I have a busy day, I'm not sure if I'll make it to the farmers' market before closing. Could you please buy me the black olive spread I like? I'll pick it up from you when I come here for lunch. What do you say?"

"Yes, Etan," she patted his shoulder affectionately. "I'll buy you the olive spread and bring it here. Don't worry."

Etan ordered an Italian salad and mushroom pizza, and of course, beer. "And what about you?" Cindy turned to me.

"The Margherita pizza appeals to me, and a large cup of hot chocolate, the largest you have." I smiled at the young waitress and handed her the menu.

Now I was quite warmed up and could remove the warm bear coat I was wearing. I hung it on the chair next to me, along with the knitted hat and scarf that wrapped me in the snowy walk, not before giving the restaurant a 10 out of 10 for the diligent warming efforts.

"So, is Keystone now home?" I continued the conversation with Etan after Cindy went to take the order from the next table.

Etan looked at me with his smiling eyes, then his expression grew serious. After a one-minute pause, he continued.

"At the entrance to my apartment, there's an old wooden board, simple and full of scratches, left by the previous tenant, with the inscription in English, 'Home is where the heart is'. So, you're asking if Keystone is home? I don't know. It's easy to fall in love with nature and peace here. The people are more friendly than people in the big city—when you live in the mountains, there's something that brings you closer to all the other mountain dwellers, a kind of 'we're all in the same boat'. They'll always help you; if you get stuck with your car, if the heating in the house breaks down, if the electricity goes out, if an animal gets inside because you left a door open, or any other situation where you need help from your neighbors. For example, I don't know if you've heard about this, but there's a strict law here about home heating. The law requires you not to stay in an unheated home, and there will never be a neighbor or acquaintance who would let you freeze outside or in an unheated house. They will immediately arrange for you to stay in a heated place until your heating is fixed. Do you remember the famous saying, 'All Israelis are responsible for one another'? That's how the residents of the Rocky Mountains feel. Everyone helps everyone."

Etan picked up the phone from the table and scrolled through it. "Look," he brought the device closer to me, "a landscape photo that the most beautiful postcard won't show you. I took it this morning on top of the mountain, right before skiing with my student."

Before my eyes, a breathtaking landscape of snow-capped Rocky Mountains surrounding the town of Keystone unfolded, standing tall in their full glory and power, sending out a dazzling white glow in every direction, as if embracing one another in a powerful and authoritative embrace. The mountains cast a dim, mysterious shadow over the large mountainside on which the town of Keystone nestled. It was a powerful image, reminding you about the forces of nature we live alongside them in a harmonious convention, as long as we show respect for nature's beauty and the dangers it holds, and filled with admiration for the nature's artisan above who sought to reveal beauty and serenity in this enchanting gaze, but also conveyed the message hidden within the wild and dangerous nature.

"Keystone is located at an elevation of eleven thousand feet above sea level," Etan continued to describe. "The oxygen here is thinner because of the altitude. In the summer, this is a vibrant town full of life, and if you are lucky, you might catch a glimpse of mountain animals, such as mountain lions, bears, or ibex with their intricate horns. I'm always amazed at how the divine hand of nature crafted such beautiful, enormous horns, horns that no human hand could perfectly replicate."

Cindy returned with a tray of drinks, and I happily wrapped my hands around the warm and comforting cup of hot chocolate.

"Etan, do you have family in Israel?" I asked, venturing another personal question. "Do they visit you from time to time?"

"Of course," he said, taking a sip of his beer.

"And do you visit your homeland occasionally?"

"Not enough," Etan replied, his tone tinged with disappointment. He took another large gulp of his fizzy beer and wiped his lips with the back of his hand. "Look, it's not easy. With every trip to our homeland, I lose almost a month of workdays, so I must always account for a month without income. And of course, when you're in Israel, it's difficult to leave your family and friends, and at the end of the visit, you climb onto the plane feeling heavyhearted, wondering if this will be the last time you see your parents. On the first day of my visits, I always observe my parents, who have aged a little more and have more white hair than in the previous visit, and I know that they will not be getting any younger. All of this causes a tightness in my throat and the realization that this is a gift of time I could have spent with them, and instead I chose to go back to the other side of the world."

He took another sip of his beer. "For example, I couldn't embrace my sister, Mimi, when she excitedly told me she was about to enlist in the army and wanted to talk to me about her enlistment plans—she wanted to be an officer or try to get into pilot training. And I'm thinking to myself, how can it be that I won't be able to attend her graduation ceremony? And I feel a surge of immense pride, and I want to go tell all the guys in the unit and boast about her, even brag about it...

"But while I'm trying to get used to the idea that my little sister is now a soldier, I arrive for my next visit, and she's already a discharged soldier, starting university. Do you understand? Do you understand how time flies?"

I nodded. Who else could understand what he was talking about? Only people like me who were going through the same thing.

"I also have a younger brother," Etan said. "He was always my little brother, studying in middle school, and suddenly now he tells me that this is his last year of high school and that he's considering a pre-military program or enlistment. And I'm standing before him, my eyes wide with disbelief, asking myself when all this happened, how did he grow so big and mature? And I think these are conversations and questions my younger siblings wish I were a part of, but I won't be, because time and distance do their work, and the closeness we had before I left has vanished. I understand that in a way, I'm no longer part of them, and every year the distance grows more, and that breaks my heart.

"Suddenly, you begin to understand what happens when you leave your family and friends. What a disconnect is created between you and everything you have in the homeland, and what you're miss-ing, from family experiences you'll no longer share with them to family crises you're no longer a part of, and who knows if you'd have helped to solve them if you were, or if they'd even happened. And I'm not even talking about the joys you miss out on—you hear that she got married and he got married, that she had a child, and she already gave birth to her second child... You're no longer part of the daily lives of your family, friends, or the unit you were connected to, and the expe-riences and events that take place within it, and even if you try to be, you won't be able to; you're merely a visitor. That's it! The moment you decide to leave the homeland, consciously or not, you change your status within the family and among friends, and a barrier, in a sense, a cruel barrier, is built between you and everything you once had."

Etan fell silent. I could sense that this was a sensitive and painful point that bothered him, and now he allowed a narrow door, usually kept closed, to open in him. He let things break forth. I wanted to embrace him and tell him how much I understood him. It felt important to me that he knew that we, too, experienced what he described, and more than that. We, too, left long before him, and every time the moment came to decide whether to stay or return to the homeland, we chose to stay for various reasons. Sometimes, because we were busy establishing the first business, which led to the establishment of the second, and when our eldest daughter started high school, we justified staying by saying that we wouldn't ruin her high school studies. When we looked at the clock again, the eldest was already pursuing a master's degree, and the youngest had finished high school and started her bachelor's degree, and so it continued, and we too became part of that classic story of those who "don't buy a new living room set because what's the point? We don't know if we'll stay," or "we're about to return to Israel."

Suddenly, I too was flooded with memories, mostly from recent years, and images of the year my beloved mother passed away surfaced in my mind. Five times I flew to Israel that year, five long and exhausting flights of flying 7,400 miles away, not to mention the financial expenses of all those trips, and the thousands of dollars I spent every time I felt compelled to arrive immediately because my mother was in the hospital and the doctors weren't sure she would survive much longer. I remembered one of those flights, sitting in the airport crying big tears into the coffee I'd ordered, and a sweet woman who came to embrace me and said, "I'll hug you even though we don't know each other. I'll hug you because I see that you're experiencing something very painful. I'm so sorry for you..."

And as every time I remember this painful scene from the airport, tears filled my eyes, but I quickly wiped them away before Etan noticed them. I could have shared this memory and many others with him, but this wasn't my stage. Today, this hour, and this moment belonged entirely to him.

Etan fixed his gaze at the table and quietly said, "In phone calls, everyone tells you how much they miss you, and they want you to remember that you're missed. To those who loved you and wished you were a part of their lives, but the reality that slapped you in the face was that it was no longer so. You were no longer part of their lives, but merely a beloved guest who came once a year, two years, or four years, to remind yourself and them that indeed, you were once part of them, but now all that was left for you was to try to fill the void with hugs and gifts and conversations into the night.

"And after the vacation, you returned to your own world, which you yourself created, and in the first few days, you felt a little sad, but then obligations called to you and quickly brought you back to your other reality, your other language, your new friends, and the new community you had built around you. And longing went with you, accompanying you every day and everywhere you went, and you grew accustomed to life with longing, but unable to reproach anyone. It was your choice, and yours alone. And that's how your heart learned to live between two worlds," Etan continued. "The heart is divided, and in my case, so are my feet. One foot here in the Rockies, and the other foot needs to be in the homeland, but in my case, I don't have a foot," he chuckled, "it's the foot that will always be on the other side of the world, thousands of miles away."

He bowed his head, and I could swear I saw tears in his eyes, but I remained silent and said no word. "So, I do myself a favor and remind myself in my imagination and heart that I do indeed have a foot on the other side of the world, and the foot I don't have reminds me why the girlfriend that said I was everything for her left when she realized I didn't and wouldn't ever have a left foot."

I was amazed by Etan's openness and equally pleased that he had decided to share with me the depths and anxieties that my wife and I also experienced. The cheerful waitress, Cindy, provided us with a pleasant respite when she arrived with the pizza and salad we ordered. I asked for another cup of hot chocolate, and Etan ordered another beer. When it arrived, he took a large sip, set down the glass, and surveyed the people seated to our right.

I glanced at my watch to see if I was late for a meeting with my daughter near the gondola and was pleased to know that I had a little more time. I could feel that Etan wanted to talk more. I took a bite of the pizza and savored the warmth and abundance of flavors.

We ate like that for a few minutes without speaking, each absorbed in their own thoughts. Finally, I asked, "And what about the guys from the unit? Are you keeping in touch with them?"

"Yes, I hear from them from time to time," Etan said, shaking himself from his reverie and returning to the here and now.

"Just this week, I received a picture from Moti's wedding, and Ilan sent a picture from the annual picnic they had a month ago. Listen, they too are changing. We've all matured a bit. Tsviki has some gray hairs beginning to show, and the ginger-haired Ilan is starting to grow a small belly, and I tell myself that if I were there, I would drag Ilan forcibly to the gym...

"So now you are wondering," he smiled. "How did all of this lead me to Keystone?"

Etan sighed slightly, put down his fork, and leaned back in his chair. "As I told you, I sustained a significant injury. The doctors told me that I was their project. I got many shrapnel wounds, and broke six ribs, one of which pierced my right lung. For fifteen days, I was hooked up to a machine draining fluids from my lungs, and during that time, I underwent lung surgery, back surgery, right hand surgery, and—the icing on the cake," he added with sarcasm, "amputation of my left foot."

Etan spoke now in a low, pained voice. His voice trembled again, and he stammered a little as he considered how to continue. He wiped his eyes with the back of his hand.

My God, what this young man has been through, I thought. He was the age of my daughter; he could have been my son... Again, I wanted to give him the warmest hug possible. And again, I wasn't sure, but maybe I saw another tear there. Etan didn't let it escape, immediately wiping his eyes and then bowing his head in greeting to someone who passed by us. I reminded myself that he was a local and knew all the residents of the small town.

"People think that a wounded soldier receives excellent treatment, goes to a rehabilitation ward, and then returns home, and everything is fine and happy, and life returns to its course," continued Etan. "Now go explain to them that after medical treatment, the second, long, and exhausting battle begins, coping with life at home and with yourself. Mentally, you're a completely different person. You will never be the same person you were before the injury." I nodded in agreement and waited for the continuation of his story.

"Precisely when I began to get stronger, the next major crisis arrived. As you understand, my girlfriend changed course. Suddenly, my limiting injury and the changed physical appearance, with my face full of marks from the shrapnel I incurred, upset her, and I was no longer the handsome and strong guy she knew. The new situation changed our relationship, not to mention the vanished sex. I think that if they hadn't amputated my leg, she hoped I would recover and get back to being who she knew. Therefore, after the amputation, when she didn't come to visit me for two weeks and told me she was home, sick with COVID, I didn't suspect anything.

"Only when my mother and sister came to visit one day and told me they saw her in a restaurant with friends did I begin to suspect something wasn't right, but I didn't say a word about it. Later, when she finally came to visit, she started through the conversation we had, hinting that she didn't know how to deal with a partner without a leg, and that she wasn't able to see blood and wounds, and it made her sick… What should I have understood from that?

"I took a moment to think and said to her that I needed some time for myself to regain my strength, and that it would be good for us to take a break to decide on our future steps. I don't blame her," Etan continued, "I know I wasn't an easy person after the injury and during rehabilitation. When I told my parents that we had decided to take a break, they were sure we were on our way to marriage.

"My father called his brother in Austria, in Arlberg, and my amazing uncle suggested that I come for a vacation at their beautiful ski resort in the Alps. I remember asking myself on the first day I arrived there how I didn't know about this little piece of paradise until now."

"So, there in Arlberg, did you learn to ski?"

"Yes, I arrived in Arlberg, and for two weeks I did nothing but get to know the area, eat a lot of fish, and chat every evening in the hotel lobby with the skiers staying there. One day, while sitting in the lobby, Johan, one of the resort's ski instructors, sat down next to me and told me that his son was coming for a visit for a few days. The next day, I joined them, completely captivated as I watched them ski with such ease. The son was as much an accomplished skier as his father, and witnessing such professional skiing was truly an awe-inspiring experience.

"After skiing all morning, I went with them to a local pub for lunch, and, as a treat, Johan surprised me by asking why I wasn't skiing. I looked at him in surprise. 'Me? How could I? I have a prosthetic leg!'

"Johan smiled and said to me, 'Why don't you try? If you can walk well on your prosthetic leg, you can also ski. It's a matter of control and balance. I'm happy to teach you.'

"I took up the challenge, figuratively speaking and literally, and after four months of dedicated practice and instruction from Johan, I became a skier. Certainly not on the black diamond runs, which are challenging and treacherous with their steep slopes, but on the other runs. The real turning point came when one of the hotel guests asked me to teach his daughter to ski. I remember looking at him, utterly stunned, but a voice inside me said, 'Yes, I can, I can!' I completed a short refresher course and certification in ski safety and began teaching children to ski. I quickly fell in love with it, this time with something that filled my heart and soul."

"What a powerful story, and what a wonderful person you are, Etan," I said excitedly, "Look how you found a way to fall in love again."

He laughed. "That's how I stayed in Arlberg for another two years, until I heard one of the ski instructors say he was going to

Colorado to experience skiing in the Rocky Mountains and asked who wanted to join him. And as you can see, I came, fell in love, and stayed."

"Look, Etan," I moved my head from side to side. "You're truly amazing. You've been through a difficult, complex, painful—what more?—and now you've found a focus, a passion for life, and a new love. I take my hat off to you," I gestured to a pretend removal of a hat. "You're an inspiration, and I'm very happy for you."

"I don't know, Marom," he wrapped himself again in slight melancholy. "It was hard for me when my girlfriend gave up, didn't believe in my recovery, not even in basic physical recovery, and simply abandoned me. But out of that came a project that I took upon myself as a goal—my recovery, and I did it in the most absurd way I could think of," he smiled, "becoming a ski instructor!"

I placed my hand on his shoulder and quietly said, "I read somewhere that you never know how strong you can be until the moment when being strong is your only option."

Etan raised his beer glass, and I raised my nearly empty cocoa, and we toasted, "Cheers." Then I got up and embraced him warmly and affectionately. We exchanged phone numbers, and Etan promised to visit us in Denver.

I wrapped my warm coat around me, put on my knitted hat, and covered my ears so they wouldn't freeze. I wrapped a scarf around the hat. I opened the heavy wooden door of the warm pizzeria and immediately sucked in the cold air.

The wind brushed my face outside. It was already noon, so the temperature usually peaked at 20 degrees Fahrenheit (-7 degrees Celsius), and obviously, the snow wouldn't melt today. I walked quickly to overcome the bone-chilling cold, but deep inside, a warm feeling flowed within me. I thought about the amazing Etan, about the injury crisis he had gone through, and about the real struggle he began after the injury—how, with motivation and strengths he didn't know he possessed, he stood back on his legs and regained the leg that had been taken from him. This was his skiing leg, which returned to him with the superhuman strength of a determined lion, a fighter who wanted to prove to the pride that...

...not only did he get a new leg, but he also gave himself a steel leg made of determination, consistency, and strength—a leg that helped him even overcome the feeling of division within him and cushioned his longing for his homeland with the new love that blossomed within him.

ELEVEN
BELONGING? / NOT?

WHAT HELPS us feel a sense of belonging to the homeland? What is it that moves us every time we think of it in the context of Israel?

What is it that makes our hearts pound when we think of the Land of Israel? Is it a geographic location? Recognition of historical roots? Childhood memories? Identification with the language? Family? Food? Friends? Military service? Perhaps the answer is a combination of all these reasons, or at least a large part of them? Have you asked yourselves?

I never asked myself these questions until a conversation I had with an Israeli Uber driver in Florida made me begin to delve into the depths of my being to find an answer, but even now, as I write these lines, I have not yet reached "my peace of mind," and I have no answer.

It all began when, to celebrate our wedding anniversary, we treated ourselves to a vacation to Deerfield Beach, a small town about an hour and fifteen minutes from Miami, Florida. A quiet vacation by the turquoise-blue sea that I missed so much in Denver, Colorado.

We landed in Miami and ordered an Uber, which arrived within minutes, so we didn't even have time to enjoy the warm March sun in the waiting area.

The driver was an older man, in his late sixties, tall, tanned, and smiling, with silver hair and warm brown eyes. After helping us load the suitcase and bags into the spacious trunk of the car, we thanked him and settled comfortably in the back seat.

It was midday, and although it wasn't too hot outside, the driver turned on the air conditioning. I inhaled the pleasant, cool air emanating from the vents with joy.

"Is this the typical late-March weather for you?" I asked the friendly driver in English while he was fastening his seatbelt.

"More or less," the man replied with a foreign accent. "Usually, March is still pleasant, but in April and May, the skies open aggressively, and we get the strongest rainfall. In these months, nature reminds us of the true meaning of tropical weather, and then Florida enjoys one day of quiet before the hurricane season begins, usually between June and September."

I noticed that the driver's accent sounded familiar to me, but I still couldn't decide what it was.

"Are you originally from Florida?" I continued to ask in English. To avoid awkwardness in asking directly where he was from, I used one of my tricks, simply asking if he was a native Floridian or came here from another state. It always worked, and nobody got offended.

"Oh, no," the man replied. "I've lived here for many years, but I'm originally from Israel."

Boom! That was what his accent signaled to me, but I preferred to be sure. "Wonderful," I said in Hebrew, "so shall we speak Hebrew? Nice to meet you, friend."

I smiled happily.

"Oh, hello there, friends," the friendly driver also replied in Hebrew. "You still have a slight accent, and I really thought perhaps you were Israelis. Also, by the name, but I wasn't sure, and at work, there are rules, and one has to be careful not to offend anyone."

"Oh, yes, of course," I smiled. "Everything is fine. Tell me, how long have you lived in the Sunshine State?"

I remembered that someone once told me that "Floridians" like it when their state is called the "Sunshine State."

"Since I left Israel," the driver replied. "Thirty-seven years, and time flies."

Later, I learned that his name is Micah Cohen, that he is already retired from his job at one of the largest and most luxurious hotels in Miami, where he managed the hotel's waitstaff and food department, and that now he volunteers three days a week at the Jewish community center in Miami and two days a week works as an Uber driver, "to fill my pockets with pocket money," as he called it, in addition to the income he receives since he retired. Micah also told us that he has four children who have already grown up and left home, and that his wife, Ilana, who is also Israeli, still works at the same hotel where he worked for more than thirty years.

"Did you come to Florida from Israel on vacation?" Micah inquired, sending us a look from the rearview mirror.

When I replied that we have lived in Colorado for three decades, Micah laughed. "Colorado, huh? Now I understand what you're looking for...There you get a lot of snow even in spring, right? Are there many Israelis in Colorado?" he continued to ask, slowing down the drive due to the annoying traffic jam we were stuck in.

"There's a small community," Rafi, my partner, replied. "Up to two thousand people, mostly people coming for work."

"We can't compare our small community to the large Israeli community you have in Florida," I added.

"Yes, the community here is large, more than half a million, I think," Micah replied.

He squinted at the sun striking through the car's front window. "Florida is full of Jews, actually," he continued, "the latest statistics show that seventy percent of the population in the southern half of Florida are Israelis and Jewish-Americans moving here in retirement.

They're escaping the New York and Canadian winters," he added with a laugh.

Rafi emitted a whistle of amazement. "Wow, that's a striking statistic," he said. "We had no idea."

We continued driving in silence, each lost in thought, but my curiosity wouldn't let me be.

"Thirty-seven years is a long time," I asked Micah again. "Do you have family in Israel? Do you visit?"

He sighed slightly. "We traveled more when the children were younger. Now that our children are busy building careers and raising their own kids, we're busy helping them whenever they need it, and they need it. Besides, there are a thousand other reasons why we can't plan a trip to the other side of the world. You know how it is; sometimes you want to travel to places you haven't been yet, sometimes you plan a vacation with friends.

"When our parents were alive, it was very important for us to see them as much as possible, but it's a bit different with siblings," he sighed slightly. "All of this, of course, doesn't change the fact that we miss Israel constantly and find it hard not to visit for a long time. But believe me, it's also hard when you travel. In recent visits, it hasn't been so enjoyable. We no longer feel comfortable in Israel."

"Really?" I wondered. "What do you mean when you say it's hard and not enjoyable?"

"Look," he hesitated slightly before speaking, as if weighing his words. "Many things have changed in Israel in recent decades. Of course, I know you'll tell me that we've also changed over the years we've been here, and therefore it's only natural that we start to lose touch with the years and feel a bit uncomfortable."

"But still, you are Israeli. Can you explain what's uncomfortable about the country? What do you find difficult?" I pressed.

Micah gripped the steering wheel and began to speak. From that moment on, I couldn't stop him, even if I wanted to.

"Ilana and I left Israel almost forty years ago. We arrived directly in Miami and settled here. We had four children, two sons and two daughters, and so time passed—work, building a home, raising the children, building a social circle... like everyone else. You know how it is."

"Yes, Micah, of course," I replied.

"Throughout those years, we made sure to visit Israel, approximately every two years, when the children were young. There were times when I visited twice in the same year, especially when significant family events occurred, such as saying goodbye to Mom or Dad. Even earlier, whenever one of them felt unwell, I felt guilt, and I would book a ticket immediately and travel. What can you do?"

"We all have parents, and it's sad when they are ill, especially as they age and you're on the other side of the world," Rafi commented.

Micah, lost in memories, ignored Rafi's words and continued his story.

"I still remember with mixed feelings our first visit to Israel, a year and a half after we left the Homeland," he said. "We had to coordinate the visit with the 'green card' interview scheduled for me at the US Embassy in Tel Aviv, and when the letter arrived with the interview date, we immediately booked plane tickets.

"The first visit to the homeland was the most emotional experience I've had. Imagine I was a 'fresh migrant,' as we're called, and at the same time, I was already beginning a new chapter in the new life I'd built here. We toured Tel Aviv and Jerusalem, and I felt as if I were still living there and had never left. I hadn't looked at myself as someone who already belonged to another world. It only began to hit me after years."

Rafi and I nodded in agreement. We were familiar with that feeling.

"Do you remember the time when airlines allowed two suitcases per passenger? Wow, we happily packed four suitcases and a stroller for our eight-month-old daughter, and four of them were filled with gifts. Back then, we still followed the tradition known as the 'gift-giving ritual before the flight to Israel'. What madness. 'My uncle from America brought me...' was the famous saying in every home back then. As if, what did they think? That money grew on trees." Micah, sounding frustrated, made it clear that the gift-giving bothered him.

"So, imagine, four of our eight suitcases were filled with gifts for the two large families, mine and my wife's, and as you know, because you've experienced this, buying gifts takes time and a lot of money. In the month before the trip, every day after work, we ran to shopping malls and stores to find gifts, not to mention the financial expenses... I'll tell you the truth, it was pure folly.

"In my family, we have ten siblings, and in my wife's family, nine. So, I had to give half my salary just for the gifts. Wait, that's not all. Do you think the gifts always fit? The size? The color? Or did they not even like what we brought?"

Micah shook his head from side to side and ran his hand through his hair in frustration. "Over time, we stopped going crazy like that. When our parents were alive, we bought presents only for them, or for someone celebrating a significant event like a wedding or bar mitzvah, and that was the end of the crazy gift-giving ritual. In any case, the first visit to the country was long and full of excitement, tears, hugs, late-night talks with the people dear to me, trying to make up for everything I missed during the year and a half I wasn't there, because everything was still fresh and truly the longing I felt was genuine; all the memories were vivid, the connection strong as it had been before we left.

"And still, I felt I cared about Israel and everyone there, that I wanted to be involved, and that I was a part of everything happening in the country. There's no describing how my heart pounded as the tiny car we'd rented at the airport sped down the coastal road toward Haifa, and passed by Atlit. Oh, the memories of the little apartment we bought in Atlit will always stay with me, and how I always told myself that there was no way we'd move from a fifty-square-meter apartment in the old block, a two-student apartment with not a penny to our name, and how excitedly I kept repeating, 'Soon I'll see my mother,' and my wife, wanting to calm me, offered me a can of 'La Croix,' sugar-free soda, and I couldn't swallow it. The soda sat like a stone in my throat.

"We spent four weeks in Israel. The four weeks passed quickly. It was also the most delicious visit I remember from all the visits I'd had all these years. Even now, my mouth fills with saliva as I recall how I dove into the food I'd missed so much, my mother's kitchen and the spice rack, the Moroccan delicacies, or the sweet baklava I plucked with my fingers straight from the bowl of hot syrup. I ate until my stomach almost burst, with no more room for the courses that followed the salads..."

"My mother's Moroccan fish on a Friday evening," I added with a smile. "And the pastries, and the stew with a sweet onion sauce, and how could I forget the spicy meatballs as a first course or the filo pastries filled with ground almonds and dripping with sweet and tangy syrup," I was drawn into the memories myself. "Just thinking about the red and orange colors of the most seasoned fish in the world, I want to be there now, in my mother's kitchen."

"And the pastries with Bulgarian cheese and hard-boiled egg that you buy from the street vendor on Independence Road near Haifa port?" Micah chuckled.

"The one with the old cart? With the torn roof?" Rafi joined the conversation with a smile.

"Yes," Micah replied, "But forget about the torn roof. From two blocks away, I could already smell that magnetic aroma, the smell that no other pastry in the world could compare to. And the taste...Already on the first morning in Israel, we woke up and went down Independence Road to buy Bulgarian pastries. I tell you, there's nothing like the food of the homeland. We missed it a lot during the first year and a half we lived on the other side of the world."

Rafi and I looked at each other. We knew exactly what he was talking about.

"Now, understand," Micah continued as we were stuck in a long, quiet traffic jam, "Even the second trip, two years later, was filled with unsettling anticipation for the day of the flight and impatience from the excitement. I missed and was excited, and already pictured how it would be to see my mother again. And with every image of her in my mind, tears came to my eyes, and the excitement grew. In retrospect, it might be that even then, there were not only tears of longing but also tears of guilt. At that time, I acknowledged some responsibility for my situation, as I had chosen to relocate to a place requiring long flights between continents, frequent transatlantic phone calls, and distance from family and friends. These circumstances were the result of voluntary decisions. No one forced me to leave Israel. It was I who wanted to move and embrace a life of constant longing. So yes, to be honest with myself and with you, I admit that perhaps even then there were some feelings of guilt, but I denied them. A year or two abroad still hasn't shown me how much I really decided to punish myself. I treated the first and second visits like a visit from someone who lives in Israel, but in a city far from the rest of his family, perhaps a place like Eilat, and came to visit because he hadn't seen his family for a long time.

"Meanwhile, our lives in the state of Florida continued to flow, and between raising children, establishing ourselves in our work, and cultivating new social lives, I became a busy person. How busy? Very. I became a person who wants to dedicate all of his life to financial stability and career development. From waking up in the earliest hour possible to turning off the lights in the house in the late hours of the night, and in between, daily dealing with the various problems that life throws at us. After all, I promised myself that I would reach the peak I desired for myself, to get the position of manager of the waitstaff and food department in a five-star hotel, and I achieved it."

"Micah," I said quietly, "This is a slightly more personal question. Do you think that when you lived in Israel, you didn't believe that you had the ability to achieve the goals you set for yourself here in America, and that you achieved them because of yourself and your abilities, and not because you left Israel?"

"That's a good question," Micah replied after a brief reflection. "I was young, I hadn't experienced enough life, and it's quite possible that I didn't believe in myself back then. I didn't think I had the ability to go far. Today, in retrospect, I know what I'm capable of and what I can do, and that's a lot."

I wasn't sure it was appropriate to ask such an emotional and personal question (and I also received a nudge on the shoulder from Rafi, who was sitting next to me) and decided to relax a bit, to remain silent.

In those moments of silence, Micah took out a plastic container filled with granola from a black bag that lay next to him in the passenger seat and said to us with a smile, "Blessed be my wife, Ilana. My sweetheart always remembers to put more food in my bag. I haven't had lunch yet. Would you like some granola that she makes?"

"No, thank you, Micah. Cheers," I replied with a smile.

Micah shoved a handful of granola into his mouth and chewed it with enjoyment, but wouldn't give up on continuing his story. He continued speaking while the sweet, dry granola crunched between his teeth.

"Thirty-seven years have elapsed, which marks a significant passage of time since I allowed it to take its course," he remarked. "During this period, time consistently contributed to constructing a barrier between myself and my previous life, gradually widening it without my awareness. In this instance, time proved to be unrelenting.

"Over time, a growing wall separates me from the life and home I once had. Each passing day makes the distance between me and my former home in Israel feel even greater."

Though Micah was immersed in driving, I felt as if I had opened a spring within him, eager to overflow but finding no time or place to do so. And I, with my curious encouragement, helped him open something that burst into a genuine torrent of confessions. I don't know how open Micah was with his wife or friends, but it was clear to me that I had touched a very sensitive point, and that this was the first time he had chosen to speak so honestly about something that troubled and tormented him.

Above all, Micah seemed even more open with us—two Israelis living in a divided world—seeing us as "fellow boat riders." Micah took two small water bottles from the cooler that was in the front seat and said, "Take them, drink, friends. The heat here dries the body and soul."

We thanked him and took sips from the cool water while he continued speaking.

"There are many moments in which I feel that, in reality, the only thing I have in common with the homeland where I was born and raised is the Hebrew language. And even here, from time to time, I no longer remember certain words or write with some errors.

"When you don't use a language, this is the price you pay, just as when you don't use a phone number for a long time and forget it. There are many words I don't use and therefore forget and find in English. I'm not even talking about coming to visit Israel and hearing words on the street or in the supermarket that have been 'impregnated' with English, distorted words that people adopt because this is the new fashion in the country, and Hebrew words that even the Hebrew dictionary doesn't recognize. Today, when I visit Israel, on the very first day, I am torn within myself, because on the one hand, I am happy to visit my brothers and sisters—and what to do, the parents have already gone to paradise—and to see the changes that have occurred with them and the growth and development of our families. And on the other hand, reality slaps me again in the face.

"I am no longer part of the changes taking place in the world that was once mine, nor part of the country that was mine, and again, I am gripped by depression from the feeling that I am a stranger in my homeland! I feel that I do not belong to the environment I am visiting, that it is no longer my place. I look around and feel alone, even if I am on a bustling and crowded street, because I know that I am no longer part of them; I am just a visitor. Call it a tourist if you want, and it is a difficult feeling. I will be honest with you, I feel alone, a stranger.

"I am no longer familiar with the roads; the trains are more modern, the buses have improved, and there are new highways I don't know. Driving is becoming more complicated for me, and thank God there is 'Waze' now, because that turn from my parents' house, which I used to make with my eyes closed every time I returned home from the base, is now closed. They turned it into a one-way street on the other side.

"And the most significant thing is the people in the country. Once, I went with my sister to do some shopping in a supermarket in Haifa, and everything there seemed so different from what I'm used to seeing here. The people were agitated, angry, not always friendly, and I am already so used to people greeting you even if they don't know you. I am used to a different mentality, and I don't know... I just wanted to get out of there as quickly as possible."

Our trip was ending. I could sense that Micah had much more to say, but time was short. I saw him thinking about what to say and did not interrupt him with questions. He paused for a moment and then said in a quiet voice, "It's hard for me to say this, but again, I want to be honest with myself. Perhaps the feeling of strangeness I experience every time I come to the country was created by me? Perhaps, as a result of the great effort I made to belong to another country, to learn the local slang so as not to sound so different from the locals, to adopt the local customs here, so as not to appear strange, not to feel strange, and not to be different from the people around me in the new world I chose to live in—all of this has become deeply ingrained in me, to the point where I feel like a stranger everywhere else, and the most painful thing is—I feel like a stranger in my own country, in the land of Israel. A stranger to the bread that I once loved, a stranger to the 'Baron wine' drink I used to buy, a stranger to almost everything that was once my cornerstone.

"So, it's true, in my first, second, and even third visits, I still haven't seen the barrier that begins to build around me, and I haven't foreseen the large wall that time will have created in the almost forty years I've lived here in Florida.

"I was young, and all I saw was the dream I had. And to say that I succeeded in realizing the dream I had. Yes! I have a good home, I raised four children, and they all graduated with degrees. Overall, we're fine, thank God. But today, at a moment like this, I ask myself—could I not have succeeded to the same extent in Israel?"

TWELVE
TWO ANCHORS FOR ONE SHIP

"EVERY SHIP NEEDS AN ANCHOR, RIGHT?"

"Yes," you reply, looking at me quizzically. A strange question.

I shake my head negatively and say to you, "Friends, you are mistaken. A ship can have two anchors."

You wonder, asking for an explanation, and I respond with questions: "What is an anchor? What is an anchor made of? What is the purpose of an anchor? What happens if a ship has no anchor? Does an anchor signify belonging to the place where the ship is anchored? Does an anchor express identification with the place where it is anchored? Does an anchor provide a sense of security? Is there a connection between the anchor's weight and the feeling of identity?"

The following story helped me illustrate a situation where a ship has two anchors, in terms of feelings, identity, security, and a sense of belonging.

As every year, the Jewish community in Denver commemorated Israeli Memorial Day for all the fallen soldiers. We excitedly entered the large lobby of the auditorium at the Jewish community center and joined the long line for the traditional pre-ceremony lighting of the candles.

Ahead of us in line stood David and Aayla Lugsy, a lovely couple whom we have known for many years and who are part of the Israeli community in Colorado. I recalled they arrived in Denver more than thirty-four years ago, so they likely came before us. Although they tried to keep their voices down, I couldn't help but hear what they were saying to each other; in the heat of their argument, they were oblivious to us standing behind them. I noticed that Ayala was trying to hide the anger that was evident on her face.

"This is the last time we're coming to the Memorial Day ceremony in Denver, David," Ayala declared firmly. "Next year, I will be at the Memorial Day ceremony in Israel, with the boys and the grandchild to be born."

"Ayala, enough. Stop pestering me. I'm not returning to Israel this year," I heard David whisper back to her without turning his face.

"I want to be near Kfir and Lavi," Ayala persisted. "Especially now that Kfir told us that his wife is pregnant. I want to be with my grandchildren! Did you hear how Kfir laughed when he asked us if we wanted a good reason to stop being 'American' parents? Clearly, he meant he wants us there with him for the birth of his son or daughter soon."

David remained silent, his gaze fixed on the line in front of him.

"David, are you processing this?" Ayala's voice sounded slightly sad. "Soon we will have grandchildren who will call us 'American grandparents.'"

"Oh, stop it. You shouldn't take every little thing the children say to heart. And besides, perhaps you could find a funny name for Kfir as well? Really, Ayala, just now that I've become a partner in the business, do you want me to abandon everything and return to Israel?"

"Exactly," Ayala nodded. "I want to be near our children and near the grandchildren we will have. If they have decided that they want to live in our homeland, well, it's time for us to return and be meaningful grandparents and parents."

"Ayala, calm down," David said quietly, annoyed, "You don't

decide something like this so easily. I'm not a twenty-year-old looking for adventures. Do you know what it means for me to pack up my bags and go back to the country at sixty-five? I can't even remember what it feels like to live in Israel."

"David, you're talking about our homeland, the Land of Israel. So, we can get used to it again. What are you worried about? Family and friends? They are there, or most of them anyway, and they survived all this time. What, is it so bad for them? No, listen to Lavi and Kfir. They say it's nice in Israel, and did you hear that Lavi told me today that he doesn't understand why we even left...?"

"Listen," David turned to her sternly. "No one is happier than me that our American-born son is successful and doing well in our homeland. Lavi isn't in our situation. We are almost at retirement age, and he has his whole life ahead of him. Lavi reminds me of us when we were his age. We also had dreams; we also moved here to experience a different life than the one we were used to. We wanted to improve our halting English, to build a business that would bring us a lot of money. We wanted to experience a different life, right?"

Ayala nodded, and David continued.

"So, I ask you to understand that I want to retire with something in hand. I worked hard to build what I built, and now, as a partner in the business, I want to hold on until the business is sold. At least I will have a share of the profits, and I will leave with a nice sum of money and be able to provide us with a comfortable retirement, without financial worries."

"David, are you hearing yourself? Leave the money alone; it's not everything in life. There are things you can't buy with money," Ayala said angrily, pushing her long black hair away from her eyes.

I could see David fidgeting. He rose on his toes and nervously scanned the people in front of him to see if the line was getting shorter.

Ayala wasn't about to give up. She approached him and pulled on his elbow to get his attention.

"David, life is short," she almost pleaded. "Let's go back to our homeland so we can help them. Kfir told me that Daphne's mother is not feeling well and can't help her, so I need to be there for them. Our son, Kfir, needs our help now. How can you not see that?"

"And what about me? And what about all the investment I made in the business?" David looked at her angrily, "You don't have a heart for me, you know? You want me to throw everything away and go back to live in Israel just because our two sons, who were born here in Denver, decided they wanted to try living there? Don't forget that their mentality is American. They are used to living here, in America. So, what will you do if they suddenly decide that living in Israel doesn't suit them and that they want to come back here? What will we do then? Pack up our bags again and go back because they are returned, and we need to be near the grandchildren. And what if Lavi gets a job in Australia or India, God forbid? Do you want us to move there too? Do you think that every time our children move somewhere, we must drag ourselves behind them?"

Ayala was silent. It seemed she was considering her words.

"You know very well that I'm talking about Kfir, especially," she began again, this time in a softer tone. "Soon he will have a child, and we will be grandparents. So why should I sit here in Denver and suffer from longing for them when I can be there and enjoy them and be part of their lives? You know that I'm happy that Kfir decided to try living in Israel. He is the child of Israeli parents, and fate willed it that he fell in love with Israel and wants to live there. Aren't you happy about that?"

"Of course, I'm happy," David replied, without much enthusiasm in his voice. "But we are in a different phase of life. We are almost sixty-five years old, at retirement age. I need to provide for us for the years after retirement. If I leave the partnership in the business now, I won't get anything, nothing!

"According to the new contract, the three partners must make an effort to grow the business and manage it until the sale and transfer of ownership, and whoever leaves first gets nothing. Do you want us to return to living in Israel while the business is working for my benefit, growing nicely, and the share I will get from the sale is excellent to allow us to live with dignity in our retirement years? Think about it."

David paced nervously. I knew the conversation with Ayala was difficult for him, and this subject, which they had argued about for the past week, came up from time to time, but he always pushed it into a forgotten corner of his heart.

He feared this would happen; he always remembered the story of his good friend, Tzahi, whose daughter moved to Israel to enlist in the army and married a man she met while in her service year. Tzahi's wife, unable to stand the longing, returned to Israel to be near the grandchildren, and Tzahi remained in Denver because of the excellent work that gave him a good income. Then the sad thing happened; after two and a half years of living separate lives, Tzahi and his wife separated and divorced, and he remained in Denver. Years passed, Tzahi retired, and he still lives in Denver, in financial comfort, and alone.

I thought that Tzahi's memories were also passing through David's mind. He certainly thought he didn't want what happened to Tzahi to happen to them. But Ayala insisted. Why didn't she understand him?

"You're terrible," Ayala said to him, trying not to raise her voice too much. "You have no feelings; your heart is made of stone. I always knew that money was important to you, but to this extent. Are you willing to sacrifice love for grandchildren? Do you prefer to stay here to save your share in the business? Forget the business and forget the money. Don't you want to help your son? Do you want to be one of those grandparents who see their grandchildren once every few years, at birth and then at a bar mitzvah? And if it interests you... Perhaps you'll also attend their military basic training graduation ceremony or something? Your grandchildren won't have warm and loving memories of their grandfather. Ugh, you're disgusting."

Ayala appeared very agitated and could no longer contain herself. With tear-filled eyes, she rummaged through her purse to get a handkerchief, and when she found nothing, she left the long line and strode away resolutely, her gaze fixed on the ground. It was clear that the last thing she wanted was to encounter acquaintances. She walked quickly, her hair covering her face to conceal her wet eyes, and headed toward the restrooms.

David did not follow her. He remained standing in line, his face impassive.

Without hesitation, I decided to follow her and try to calm her down. I signaled to my friend that I was going to the restrooms and left the long line.

I could see Ayala opening the door to the restroom, which was in a corner of the lobby. I followed her as she approached one of the sinks to wash her face, which continued to stream with tears. Sobbing, she splashed cold water on herself to try to calm down, but she couldn't control the escalating sobs.

Then, she forcefully pulled two paper towels from the dispenser and began to dry her face. I approached her and gently placed my hand on her shoulder.

"Ayala, it's me, Anat. I'm sorry you're upset. We were standing behind you and couldn't help but hear the argument you had with David."

Ayala's sobs intensified. She remained standing, facing away from me, then turned and buried her face in my shoulder, as if finally finding a shoulder to cry on and release her pain.

"Oh, Anat, everything is terrible," she whispered, her voice full of tears.

"Oh, sweetie," I hugged her warmly.

"Ugh, the whole thing is awful," Ayala whispered, "It's the constant argument about returning to Israel. David isn't willing to hear about it, and I'm already at my wits' end."

"I'm sorry to hear that," I said, hugging her again.

"For a long time now, I've been trying to convince him to return to the homeland. You know that Kfir and young Lavi decided to try living in Israel, and this week, Kfir told us that his wife, Daphna, is pregnant.

So, that's it; I want to be there for them. I want to help them with the grandchildren; I want to be part of my grandchildren's lives, but David isn't willing to hear about returning to Israel. He wants us to stay here for a few more years until the business is sold; otherwise, we'll return to the homeland without a penny. What a terrible situation."

"This isn't a conversation to have in a public restroom," I tried to calm her. "Come on, let's get out of here, find a secluded couch in the lobby, and talk. Besides, I don't think the Remembrance Day ceremony will begin on time. There's a long line for the candle lighting. Relax and let's go."

I took Ayala's trembling hand and led her to a seating area in the lobby.

We sat in a couple of the red, padded armchairs, and Ayala sniffed again.

"Now tell me, David doesn't want to return to the homeland at all?"

"No, it's not that," she explained. "He wants us to stay in Denver so he can continue to develop the business until it generates enough profit. Only then will it be justified to ask for the high price the three partners want to sell it for."

"And what happens if the business doesn't succeed?" I asked. "No one guarantees him that the business will grow and thrive in the coming years."

"Exactly," Ayala began to cry again. "Do you think I haven't asked him these questions? He says he feels optimistic."

"Hoping, I know, it sounds familiar," I said softly. "The question is whether the business has growth potential and what he's doing to increase its income."

"Exactly," Ayala sniffed again, her nose red. "You understand, Anat, David lives on hope, on aspirations; he invested everything we saved to start this business... As a partner in this venture, they agreed among themselves, the three partners, that none of them would leave the business until it was sold. So David is bound by this agreement, and I have to wait until the business is sold, and in the meantime, suffer quietly."

I paused for a moment. This entanglement wasn't simple, I thought. After all, I am entirely dependent on my small business. I am a real estate broker, what is called in Israel a "house broker," a single mother to a child I gave birth to at the age of forty-two, and my son is currently in high school. I know very well what it feels like when a business isn't working, and the frustration when there's no income that month, more than once.

"Ayala, listen," I said to her, holding her cold hands, "you and David built a great life together. You have two wonderful sons who fell in love with Israel and decided to move there, and we admired such a brave decision from your children. On the one hand, I understand David; he wants to succeed here, it's his dream. Everyone has a dream, and I have a dream too, for example, to sell ten houses every month. But all my efforts haven't yet brought me to fulfilling this dream, and imagine that I work very hard, how do we say it here? From sunrise to sunset, right?" I wanted to make her smile, and I raised my eyes to the ceiling, raising my hands. "Who knows, maybe one day I'll achieve such achievements. What do you say, Lord of the planning of the heavens, you, who plans everything for us, right?

"On the other hand, I also understand you. You have the warmest and biggest heart I know, Ayala. Everything you see in front of you is the joy of taking a walk on a pleasant sunny day with your newborn granddaughter or picking up your grandson from daycare. When they ask you to babysit, you're always there to help, and on Fridays, you want to cook for your son Kfir, all the delicacies he is used to and fill the Shabbat table with your delicious food and songs with your grandchild, songs she learned at daycare. You're probably already planning on sewing costumes for Purim and taking measurements, and as I know you, you've already rushed to buy the newest magazine for knitting for babies, and you're already knitting clothes, and it bothers you that you won't be there to measure them for the prince or princess who will be born."

Ayala nodded, and her eyes filled with tears again. I knew my words touched her pain directly. "I don't know if you'll feel good about what I'm going to tell you," I continued, "but think about the moment you left the country with David. You didn't have children yet, and then, in a transatlantic phone call, you told your parents that you were pregnant. Over the years, Kfir and Lavi were born. How do you think your mother felt?"

Ayala raised her face in surprise. She didn't expect this question, but quickly recovered and replied, "My parents flew here and were with me for eight weeks after Kfir's birth and six weeks after Lavi's birth."

"Exactly," I said without reproach, "They came for a period they could allow themselves. They also worked and had various commitments, so they compromised and did what they could, and you didn't blame them, right? You just accepted the facts as they were."

"Yes," she nodded sadly, "I remember asking them to stay longer, but they couldn't."

"That's exactly right," I said. "There will always be situations in life that require you to compromise, to sacrifice something, and it may be that you're approaching such a situation as the birth of a child. You chose to move to Colorado from Israel, and many years after your decision, your children chose what they thought was right for them now and moved to Israel. Perhaps this will change." I tried to encourage her again. "Do you remember the case of Steve and Gail, who decided to try living in Israel? They even moved a large container of all their household belongings, but the move wasn't successful. I remember that Steve, the tough lawyer, was really frustrated. He couldn't get used to the mentality, and certainly not to learn the language. How we laughed when he didn't understand the difference between the words (Itriyot, Mitriyot, and Pitriyot) pasta, mushrooms, and umbrellas..."

"In the end, they returned to Denver," said Ayala.

"What I'm saying here is that it's possible that your children won't get used to the country, the Hebrew language, the mentality, and perhaps the work will be the reason, you can't know, that they'll want to return here, to Denver. So maybe you and David shouldn't rush to a decision. Give yourselves time. And if the children decide definitively after a year or two that they're staying in the country, you can start thinking about it again."

"But understand, Anat," Ayala's voice was almost desperate, "it hurts me so much that I won't be present in my grandchildren's lives on a daily basis. Look," she looked directly into my eyes, "you're not yet a grandmother, and neither am I, just a grandmother-to-be... But how do I describe this feeling? You know, they say that the love of a grandchild is greater than the love of a child. I don't know if it's true, but I know how frustrated I feel right now."

We sat there for another long hour, and in the meantime, the memorial service was over, and the large audience began to leave for the lobby. I remembered from last year that this was a moving and heartbreaking ceremony, the sad music and the video about the brave soldiers who fell in Israeli conflicts during the past year broke my heart. I took a deep breath.

I saw my partner quietly leaving with everyone, wiping his eyes. How could it not be?

Several months after that evening, I went shopping at the supermarket and ran into David in the fish department, where he was hesitating and asking the attendant about the fish he wanted to buy.

"Hi, David, how are you?"

"Hi, Anat, how are you? Didn't you travel to the homeland this summer?" he asked.

"No, this year I have guests from Israel. How's Ayala?"

"Don't ask," he smiled a big smile, and his brown eyes lit up. "She's been in heaven since our granddaughter was born. She went to Israel for a month and a half... to help at Kfir's house, and we'll likely travel together again for Sukkot. I'll stay in the country for two weeks, and she will stay for another two weeks after me. This will be our compromise for now."

"And how's business going? How's it progressing?" I inquired.

"Working hard and starting to see some results," David replied. "We hope the business grows further. But health is paramount, right? And peace of mind..."

"Right," I confirmed, "Health first. Good to see you, and warmest regards to Ayala when you call her."

I continued with my weekly shopping, pushing the cart through the aisles of the vast supermarket, and reflecting on the heated argument I witnessed on Memorial Day. I was pleased to hear that Ayala was in the country to help with her first grandchild, even if it was only for a short time, and that she and David had found a temporary compromise that was helping them maintain their family unity and the strong relationship they had enjoyed all these years.

I felt immense relief that they had managed to find the "golden path" that worked for them under the circumstances, helping them to navigate the challenge that had arisen in their lives. After all, who better than me understands how challenging life can be when one chooses to live on the other side of the world, and out of necessity, not choice, must shift one's steadfast anchor to a different one.

THIRTEEN
A MARITIME REMEMBRANCE

"HEY, hello, what are you doing there? Do you want to die?" someone shouted, their voice anxious and loud.

Rami turned his gaze toward the source of the voice. The caller was an officer, one of the crew members of the massive ocean liner, *Fantasy of the Sea.*

The officer stood at the end of the stairs on Deck 15, his face etched with worry. He wore the white uniform of a sea officer, and three gold stripes adorned his shoulders. Since Rami wasn't familiar with the ship's officer ranks, he could only guess that this was a high-ranking officer. The man wore dark sunglasses and held a pressure gauge or something similar.

"Oh, no, don't worry," smiled Rami, "I don't intend to jump or fall. I'm just looking for something my friend carved onto this particular railing three years ago."

"Look," the officer approached him decisively. "You're dangerously close to the railing. Why did you come up here? This is off-limits to passengers. Didn't you see the sign, 'Crew Only'?"

"I admit," Rami lowered his eyes for a moment, "I did see the warning sign. But let me explain. I didn't come up here to perform stunts. My friend and I were on this ship three years ago, during a voyage. He fell overboard from this deck, right here."

"Wait a minute…" the officer said. "Now I remember. When I joined this ship a year and a half ago, someone told me about a terrible accident here. Yes, I recall. One of the senior officers spoke of someone falling here about three years ago. You say the man who fell overboard was your friend?" He looked at Rami with curiosity and a desire to know more.

"Aha, I found it. Look here," Rami pointed at the ship's side, and the officer removed his dark sunglasses, bent down to the outside of the railing, and tried to see what was there. He examined it and immediately straightened up, putting his sunglasses back on. "I see something carved there, but I can't quite make out what the message says. Why is this so important to you? What did your friend write there?"

"My friend engraved his name," answered Rami. "In Hebrew. His name was Moshe. We're originally from Israel. My friend had a habit—everywhere he went, he'd carve his name."

"And you came all the way up here just to check if his inscription is still there?" the officer wondered. "Was he a close friend?"

"Yes," sighed Rami, "a close and dear friend, whose foolish and fatal mistake I still can't process."

"A mistake?" the officer wondered. "Now I truly don't understand. Wasn't it an accident?"

"I couldn't believe he would actually dare to climb the railing and risk it all just to carve his name," explained Rami. "Moshe and I booked this trip together. We wanted to celebrate his return to Israel after twenty years of living in Colorado. This was supposed to be our last vacation together before he returned to Israel."

The officer adjusted his blond hair, touched his sunglasses for the tenth time, smiled pleasantly, and straightened his hat.

"Valuable friendships are a thing to be cherished," he said. "There's an English saying that goes: 'It takes a long time to cultivate genuine friendships with a good friend'. I even share such a fraternal bond with a childhood friend in Florida, where I grew up…" For a moment, his thoughts drifted into the distant horizon, then he shook himself and extended his hand to Rami.

"Nice to meet you, I'm Ray."

"Nice to meet you, I'm Rami," Rami replied, smiling and shaking the offered hand.

"Moshe wasn't my childhood friend. I met him when he came to Denver, Colorado, due to a work contract. Our first meeting was at a 'Mimouna' party—a celebration held by the Moroccan Jewish community to mark the end of the seven days of Passover. One of the Israeli women in Denver, Yaffa, a woman of Moroccan descent, organized the celebration. This party brought together all the Israelis in the area. She heard about Moshe, who had already settled in the city and lived alone, and invited him to meet other Israelis. That is our tradition," he explained, "Israelis always want to meet other Israelis and build friendships to avoid being alone on the other side of the world."

"I understand," said Ray. "Please continue."

"When you leave your country and move to the wider world, the friends around you become your family," Rami said.

"Both when things are good, and especially when they are bad. You celebrate birthdays and Jewish holidays with them, you go to soccer and basketball games with them, you go to pubs with them, and you invite them to Shabbat dinners. These are the friends who will visit you in the hospital, God forbid, and those who will prepare home-cooked meals and provide round-the-clock support if you have a sick child."

"I'm sure it's not easy to choose to live far away from family," Ray shook his head. "And especially to drastically change your framework, to move to a completely different world. And I'm not talking about mentality and language. I have to say, it takes courage to take such a step."

"Thank you," Rami replied. "I see that you understand what I'm talking about."

"Of course," Ray replied. "Look, I'm the ship's chief engineer and supervisor of a crew of more than fifty. I think perhaps four of the crew in my department are American; the rest came from all over the globe, for example, from India, South Korea, many from the Philippines, and Malaysia. They all miss home, familiar food, and family. Some are married; some have young children. But working on this ship helps them. They don't pay for food or accommodations, and they also get a salary that in their own countries they wouldn't have gotten even half of, and so they even send money home to their families. Here on the ship, the crew is their family, so I imagine that in your small community in Denver, you are also a kind of family, with everything that implies."

"Precisely," smiled Rami. "You know, some people connect easily, some people don't. Moshe and I found that we had much in common and connected immediately. Moshe was an excellent athlete. I remember that in the week he arrived in Denver, he immediately asked to join a mountaineering group for rock climbing in the beautiful Rocky Mountains. He skied and loved nature walks, obtained a hunting and fishing license, and visited the most remote and forgotten places in the mountains. Once we even crossed the continental divide in the Rocky Mountains—an experience not to be missed. He wasn't just athletic; he loved sports and didn't miss any home games of the famous Colorado Broncos soccer team. So, we even had a shared season ticket to see all the games. I can tell you he was also the first to know about every popular artist who came to perform and the first to book tickets for all the major shows at the Red Rocks Amphitheater."

"Oh, yes, I've heard of Red Rocks," noted Ray. "It's the beautiful amphitheater carved into Red Rocks Park."

"Exactly," nodded Rami, "near the small town of Morrison. This amphitheater is considered a natural wonder. The sound quality there is so clear and distinct that there is no need for artificial amplification. It's a wonderful musical experience, and if I'm not mistaken, it's also considered one of the wonders of the world."

"Here's another place I've added to my sightseeing list," smiled Ray. There was a moment of silence, then Ray gently brought Rami back to the story. "You said that Moshe came to Denver for work. What did he do?"

"Moshe was a systems engineer at a large Israeli company," replied Rami. "He was an excellent, dedicated, and loyal employee, and so he was constantly promoted. Every year in May, when the time came to extend his work contract by another year, Moshe always hesitated. Although his family strongly supported his decisions, he remained in close contact with them—morning calls with his mother, a phone call to say Shabbat Shalom to his father every Friday, and video chats with his nephews and nieces every week. If his parents were healthy, and his siblings were living not far from them, he would have never considered returning to Israel, and he extended his work contract for another year. Thus, one year followed another, until twenty years passed, or as Moshe used to say, 'What's going on here? This isn't fair. We're playing tag with time, but time always wins.'"

"You're touching on a very familiar sore spot," smiled Ray. "I also told myself that my seafaring career wouldn't last more than ten years, and here I am, counting my fourteenth year at sea. And the longing for home? For family? Familiar. I lost a girlfriend because of work at sea; she didn't like the initial periods when I was away from home, and eventually gave up."

"For Moshe, the longing was less significant," Rami continued the story. "He traveled to Israel every year to present his two-year work summaries and sign a contract for another year with the company back home. Every visit, he saw his family for a few days. Not a bad compromise, and everything proceeded smoothly. But all that changed when his father suffered a stroke that left him paralyzed in his limbs and hands. Moshe's mother was the primary caregiver for his ailing father, because Moshe's siblings were each busy with their own lives. Two months later, she collapsed and was confined to bed herself.

"The collapse was physical and mental, the doctors said, and would take a long time to recover. Moshe was torn within. If he stayed in Denver, he could get the promotion he had longed for over the past four years. He had invested a great deal of effort in his position and wanted to build excellent work references. We discussed the options available to him, and he pondered them night and day. And that year, he traveled to Israel and returned to Denver at least three times, to help and support. This only reinforced the understanding that there was no turning back, and the final decision would be to return to the homeland. The only hesitation was regarding his work—where could he find a job with such an exceptional salary and benefits? The company where he worked agreed that he could submit his resignation as soon as he found a suitable replacement, and he even started exploring work that could primarily be done from home, so he could help with the heavy family burden."

"He undoubtedly felt divided between two worlds," Ray nodded thoughtfully. "On the one hand, he wanted to continue living in Denver with all its comforts, quality of life, and high standard of living that his high salary enabled. On the other hand, he understood that his family in Israel needed him now more than ever."

"Indeed, that's how he felt," Rami agreed, "but once he made the decision, he began to finalize matters in Colorado. And I'll tell you, it wasn't easy. There was a lot to do to wrap up twenty years of routine in a place. He sold things, donated a lot of equipment, canceled personal phone lines that would be closed a week after flying to the homeland, and sent personal belongings in a container to Israel. I felt sorry for myself, but happy for his family. I understood that in Israel, he was considered the heart of the family. When everything was finalized and organized, I offered him a little vacation before his departure—a five-day cruise in the Caribbean. He was happy and excited, and laughed that it was an opportunity to buy a few more gifts for his nephews and nieces from the Caribbean islands."

"Sounds like a nice and cheerful fellow, your Moshe," the officer smiled. "By the way, I've never heard the name Moshe. Was that his real name? What does the name Moshe mean in Hebrew?"

Rami smiled. "Moshe is his real name, and in English it would be Moses, and in Denver, I adopted a nickname for him, Mushon, and before long, everyone knew him as Mushon. No one called him Moshe."

"Oh, that's clearer now," Ray smiled. "Now tell me, what happened? How did this tragedy happen that Moshe lost his life?"

"Moshe had a hobby that sometimes troubled me and my other friends," Rami sighed. "Wherever we went or traveled, whether it was a skiing trip to Keystone, Vail, Morrison, or Aspen, he would impede us just to carve his name into trees, concrete, iron railings, bridges, and the like. Not only that, if we returned to the same place to travel again, he made sure to look for where he carved his name and wouldn't leave until he found what he was looking for. He loved carving his name so much, you know, a kind of hobby or an unexplainable complex. And that's exactly what happened here on this beautiful ship. On the first day, we went to the dining room to grab some lunch, and immediately after that, we ordered our first cocktails at the bar. With the cocktails in hand, we began to survey the ship, with all its fifteen decks. For Moshe, this was his first cruise, and as you can imagine, my curious friend wanted to see everything and check out every attraction on the ship. We started from the first deck; the first few decks only had rooms, so we went up to the fourth deck, where it started to get interesting. We passed the restaurants and bars, walked around, and reached the highest deck. Moshe always loved heights, whether it was admiring the height of the Empire State Building in New York or standing on the top of a mountain after a long climb, and so when we got here, which was actually the highest point on this ship, he was so captivated by the view he saw, that his eyes widened with the magnetic charm of the endless blue sea and the horizon that stretched out in every direction. He let out cries of surprise and wonder at the marvel that unfolded before his eyes and the mysterious beauty that the sea conveyed. 'Wow, man, to see something like this, I can't believe it, we're on top of the world,' he couldn't stop marveling, 'I can shout... And cry out or sing in a high operatic tone, a vociferous sea opera in my hoarse voice, and no one would hear me from this high deck.'

"'Yes, yes,' I'd laughed at him. 'Hope the wind wouldn't blow us off the deck. See what a thin railing this ship has. How could it be that on the railing of this deck, they did not also add a wide safety railing of glass? It's dangerous here, and I need to return you to shore whole, not in pieces, remember?' I'd warned him as he touched the white metal railing opposite him.

"'Rami, you know we're not supposed to be on this deck at all,' Moshe had commented to me. He looked like a small child who had played a trick on his teacher. 'There was a sign at the bottom of the stairs that said, For crew only, did you notice?'

"'I know, that's why there aren't any safety railings for passengers here,' I'd replied in a reproving voice.

"'It's okay,' he'd said. 'Let's just peek here a bit and go back down to deck 14. It is safer there, okay?'

"'Good, so be it. Let's enjoy a delicious cocktail, soak up some of the deepest blue scenery, and go to the pool.'"

"And all this time you were next to your friend?" Ray asked.

"Yes," Rami nodded. "Meaning we talked, and with that, I surveyed the high deck. It's not every day that I get, unlike you, to stand on a deck fifteen stories high and look out at the endless expanse of the ocean, right? More than anything, I was fascinated by the huge chimney on this deck, from which a strong stream of white smoke was issued incessantly, with the roar of enormous bellows into the sky. I stood next to the chimney, the noise of the pistons that drove the huge engines below was monotonous and deafening even at this height, and I asked myself why white smoke came out of the chimney and not black, a question from someone who understands nothing about mechanics. Then I moved a little away from the chimney, which, as you know, emits immense and unbearable heat, and surveyed all the clocks that were attached to its right wall, trying to learn what the clocks were saying, but I couldn't understand anything."

"Don't be surprised you didn't understand," the officer smiled. "If you're not a ship mechanic, it will be very difficult for you to understand the intricacies of a ship with such power."

"Moshe still stood by the metal railing, surveying the blue scenery, completely captivated," Rami continued his story. "I looked at him for a few moments. I imagined him thinking of the homeland and of his father, who was a big and strong man and now needed care, and how much it hurt him to know about his beloved and strong mother, who also now needed treatment and strengthening. When you know a person like how I knew Moshe, you learn to recognize his expressions, and I could see on his face that he was troubled but also at peace with his decision. Since he made the decision to return to Israel, a heavy burden had been lifted from him, and there was no chance that he would have made a different decision. For this, I appreciated him even more.

"I gave him the time and space. I thought that in a few minutes we would go down to the bar, order another cocktail, enjoy the scenery of girls in bikinis, and go to the jacuzzi. Then I called him from a distance and said I was going around the chimney to see what else was on this deck. I started walking around the hot chimney, and when the first round ended, I saw Moshe checking something on the railing deck.

"'What are you checking there on the railing?' I called him.

"'I'm trying to check where it's best to engrave my name,' he'd replied in a shout. 'I don't have a key or an engraver in my pocket, only the magnetic room card, and it doesn't engrave well.'

"'Are you serious?' I'd asked in return. 'Even on the ship, you want to engrave your name. Forget it, no need. What are the chances you'll return to this ship to see your name engraved? Besides, you know that the ship's maintenance people won't be happy if they see engraving on the railing that will further cause corrosion from the salt on the metal, and they will have to paint it again. Come on, forget it, let's go down.'

"'Let me write the name at least,' Moshe had grumbled. 'You

know that's my fingerprint everywhere I go, come on, give me two minutes in your life.'

"Moshe tried again to engrave with the magnetic room card without success, and then it seemed that an idea came to his mind. He bent down to check the other side of the white metal railing, the side facing the sea. I didn't quite understand why the other side worked better for him for engraving—and then he bent his body even further so he could see what he was trying to engrave. It seemed that the engraving wasn't strong enough for him; he tried again to draw each line several times. When he didn't succeed, he suddenly climbed onto the railing, turned around, and sat down with his face turned toward the ship and his legs held between the bottom and top railing, in a position where his left hand and legs held the bottom railing, and with his right hand, he could engrave on the railing. Of course, there was another reason for him to do this risky, looping exercise. He didn't want the ship's maintenance staff to see the engraving on the inner side of the railing, so they wouldn't paint over and erase it ever."

Ray's face was strained. He didn't utter a word; he just nodded at Rami to continue.

"Suddenly, we heard a small scream and the rolling laugh of a young woman. I turned my head toward the sound and saw a young man and woman who decided to climb up and see what the view was like from the highest deck. The girl didn't stop laughing, and the boy chased after her, tickling her on her waist, and she made little screams of pleasure from time to time. Suddenly, she screamed with surprise when she saw Moshe hanging on the other side of the railing, supported only by one hand on the lower railing."

And then... Rami's voice weakened, "And then Moshe's call for help was heard.

"All I could imagine was Moshe being startled by the young woman's scream, and his left hand slipping and no longer having support on the railing. Everything happened so quickly... he didn't have time to bring his left hand back to hold onto the railing again, and he slipped and fell into the sea.

"I heard something like, 'Oh, oh, damn it, Rami,' and when I reached the other side of the railing, Moshe was no longer there. In the first few seconds, I looked at the deck, an immediate instinct to make sure he'd gone to the safe, solid deck floor, but all I saw was the young couple screaming for help and looking down at the sea. I turned my gaze there and saw Moshe in the water. The weight of his body and the force of the fall caused him to dive deep; he sank to a depth of at least ten meters before surfacing. I ran to call for help, while the young couple tried to calm down from the shock of what they had seen. They both stood there helplessly, shouting at Moshe to try to hold on and float until help arrived."

"Remember that the ship was underway at a speed of about fifteen knots..." muttered Ray.

"Precisely," Rami nodded sadly. "The ship began to pull farther and farther away from Moshe. I don't know how I leaped all those steps on the way to Deck 14, and from there to 13, and then to the first corridor I saw. I grabbed a steward who worked on the suite level and, in a panic, asked him to summon help. The steward immediately pressed a button on the cordless phone he carried in his jacket pocket, and it emitted a high-pitched, long beep. He began shouting into the phone: 'Man overboard, man fell from Deck 15, quickly, yes, Deck 15. Emergency, emergency...'

"I left him there, continuing to shout into the radio, and I started running back upstairs," Rami continued his story. "I skipped four steps at once, almost out of breath, leaning on any possible railing to prevent myself from falling, continuing to jump, run, and sprint back to Deck 15.

"When I arrived there, breathless, rescue boats and divers had come—because I could not explain otherwise how they got there so quickly—security officers and rescue divers. One of the officers was already giving instructions over the intercom; I could see below three men in rubber suits preparing to enter the water instantly.

"From the ship's side, I saw the white cranes beginning to lower a yellow life raft, and a small speedboat, which I immediately recognized from my Navy service. It had almost reached the first deck of the ship and landed on the water."

Rami took a deep breath. His face was strained, and tears welled up in his eyes. "The divers plunged into the water and began swimming swiftly toward Moshe, but he was quite far away, at least a kilometer, I think. Only then did I begin to grasp the size of the event, and reality struck me. Moshe, my best friend, was in grave danger. In those moments, terrible, dreadful thoughts raced through my head, that a shark might devour him, or that he might drown in the depths of the immense ocean."

"What did the other passengers do?" Ray asked, "I imagine there was panic on deck."

"The news of the fall spread quickly to many of the passengers," Rami shook his head. "Others saw all sorts of illogical things happening around them—crew members running frantically from one side of the ship to the other, bartenders instructed not to use blenders—later I understood that all of the ship's electricity was dedicated to the energy the electric cranes required, and other unusual activities. Within minutes, a rush of people headed to Deck 15. Everyone wanted to see, to participate, to offer advice. The ship's security personnel set up a human barricade to prevent people from reaching the area and tried to calm the astonished 4,500 passengers who understood that a great disaster had occurred."

"I can only try to imagine what you went through," Ray said empathetically.

"I just stood there, near the officers, and in a fractured voice and panic tried to explain to them that this was my friend, who just wanted to carve his name into the hull of the ship," Rami continued his story. "At first, they didn't understand what I was saying.

"I cried and spoke, sobbed and screamed, covered my face with my hands, pulled my hair—I was seized by terror as my body trembled and my mouth mumbled unintelligible words. Then someone pulled me aside and attached an oxygen mask to my nose and mouth. Later, I understood that it was a paramedic who was called to calm me down.

"A doctor in the ship's uniform injected me with a sedative, and after that I saw and heard nothing."

Rami paused for a moment, his thoughts drifting. He hugged himself with both arms as if he were suddenly cold. "I lay in the ship's infirmary for two days," he said quietly. "Every now and then, I woke up and fell back asleep. I don't know what the medicines they gave me did, but they made me sleep all the time. Until one morning, a nurse entered my room and saw that I was awake. She checked me, and then I could no longer bear the uncertainty. I grasped her hand as tightly as I could, crying bitterly and begging her to tell me what had happened to my friend... 'Tell me they managed to save him,' I'd pleaded. 'Tell me, I have to know, please.'

"The nurse looked at me, and her eyes filled with tears. Someone called out her name, and she left the room. I tried to get out of bed, but I fell back down immediately because I felt awful dizziness. A few minutes later, a doctor and two nurses, accompanied by one of the ship's officers, entered the room. I looked at them, trying to understand what was happening from their expressions.

"I pleaded with them, 'Tell me my friend is alright, tell me you managed to save him.'

"The four of them just looked at me with compassion and did not speak. Then the ship's doctor approached me and, in a quiet voice, said, 'I'm so sorry to tell you that your friend did not survive. The ship was underway, if you remember, and it took time to stop such a large ship. Your friend likely swallowed a lot of water when he fell; he didn't float for long. The life rafts reached the area where he fell and sank within minutes, but in that short time, we speculate that one of two things happened—either he drowned because he swallowed a lot of water...

"'Water had entered his lungs, or he had been attacked by the large group of sharks here.'

"I'd looked at him and couldn't utter a word.

"'I'm truly sorry,' the doctor had continued. 'We are all sharing your sorrow. I want you to stay here in the clinic to recover for a day or two, and then we can try to help you with any messages or calls for his family and anyone you need to call. But please, you've been through a severe trauma, and I ask that you stay here for another day of recovery and strengthening. And again,' he'd gently patted my shoulder.

"'Don't worry. The entire staff will be with you until the ship returns to Miami port, and we'll ensure you're okay until you get home.'

"The doctor had prescribed a calming medication for me. I didn't argue. I tried to stay strong for Moshe, for the most special and wonderful friend I'd ever had."

Rami fell silent. Ray looked at him and saw that his eyes were full of tears.

"It's been three years since then," Rami said. "And as you can see, Moshe doesn't have a grave. In the first year after his death, I flew to Israel and was there with his family. I think the hardest thing for his parents is the fact that he doesn't have a grave and tombstone, and that they have no place to come and light candles for him, and to recite Kaddish and bring fresh flowers, or to fill water bottles from the tap that is in the corner of every cemetery and do the traditional washing the grave that is done in Israel for every grave—washing the grave of the accumulated dust, refreshing the deceased's name in fresh water and making sure that the wind did not extinguish the candles lit in the box attached to the tombstone, where they also leave matches and candles for anyone who comes to honor his memory.

"I pondered what would be the best way to perpetuate Moshe's memory, and the idea for the most meaningful memorial service, given the circumstances of his death, occurred to me. Since then, for the past three years, I've arranged a cruise on the ship from which Moshe fell, and on his anniversary, I stand here, talking to him and verifying that the name he engraved is still on the side of the ship's railing.

"I tell him how life continues without him, update him on what's happening with his father, and tell him that every time I come to Israel, I make sure to visit his family and share what's happening in my life as well."

And so, they stood on the 15th-floor deck, Ray and Rami, and their thoughts soared beyond, into the depths of the blue horizon, allowing the warm Caribbean breeze to blow strongly and pat their faces, as if reminding them that despite the beauty and magic of this amazing landscape, it was not the most sympathetic place to be standing. Ray was silent for a moment, then reached out and shook Rami's hand again.

"I greatly appreciate you sharing this difficult experience with me," he said in his gentle voice. "Will you join me for a beer on the promenade?"

FOURTEEN
GRAVE

EVERYONE EMBRACED EVERYONE ELSE, and here and there, tears welled up in their eyes. In the small "Feldman Mortuary" hall, located north of the bustling Colfax Street, at 1673 York Street in Denver, Colorado, an atmosphere of sorrow and grief hung heavy, and like everyone else, we mourned quietly. It was hard to accept that Itzik was no longer with us. The smiling, loving, and considerate man, who was kind to all, the brilliant inventor of patents, the modest man who made no fuss about his professional achievements.

Itzik, the man with the guitar, the one who lifted the spirits at every Hanukkah and Mimouna party, the one who reminded us of the songs we grew up with and missed, like "The City in Gray," "Next Year," and how could we forget "Beautiful and Flourishing Land of Israel...?"

He had passed away.

I stood there quietly, surveying the people who had come to pay their final respects to their beloved friend. I hoped Itzik had seen and understood just how much he had touched everyone's hearts at every singing gathering, and how through his guitar strings, music, his endless smile, and the positive energy he radiated, he lifted the spirits of all of us in exile, and helped us feel a little bit of what we had left behind, a little bit of what was missing in each and every one of our personal identities who had, for now, chosen the diaspora as their home. We needed these reminders like air to breathe.

Gradually, the guests began to settle into the dark-blue upholstered chairs arranged in rows. A small stage stood before us, and additional chairs were placed behind it, likely for people who wished to speak about the deceased or community leaders.

Now, the small funeral hall was filled. Everyone who knew Itzik came to say goodbye, and everyone who knew Neta, his wife, came to offer her a warm embrace and to remind her that she was not alone, that we were here with her, for better or worse, because we were the family we created for ourselves, out of necessity, in the diaspora.

I sat there with everyone else, thinking about Itzik and how he had met his untimely death. Although I didn't know all the details, still, to die from slipping on black ice right next to his home?

Slipping on black ice was the nightmare of anyone living in Denver. It occurred on sunny winter days, after the sun melted the large layer of snow and a small amount of snow remained on the concrete, the water would refreeze in the evening and throughout the night, turning into transparent ice that allowed one to see the concrete or asphalt of the road. Thus, the frozen water and sidewalks earned the nickname "black ice." It was very dangerous because it was not always noticeable due to its transparency, and slipping on it and getting hurt was very easy.

The farewell ceremony for Itzik began with quiet guitar music, and, as in similar previous sad events, everyone shared their last memories of Itzik, what music he played at the gathering two weeks ago, and other things that would now become memories and would provide all of us with food for thought about Itzik and the fact that he did not have time to say goodbye to the ones dear to him in Israel.

Between speakers, an atmosphere of sorrow and tense silence reigned in the hall. Here and there, I saw someone who couldn't hold back and wiped a tear; one person coughed to disguise the impending cry. Anyone who wanted to speak to the grieving audience stood up from their chair and shared something about Itzik or shared anecdotes that tried to bring a little smile to the audience. Some people smiled, even if only out of politeness.

I also shared with the audience my acquaintance with Itzik, and at the end of my brief speech, I felt it was important to remind everyone of the well-known saying from the song "It's not what you took with you when you left, but what you left behind," and "How true this is about Itzik, the considerate, friendly man."

As the ceremony ended, the attendees wrapped themselves tightly in their coats and went outside to the freezing air. It was already dark outside, and the 28-degree Fahrenheit temperature, which was minus two degrees Celsius, reminded us that winter was still in full swing in Colorado. We quickly walked toward the car parked far away in the fully occupied parking lot, and I asked my partner, Gabi, for his jacket too, so we could warm up until we reached the car. We circled Feldman Mortuary and walked toward our car. The only noise on the dark street was the click of my heels on the pavement. I intertwined my hands with Gabi's to warm up a little.

When we finally sat in the car, I felt I couldn't hold back. I covered my face with my hands and burst into tears. Gabi took my left hand and gently stroked it, trying to calm my spontaneous breakdown.

"It's okay, everyone's sad today," he said. "We received another reminder of how fragile lives are. Today we are here, and tomorrow? Who knows," he added sadly.

"I'm cold," I shivered from the cold and sadness, rubbing my hands together and bringing them close to the vents to feel the weak heat emanating from the car. We started driving and were soon stopped in traffic at the exit from the parking lot, to allow all the other mourners to leave.

"It hurts me every time I look at Neta," I replied, wiping my eyes again. "Did you see how strong she was?"

"She has to be strong," Gabi replied. "She is going through a serious crisis, and so are her children, even though they are already grown. It's not easy to be strong in front of the audience that came to comfort them. Neta tried to show us all that she is holding up with courage in the face of the tragedy. Imagine what immense fortitude she needs now, for the funeral back in the homeland. I heard her tell Tzipi that their flight to Israel departs at four o'clock in the morning, because they couldn't find another flight that would allow them to transport Itzik's coffin."

I wiped my face and sniffed my nose for the tenth time. A silence fell between us for a few minutes, but I wanted to speak, to unload more of what was within me.

"Do you have any idea how much it costs to fly a body from here to Israel?" I asked. "I imagine it's an expensive affair."

"I'm not sure," Gabi replied, as he steered the car onto the main road on our way home. "Once, many years ago, at one of the Israeli gatherings during Hanukkah, I heard someone talking about a family from Boston who had to fly a body to Israel, and they didn't have the money because the cost was something like twenty thousand dollars. And imagine, that was twenty years ago. Who knows how much it costs today?"

"Wow, that's a fortune," I gasped at the sum.

We both remained silent for a long moment, Gabi focused on driving, and I was lost in my thoughts.

"Say," I began again, "have we already written in our wills that we want to be buried in Israel? Can you imagine what this will cost our children?"

"I don't care how much it will cost," Gabi said firmly. "I'm insistent on being buried in our homeland. I was born in the Land of Israel, and I want to be buried in the Land of Israel. Remember that if I die before you. You too, right? If you change your mind, tell me so that I can update our will."

"We should also remind Nurit," I said quietly. "She was delighted to hear that she'll receive the inheritance we're leaving her, until I told her that she'd have to fly our bodies in caskets to the homeland. That didn't sit well with her at all."

"Oh, but the money we are leaving her is fine," grumbled Gabi, shaking his head from side to side.

"But wait, we need to talk about where in Israel we will be buried. I want to be buried in Migdal HaEmek, next to my parents," I said seriously.

"No, no," Gabi laughed. "I also want to be buried with my family, and as you know, they are buried in Dimona." He slowed the car before a yellow light and was rewarded with a harsh honking noise from the driver behind us.

"Oh, you could have gone through that light," I grumbled.

"Why should I risk it?" he replied angrily. "And today of all days, with all the cameras everywhere? Do you know they would film me going through a red light, and then who would pay the two-hundred and sixty dollar fine?"

I could hear the anger in his voice. Whenever the topic of burial came up, Gabi became short-tempered and irritable, but I wanted to pursue the conversation.

"Why should I also be buried in Dimona?" I asked quietly.

"No, stop," he was close to being truly annoyed. "I know you're not crazy about Dimona, but I grew up there, and my father is buried there, and my grandmother..."

"Well, right," I agreed, "but your mother is buried in Jerusalem."

"I want to be buried in Dimona," he tried to end the argument. "You know I still have friends there."

"What a strange man you are," I scoffed. "What does it matter or add that you have friends in Dimona now? Do you believe your friends will still be in Dimona after you pass on to the next world?"

"Who knows, and if I go before them, there will be someone who will come to visit my grave. Don't you think so?"

"Oh, Gabi, you're talking nonsense," I protested. "Who knows who will die first. Maybe we should solve the problem by asking to be buried here in Colorado, and that's it?" I suggested.

Gabi frowned. "What's gotten into you? Have you forgotten what Jewish cemeteries look like here? They're in terrible condition. Remember when Don's grandfather passed away, and we went to the funeral at Mount Nebo Cemetery? There isn't even a decent parking lot. I parked on the side road before entering the cemetery, and we walked a full mile on foot and were late. The neglect was screaming everywhere. The busy road on one side and weeds growing even on the walk path, which wasn't paved, and the miniature space allotted to the tombstone... did you forget we walked on grass that was the grave of the tombstone in front of it? My skin crawled. It's disrespectful!"

"Right, right," now it was my turn to shudder. "And that they don't allow lighting memorial candles there? In every cemetery in Israel, there's a small metal or stone box where you can light a memorial candle and regular candles. I always leave candles and matches in the box in case someone forgot to bring them. And I always light candles for two other graves nearby. I choose the two that seem most neglected, the ones I know haven't been visited in a while. That's something I learned from my mother when I was still a little girl. I saw her do it after every visit to my father's grave in Migdal HaEmek."

"Really, what kind of thing is it that you can't light memorial candles for the deceased?" Gabi wondered out loud. "Show me one cemetery in the country that burned down because of memorial candles. You know what? Now that we're talking about it, I really feel something is missing when we leave the cemetery here. Now I know it's because we didn't light a memorial candle for the deceased, as is customary in Israel."

We continued driving, and the conversation turned to other cemeteries in Denver. Gabi mentioned "Rose Hill Cemetery" and explained that it was older than "Mount Nebo" because until fifty or sixty years ago, most of the Jewish community lived on the west side of the city, closer to the mountains. They, like everyone else during the gold rush about one hundred and fifty years ago, wanted to be close to the mining areas.

"Well, yes, that's why there's still the 'Ohr Chaim' synagogue of Rabbi Serman," I laughed. "They are not planning to move to the east side of the city."

"Do you remember, four years ago, how we volunteered to join the Jewish community expedition to weed and clean the Jewish cemetery in the town of Leadville?" Gabi reminded me, bringing back forgotten memories.

"I remember," I smiled. "How could I forget? A long journey, almost three hours on narrow, dangerous roads, to maintain a Jewish cemetery in some remote place..."

"But what a beautiful route, 'Gwanella Pass'?" Gabi said, wistfully. "The high mountains, the green trees that conveyed to us the mystery of the towns from Mark Twain's 'The Adventures of Huckleberry Finn.' Such an enchanting region."

"And do you remember the return trip?" I asked, "The Mexican restaurant where everything we ate was spicy?"

Gabi recalled it, laughed, and we continued to delve into memories of that trip and others, until we returned to the conversation we had started.

"Say, what do you think about this absurdity here in America, that every deceased person must be buried in a coffin, even Jews? In Israel, people aren't buried in coffins; why shouldn't they respect the well-known saying, 'Dust you are, to dust you shall return,' here in America too?"

"Because Colorado law mandates burial in a coffin, but the Jews found an original way to respect both the law and the halakha," Gabi explained. "They buy the simplest wooden coffin, drill a few holes in the bottom, and that way allow the earth, rainwater, and worms to penetrate the coffin and come into contact with the body. Thus, they fulfill the halakhic commandment, 'From dust you came and to dust you shall return.'"

"Wow, brilliant," I said, "there's nothing like us Jews. We pepper-minded people always find a solution for every situation. But let's return for a moment to our argument. Do you not want to be buried next to me in the Upper Galilee?"

"I didn't tell you that I don't want to be buried next to you," Gabi sighed. "I want to be buried in the place where I grew up. I want to be buried in Dimona. Why aren't you willing to accept this?"

"But I also want to be buried next to my parents," I protested. "You aren't fair."

Gabi remained silent, and I continued in the same vein. "It's interesting if Neta will bury Itzik where he wanted to be or where she chose. Maybe they even agreed beforehand where they would like to be buried?"

"I think if Itzik isn't buried in the city where he's registered in the city registry, Neta will have to pay a certain amount for burial in another place."

"Didn't you hear what Tzipi said there tonight?" I asked him. "Someone told her that Israelis who don't live in Israel don't get a free plot in the cemetery. This is the first time I've heard such a thing."

"Tzipi told you that?" Gabi was surprised. "I haven't heard of such a law either. It's interesting if it's true. Because if it's true and we don't have a right to a free burial in Israel, then our whole discussion is unnecessary. We need to examine this matter seriously."

"Yes, I understood from her words that this is confirmed—anyone who isn't registered as living in Israel for at least six months a year doesn't get the right to a burial plot in the homeland. That means we will have to buy a burial plot anyway, regardless of where in the country. Who thought of all this when we left Israel?"

"We haven't discussed this either," Gabi said seriously. "It's the kind of issue that people usually don't want to talk about."

"But in our case, we have to talk about a grave and a cemetery, and arrange this matter as quickly as possible," I declared. "We don't live in Israel, and live comfortably here, playing tag with time, and meanwhile, time runs forward and wins. We don't know when we will die, just as Itzik didn't expect... You know those who say, 'It's far from thinking,' or those who, in the most naive way, think, 'It won't happen to me soon, I intend to live a long time.' People push such conversations aside, don't want to deal with thoughts of death and burial, prefer to ignore…

"Slipping on the snow near the house, suffering a severe head injury, and dying within a week—and now tomorrow they are already flying his body to be buried in Israel. I don't know if Nata and Itzik ever discussed it."

"I hope there are people helping Neta and the children with all the burial arrangements," Gabi said, "but what about people who no longer have family in the country? Who helps them in such a situation? Most people leaving the country don't consider these things until something like this happens, and then they start racking their brains and searching for help and advice on such an important matter.

"See," he added as we approached our green neighborhood, "moments like these stir us all, but let's be honest with ourselves— will we continue talking about this tomorrow and next week until we reach a decision?"

"So, let's try to decide now," I insisted.

"How about we write in our will that we should be buried in Netanya?" Gabi smiled. "That way we'll be together, and families and friends from both sides will come to the central area of Israel to visit our graves."

"Netanya?" I frowned.

"Well, what do you want? Netanya is a city in the center of the country. If not Dimona or Migdal HaEmek, here we've found a neutral place in the middle."

I looked at him sideways. His small smile revealed he was joking.

"Gabi," I became serious again, "do you remember Victor's funeral story? We did not fly to his funeral because it happened during the pandemic, but I heard from my sister that his son-in-law wouldn't wait until they arranged a grave for him in Migdal HaEmek, next to my parents, and insisted on burying him the same day. They buried him in the city of Kiryat Motzkin because a grave was available, but I was upset since Victor had wanted to be laid to rest near our parents. I still have not forgiven that son-in-law for deciding that burying the deceased immediately on the day of death was more important. That is not what my brother wanted. Ugh, why wasn't I there when it happened?" My eyes were already moist. "This is another price we pay for not living in Israel, near family. I would have made sure and insisted that he be buried where he wanted..."

Gabi held the steering wheel with his left hand and held my hand with his right. A brief silence passed, and I recalled the shiva for Victor in Denver, where friends and strangers gathered for mincha and joined Gabi in reciting Kaddish. Gabi witnessed the shock and pain I experienced then. I could not hide the enormity of the loss I felt.

We stopped again at a red light, and Gabi quietly turned to me. "This week I'll call lawyer Glazman to update our wills," he said, "so it will explicitly state that we require our bodies to be flown to the country, and we will also clearly indicate where we wish to be buried."

"Fine," I agreed, "let's give ourselves three more days to make a final decision and not change it. Okay?"

Gabi nodded.

"I already heard our daughter Nurit complaining," I smiled with a painful memory. "She won't like these responsibilities we are leaving for her."

"Sorry, but I truly don't care how Nurit reacts to this," Gabi said. "She should respect our wishes and do exactly what is written in our wills. And I will tell you more than that, Nurit herself was born in Israel, and I would be happy for her and her children to decide to be buried in Israel after their hundred and twenty years, why not?"

"Don't get your hopes up." I felt sorry to disappoint him. "Nurit came here at the age of three. She has an American husband and American children, and they will decide for themselves where they want to be buried. I would not be surprised if she and her husband decided on a completely different decision than ours," I added with disappointment. "We are Israelis in heart and soul, and we know we want to be buried in Israel, but the feeling toward the country is a very individual matter. Nurit grew up in America and identifies as an American Jew. Although she maintains a Jewish home, her mentality is American in every way. Certain circumstances are outside of our influence, and this situation exemplifies such conditions. Remember, we brought Nurit to live here. If she decides to live in Israel... let's leave that to miracles."

A disturbing silence filled the heated car. I thought about everything we discussed, things we said for the first time in the decades since we've lived in Colorado. I thought about the people who came to say goodbye to dear Itzik today. I thought about Neta and the strength she must gather for the funeral in Israel. I thought about those who came to comfort her and the children, who would slowly return to their daily routines, and about her, left alone to deal with the sudden shock, the sorrow, the new challenges, the loneliness, and the memories.

We arrived home. I took off my heeled shoes and replaced them with soft slippers. I took off my suit and changed into comfortable, warm pajamas. A cup of tea could warm me now, I thought. I filled the electric kettle with water when a sharp ringtone interrupted the silence. It was a video from my friend, Danielle, who also came to Itzik's funeral. She shared a video she took at the last gathering she organized during Hanukkah at her home. I sat there, with tears in my eyes and trembling hands, watching the one-minute video in which Itzik, the man with his beloved guitar, smiled at the audience and straightened the white sheet music he brought with him, playing vigorously as his body moved rhythmically to the music—right and left—and we surrounded him tightly, the main thing being to be part of the feeling, part of the unity, part of something that connects us here with divided hearts, in death and in life, as we sang in raspy voices, "The land of Israel is beautiful, the land of Israel is flourishing..."

FIFTEEN
IN THIS GOLDEN CAGE

RONALD INSISTED on paying for the exquisite and indulgent meal we had. I felt embarrassed and suggested we at least pay for the tip, but Ronald insisted on footing the entire bill.

I thought it was wise that we booked and paid for the hotel room in advance; otherwise, as I know Ronald, he wouldn't have charged us for the room, since the hotel we stayed at was also part of his hotel chain.

"Let us spoil you," Ronald said with a smile when we arrived. "It's not every day you're staying with us in the mountains. When we come down to Denver for business, you spoil us with your delightful hospitality and delicious home-cooked meals, so please, allow me to spoil you today."

Ronald and Debbie, our close friends, invited us to a late lunch at the renowned Grand Rapids restaurant in the cowboy town of Grand Lake in the Rocky Mountains. Grand Lake, named by Native Americans over a century ago, is about 30 minutes from the Winter Park Ski Resort.

The exceptional restaurant was situated in a breathtaking spot, on a hillside overlooking Grand Lake.

From the enormous windows, we could gaze at the powerful water's frothy rush of the river flowing beneath us. Waves crashed noisily onto the small rocks that lined the riverbed and banks, creating swirling maelstroms that danced in a dizzying rhythm to the captivating music of the water.

The spectacle was equally beautiful, frightening, and amazing; the untamed beauty of the mighty forces of nature was breathtaking. Through the towering windows, we could also admire the enchanting beauty of the surrounding mountains that resembled imposing giants guarding Grand Lake with their unwavering and uncompromising stance, momentarily appearing as though they embraced it warmly. The sun dipped below the ridge in the west, its rays resembling golden wings of light encircling the mountains and the lake in a mysterious aura of shimmering, golden light, creating final streaks of shadow and gold on the water.

We sat at the table closest to the windows, and the conversation flowed easily. We had much to discuss, with the sound of the river's current and the pleasant restaurant music accompanying us.

"We're going down to Denver this week," Ronald said. "Debbie needs to renew her Israeli passport, and we have a meeting scheduled with the consulate in the city."

"Yes," Debbie smiled, revealing perfect, gleaming teeth. "It is time to get my 'fix.' I miss our homeland so much. Almost three months have passed since my last trip, and besides, you know," she continued, "I'm not crazy about the spices here in Colorado. I always buy a three-month supply in Israel, and that gets me through until my next trip."

"Debbie, really, to that extent?" I wondered. "True, the spices here aren't quite as good as in Israel, but isn't it really difficult for you to travel every three months? We couldn't have traveled so much; every trip for us involves lost workdays, too."

Debbie sipped her white wine and did not say a word.

"We only travel about once every two years," I added. "And yes, reluctantly, I compromise on the spices I find here," I said quietly.

Debbie coughed slightly. "In Israel, the spices have a captivating aroma, and the taste reminds me of our childhood and the fragrant dishes of the country..." She took another sip of wine and said resolutely, "Believe me, if Ronald could move his business to Israel, we'd be moving there immediately."

I was surprised by her words. Debbie did not lack anything; she was living quite well in Colorado. Debbie's life reflected the common dream of gaining financial freedom by moving abroad. The saying, "Debbie has won the money-making tree," certainly applied to her, but this victory brought with it something else that none of us would want to "win."

Debbie was an Israeli journalist who had been a successful writer for a newspaper in the north of Israel. She met Ronald in Eilat during coverage of a conference for investors interested in developing a hi-tech city in the Negev, which is the southern part of Israel. Following the interview, Ronald invited Debbie to join him for dinner at the hotel where the conference was being held; she accepted, and they spent the evening enjoying a wonderful dinner and then sat in the hotel lobby, drinking wine and talking until late into the night.

Debbie's company captivated Ronald. She had dark hair, honey-colored eyes, and freckles, and he asked her to stay longer in Eilat the next day. Debbie hesitated, but Ronald continued to ask, and finally, seeing how much he desired her company and, to tell the truth, noticing a little interest in her part as well, she agreed to change her plans. The delighted Ronald arranged a suite for her at the hotel where he was staying, and the rest, as they say, is history. It would be fair to say that, for Ronald, it was love at first sight.

Today, after thirty-five years of marriage, whenever I saw them, I noticed the love and mutual respect they held for one another, and my heart expanded with pleasure.

Their two children, Debbie and Ronald's, studied at Harvard and Duke, among the most esteemed universities in America. And how shall I describe their Denver home? A small palace, and now that they have moved into a suite in one of their hotels in the mountains, the only residents of this beautiful and magnificent mansion are their housekeeper, gardener, and maintenance man, with its elegant, winding Cinderella staircase, seventeen rooms, five large reception halls, and twenty-two bathrooms.

From previous stories Debbie had shared, I remembered their frequent excursions on their private yacht moored in Miami, Florida, and Las Vegas was always a "direct dial" away, where they delighted in watching spectacular shows and meeting such megastars as Celine Dion, Carrie Underwood, and Jennifer Lopez.

But now, when Debbie announced it was time for her regular "fix"—a trip to the homeland—a red flag went up. I wondered precisely what she meant, but I was not sure Debbie would want to discuss it during our meal with all four of us present, and I waited for a moment when we would be alone.

The moment arrived much sooner than I expected. The restaurant owner approached us and whispered something in Debbie's ear. She rose from her place and said to me, "Excuse me, my dear. The hotel's front desk manager is looking for me," and went to the cashier's area. The cashier handed her the business telephone, and Debbie smiled as she answered the call.

Ronald and my husband, Rafi, were engrossed in their usual animated discussion about renovations at the neighboring hotel, and they didn't even pause their conversation when I stood to admire the captivating view. Debbie caught my eye and motioned for me to come closer. I slowly approached the counter and stood beside her.

"Wow, you won't believe who just arrived for a meeting in the lobby of our hotel," she exclaimed, enthusiastically.

She smiled at me excitedly after ending her phone call. "It was our front desk manager. I left a message saying that we were having lunch here, so he knew where to find me."

"So, who arrived at your hotel?" I asked curiously.

"Andrew Taylor." Her eyes sparkled with excitement. "The lead singer of the Logic band. He lives in Vail, two hours away, and has scheduled a business meeting with someone staying at our hotel. The front desk manager knew how much I loved one of their songs and thus informed me. I know you are also a huge fan of this band," she smiled at me. "Would you like to meet him? Come to our hotel for coffee and dessert, and I'll introduce you to him."

My eyes widened. "Wow, we'd love to," I said.

"Great!" Debbie exclaimed and turned back to the table. I took advantage of our being alone and quietly asked, "Debbie, what's got you so troubled? And what do you mean by 'fix'? Is everything all right with the family back in Israel?"

Debbie stopped in her tracks. Her delicate face grew serious, and her gaze lowered before she spoke. She took a deep breath and said, "My dear, you're my closest friend here in Colorado, and I know you truly care about me. I am going to share something I usually don't share with our friends. But let's sit down for a moment."

She gestured toward two deep armchairs in the restaurant's now-empty smoking section.

We sat down, and she began, "You're Israeli, just like me, and I know and am certain that at least some of what I'm feeling, you also agree. With my hand on my heart, I know you understand exactly what I am about to tell you. Thank God, my marriage to Ronald is beautiful, good, and filled with love. We created a caring home, and now our two children have moved out to start their own lives in different regions of America. When I met Ronald, it was clear to me that I would have to compromise and leave the homeland. Ronald was honest with me from the start, explaining that he takes the management of the company his father bequeathed him very seriously.

"I knew how much he valued his father, who worked hard to establish the family's successful company, and it was clear to me that Ronald would not want to disappoint his parents. When he proposed marriage, I knew that if I accepted, I would also have to agree to live in Colorado. Only in my worst nightmare did I fail to understand what it meant to live with a divided heart. To miss so much and to feel something missing within you, no matter how well you are in the place you live, and no matter how much wealth surrounds you from every direction, there are things that cannot be bought by money, and material possessions do not compensate for everything. I find myself spending many years trying to get used to living with a longing for things I don't have here."

"What is it that you miss so much?" I asked. "What do you miss in Israel the most?"

Debbie sighed slightly, hesitated for a moment, and then replied in a slightly choked voice. "You ask what I miss? Obviously, my parents, my best friends, my extended family, and the warm mentality of the people of our homeland. You may think it is funny, but often I still dream of the home I grew up in, where my parents still live. There's one special dream I have, and in it I see myself as a little girl, seven or eight years old, climbing the trees in the backyard and picking apples to bring to my mother, who would prepare treats from them—apple blintzes, apple pie, and, how could I forget, the Moroccan chicken with apples and aromatic spices? And in the dream, I am careful not to step on the ground near the right apple tree in the garden, because that's where we buried a dead bird we found. Do you believe even this detail appears in my dreams? I remember that I had no patience to wait for the prunes on the only plum tree we had to ripen, and how excited I was when it happened, and I quickly climbed the tree so I could pick them when they were purple and juicy with a sweetness bordering on a little sourness... and how they smeared themselves on my face and colored my hands in sticky purple-red... and I'm also horrified in my dream to see that I stained the shirt I wore with purple-red stains from the juicy plums I ate... tell me, doesn't this seem strange to you that I still think...

"And dream of these things that were part of my Israeli world thirty-five years ago. To this day, whenever I visit my parents' house, I go check the garden, touch the green leaves of the apple trees, and then see if the plum tree looks good and if it's plum-ripening season. It is a kind of ritual, you could call it tradition, that I do regularly. My mother laughs a little at me when she sees me checking the garden, but I try explaining to her how much I miss it. She doesn't understand my desire to relive the days I lived in Israel, and I try to explain that I'm trying to make amends for myself, that I miss things that are part of me, of my memories, and of what defined me as an Israeli, and that's part of what I took with me when I moved to the other side of the world.

"Think about what you're packing in your suitcase," Debbie continued, in her heartbreaking monologue. "Clothes, books, documents, jewelry, and anything else that has meaning to you. For me, these memories are part of me and will always go with me wherever I live or reside. This is part of my Israeli identity, part of my soul. I am Israeli, and that will always be a part of me.

"I feel like I tore myself away from friends in a certain sense, and not just friends and neighbors—after all, in the period I grew up in Israel, good neighbors were part of the family. And when the neighbor's father was in the reserves, the neighbor and her children sat at our table every Shabbat evening, eating with us until the father returned from the reserves. To leave the neighbors alone? Out of the question. For my mother? It was not even an option. Where would I find such warm connections here?"

Her eyes began to well up, and she gently wiped them with a paper napkin she pulled from her jacket pocket. Then she continued to speak quietly.

"I miss friendships like the one I had with my high school friends," she said. "And how can one erase the fun connections that remained with the guys from the army? I feel like I am missing that specific kind of friendship. It is not that I do not have friends and acquaintances here. You know how it is when you live in a mansion and the entire community wants to be your friend and be invited to every event you throw—because who doesn't want to be photographed in the foyer of the house with the fountain I have in the living room and the round Cinderella staircase and say that he's a friend of Debbie and Ronald the millionaires? But you know how it is living in Colorado. The mentality here is different, more reserved, and people are not as open as they are in Israel.

"Tell me." She looked at me intently. "After all, you won't necessarily connect with people in Denver who you wouldn't have connected with in Israel, will you? People are a matter of chemistry. You connect with those you have things in common with, who you enjoy being with, who you feel comfortable with, with whom you agree with at least some of what they do and think, and I've already had a few instances where I said to myself that a certain person wasn't right for me for the same reason that I wouldn't have connected with that person in Israel."

I nodded slightly and remained silent.

"So, for all the reasons I mentioned here, I simply travel a lot to Israel," Debbie said. "I don't want to lose the connections I've built and cultivated over the years. When Ben and Millie were young, I traveled less, because it was more difficult. Now that they have built their own lives, I allow myself to travel more. Granted, Ronald doesn't like that I travel and leave him alone, but he can't be absent from his business for long anyway."

She fell silent again, then motioned for me to come with her. We positioned ourselves near one of the expansive windows, quietly observing the exterior landscape for several moments. Then Debbie spoke again.

"Yaffa, observe the remarkable Rocky Mountains landscape located across from our residence. But where is the sea I grew up next to? I grew up by the sea and deeply miss my homeland's coast. Remember, I also served in the Navy? And there was nothing like the fact that weekend and holiday outings here did not include our fun sea there. When I visit the country, I meet up with friends at the seaside in the morning, before the big crowds begin to arrive. And we order breakfast in the best cafés in Kiryat Hayyim, Kiryat Yam, or at Carmel beach. Wow..." She sighed with pleasure. "Just thinking about the crispy, hot bread they bake there, the bread that makes crackling sounds when you tear off a fresh, hot piece and spread cold white cheese and dark and purple Kalamata olives on it, with lots of original green olive oil. Tell me, where will I find breakfast like that here in Colorado? I am not even talking about Israel's good coffee," she continued enthusiastically. "I am willing to pay double to enjoy an Israeli 'cafe latte.' Here, I can only dream of the cappuccino they serve me in the country. Think about why Starbucks tried to open branches in Israel and failed. Their coffee is of mediocre quality compared to the quality coffee in Israel!

"And where's the Mediterranean music that lifts your spirits? Music that sweeps you away in an instant to move and dance to the rhythm? The music I grew up with, which I miss so much even though I have it here in the car, at home, and on my phone... It is different from going to concerts in the country and dancing to the Mediterranean rhythm. After all, it is part of the atmosphere and part of the enjoyment of us all in Israel.

"When I drive my car here in Colorado and listen to Israeli music, I open the window, and everyone stares at me strangely, and I feel that I have nothing in common with all these people. Then it hit me in the face. I am an alien, and I will always be different here, in the place I live, which I am a part of and belong to, but in a certain sense, I don't. Part of me will always belong to the place where this music comes from, on the other side of the world. That is where the other part of me is, with whom I so identify. And because I have rooted myself here, with a house, a husband, children, and a life that has already accumulated almost forty years, I will always remain divided. Because truly, I live in a cage. Yes, a golden, diamond cage, whatever, but ultimately, I am trapped."

I looked at her, and my heart ached. I had always known that Debbie loved to travel to visit the homeland, but today, there was something more. Today, Debbie shared more of the pain and longing she experienced in her daily life. Today, she revealed to me what she calls the "price" of her choice, contrasted with the longing within her, and the sacrifices that had become painful and troubling as part of her choice. This, in my assessment, explains Ronald's lack of objection to her frequent visits to Israel. In his wisdom, Ronald understands and knows that Debbie's sacrifice was not easy for her, and perhaps over the years, as the chasm grew wider between her life here and what she misses in the homeland, he tries to compensate her with frequent visits to Israel.

We concluded the excellent meal with sweet Moscato wine and thanked the friendly restaurant staff. We carefully descended the wooden stairs of the charming restaurant, and Ronald invited us to coffee and cake at the hotel where they were staying. We entered the warm lobby of the Grand Lake Lodge. The front desk manager greeted us at the entrance and updated Ronald and Debbie on the commotion in the lobby. The hotel security personnel directed all guests to one side of the lobby so as not to disturb the special guest and his entourage. We followed the manager to a corner of the lobby, where he introduced Ronald and Debbie to the talented musician. Andrew Taylor shook hands with all of us and readily agreed when I asked for a group photo. We knew he was there for a business meeting and decided not to intrude too much. We thanked him and turned to the other side of the lobby to have coffee.

We sat on black leather sofas with colorful orange, teal, and black cushions scattered throughout the lobby, a design inspired by the Indian decorations of the neighboring Indian reservation, adopted by settlers in the Wild West. We surveyed the unique setting of the luxurious lodge-cabin, like the walls covered in dark-brown wooden planks, stained only with transparent varnish, which looked as though they had just emerged from a magnificent prism. The rustic and authentic look characteristic of the small cabins in the Rockies was evident. The entire ceiling was covered in dark wood planks and crisscrossing wooden supports that connected the planks, giving it the appearance of one enormous cabin, illuminated by dozens of chandeliers inspired by the animals of the Rockies, with enormous elk antlers attached to each, each with a small lamp. These gave the huge lobby a half-dark and mysterious appearance. On the wooden walls, dozens of taxidermized animals, dried naturally, looked as if they were about to rise and move at any moment. At the entrance of the lobby, a large brown taxidermized bull welcomed us, and on the high walls hung small elk, large elk heads, a magnificent mountain lion, and two foxes—one almost black, the other a red fox. A not-so-large mountain snake served as a frame for one of the pictures on the wall near us, and this sight slightly unnerved me. Most striking of all was the taxidermized elk head above the hotel's old metal safe, staring directly into my eyes. For a moment, the direct and profound gaze stunned me, and a slight tremor ran through me.

Local homes, hotels, and cabins often blended with their natural surroundings, so Ronald and Debbie built their lodge to harmonize with the Rockies' landscape.

"Hey, Beautiful," Debbie gently roused me from my thoughts, "I see you've finished your coffee. Would you like to see the contemporary design of the hotel garden? Come, I'll show you the ideas I've had and how I chose to design it this time."

"Certainly," I quickly stood up, happy to leave the lobby filled with taxidermized animals. "I also see that Ronald and Rafi are so engrossed in their conversation that I don't think they'll miss us much."

We exited through the wide doors of the lobby toward the garden, which opened onto the west side of the hotel. Outside, a pleasant September breeze blew, and autumn was evident everywhere. In the large garden, dried leaves in shades of brown, orange, red, and faded-yellow swirled. We walked on green and brown leaves and fallen pine needles from the tall pine trees that bordered the garden, giving it the look of a mature forest.

We strolled through the enormous garden, which reminded me more of a small forest. I turned my head toward a corner of the garden and smiled. Now I knew why I heard rustling and birds chirping. In the far side stood a gazebo, a kind of round hut made of wood and completely covered with netting. In each opening where there was no netting, there was a small birdhouse made of glass or transparent plastic. Inside and outside, small birds flew around, eating the seeds and food scattered there. I saw both familiar garden birds and some new species, which I assumed were mountain local birds or seasonal birds.

Inside the gazebo, I saw two baby Bambis, small and cute, nibbling what looked like spinach leaves. Occasionally, they would emerge from the gazebo, check what was happening outside, and return to eating. Debbie asked that we not approach them so as not to scare them.

Near the fence was a large flower bed with various herbs. I observed rosemary, thyme, and a large amount of mint. Who would have believed, I thought, mint in the Rockies, and at least two types of mint. Debbie explained that mint could thrive beautifully in the mountains and even spread to a large area, but only in the spring and summer seasons.

We continued our walk and observed several elevated platforms throughout the garden, where summer lilies of yellow, pink, and white were growing.

Debbie drew my attention to a bar located in the right corner of the garden. The bar was built from reclaimed wood and surrounded by highchairs shaped like elk antlers. The chair handles were wide, and each chair back had a small wooden bowl attached. In one of the bowls, a tiny bird hopped and tried to peck at the last crumbs of a bread slice that someone had left there.

Colorado's snowy, harsh climate limited which plants and trees could thrive. So, I was curious to see what trees Debbie had chosen to plant in the hotel garden. I approached the two trees on the garden's left side—two small, vibrant saplings, recently planted, with tiny, green leaves—and drew closer to read the tag affixed to them, "These apple trees will flourish and bear fruit well in Colorado's summer season."

"This is my quiet corner when I need to escape my thoughts," Debbie whispered.

I thought to myself that our first years, living in a divided world, were what a philosopher called "a honeymoon." These were the years when we were enthralled by everything in our new world, eager to adjust to the improvements over our former home, wanting to learn the new language, establish a home and a career, or, for some, the seemingly sacred goal of starting a business and working to build it, pushing ourselves to prove to ourselves and the world the merits of our decision to relocate. During those years, because we are busy establishing ourselves, we unconsciously or consciously push aside the negative and the sorrowful, choosing not to dwell on the hardships of the transition and all the challenges we face.

But time does not wait. Time does its work, life moves on, and in moments of longing, when thoughts wrap around us, we begin to digest and understand the true meaning of "living with divided hearts."

SIXTEEN
SOPAPILLA

MY DAILY MORNING walk through Utah Park is invigorating and keeps me in good physical shape. And if I add my little secret, which sweetens my walk even more, you will quickly understand why it was hard for me to give it up.

The park was about a mile from our home, and it underwent significant renovations last year. Among other improvements, the city, thankfully (after we'd grown tired of complaining), expanded the walking path so walkers wouldn't collide, especially those who struggled deciding whether to move to the right or left when someone was walking toward them—and then, *bam*—a collision.

A city council member's efforts led to planting thirty additional trees on the lawns. The city also enlarged the pond, often visited by Canadian geese. In summer, these birds display blue, gray, and green feathers and are visible near the water along the path. The unsafe playground equipment was replaced with a new, colorful play set. The metal swings had been replaced with plastic swings that were durable and colored.

Three years had passed since the park reopened, and I had joyfully included it in my daily walk. However, as mentioned, I won't hide from you that I had another, truly delectable reason for visiting every morning. Here it was, in one word—Sopapilla.

How could I give up Señor Lopez's Sopapilla?

If you hadn't tasted sopapilla to this day, you hadn't tasted a sweet, crispy, fried delight that burst in your mouth with a boisterous crackle, easily rivaling the clucking of the turkey in my Ethiopian neighbor, Ms. Missi's, backyard, setting the molars dancing and calling all the senses—taste, smell, touch, sight, and sound—to awaken and dance to the rock and roll melodies of flavor that thrills me anew.

But wait, I completely forgot; Do you know what sopapilla is?

Sopapilla was a treat that arrived in Colorado from our neighbor, the land of tacos—Mexico, the land of quesadillas and tortillas (which I jokingly called "tortillala"). Sopapilla was prepared by pouring thin, nearly liquid dough in a spiral into hot oil. As it was fried, it filled with air bubbles, which I primarily attributed to the satisfying pops that sing their "popcorn" song in your mouth with each bite. Señor Lopez "danced" the spiral in the hot oil for two minutes on each side until it reached a deep golden-brown and then removed it, dipping it in a dreamy sauce. There was no other way to describe these flavors other than "dreamy."

Want another illustration? Please:

Imagine a food with the taste of honey, with tart hints of fresh lemon—that already tickles your palate, right? This mix combined agave syrup with alcohol, orange juice, and lemon, creating a layered and flavorful experience.

The first bite of the pastry caused it to break apart between your teeth. With each subsequent bite, the sound of the cracking rhythm, like an "orchestra," brought euphoria—no less.

After all these descriptions, wouldn't you run to try this treat, which awakened all your inner taste buds and danced every morning anew?

At six o'clock, I was already out of the house. I closed the door gently to avoid disturbing Rachel, my wife, and proceeded at a brisk pace to both counter the morning chill and expedite my arrival at the park. Indeed, sopapilla, what could I say?

Ten minutes of brisk walking, a run, and I arrived at the park. From a distance, I already smelt the aroma of Señor Lopez's pastries, which he sold every day in his worn-out, creaking metal cart. Señor Lopez stood there, waving his hand back and forth without pause, trying to chase away the insects and flies who also wanted a taste and to stick to his sweet delight.

Señor Lopez, bald, elderly, and charming, permanently parked his cart next to the colorful playground. Well, it was understandable, saying "no" to kids wanting the sweetest of the sweet, was difficult, wasn't it?

Admit it, when it comes to Señor Lopez's Sopapilla, call me a grown-up child. But how could I resist?

I must swiftly approach Señor Lopez's cart. The friendly elder recognized me from afar, and as a regular customer, he waved hello to me enthusiastically, and I, naturally, waved back.

And then, whether I wanted to or not, with a smile stretching from ear to ear and eyes sparkling with excitement, I suddenly became a mesmerized magnet, and walked even faster, following the scent of the sopapilla that led my nose down "the golden path," completely wrapped in the excitement of a child about to receive the tastiest bonbon.

"Hey, Señor Lopez, how's it going?" I asked. "How's business today?"

"Hey, amigo," the vendor replied, adjusting to the long raincoat that reached his knees, "You know, I have got to sell everything, but today's still long."

Usually, Señor Lopez sold at least a third of his treats early in the morning, because all the regulars in the park knew they needed to help Señor Lopez—after all, it was his only livelihood, and to support the kind, elderly vendor, we all bought at least one sweet sopapilla on the way home (and another to treat the children before they went to a long day of school).

"The Broncos are playing today," continued Señor Lopez. "What do you say? Do you think they will finally throw us a good bone with an unexpected victory?"

"Well," I replied, "it remains to be seen if their new striker, Mathews, will get moving and help them out."

"Look," Señor Lopez placed his hand on my shoulder encouragingly, "if the new striker, Mathews, doesn't contribute his skills, they're in serious trouble, right?"

"Yes, I agree with you," I replied. "But now, Señor Lopez, give me a fresh sopapilla. I need my morning energy."

I pulled out a five-dollar bill and handed it to him.

"Thank you, Mr. Ralph, thank you truly," he handed me a sopapilla wrapped in white paper. "Business is slow this morning. Have a Merry Christmas, all right?"

"Señor Lopez." I smiled at him, "I've told you this several times. I do not celebrate Christmas, I celebrate Hanukkah, remember?"

"Oh, what does it matter," Señor Lopez replied dismissively, "the one and the other. Celebrating is the important thing."

"Well, alright, fine," I concluded the conversation and turned my attention to the sacred treat. I tore off the sticky paper wrapping from the sopapilla, which was already beginning to melt, and continued on my way, waving goodbye to Señor Lopez. It would not help, I thought, as I walked away, if Señor Lopez had no idea about Jewish holidays, no explanation would work.

One morning, when I lingered to chat with him a little longer, Señor Lopez told me that he grew up in a tiny mountain village somewhere in Mexico and never left. Now he was here because his son had moved to Colorado and decided to bring him, so that he wouldn't be alone in the remote village, and also because it was hard for his son to visit him in Mexico, as each visit cost his son two weeks of work.

So now he lived in Denver, making a living selling sopapillas, and thinking that the entire world celebrated Christmas. I would not forget how I laughed when I tried to explain to him that I was from Israel, and he asked me in which Colorado city Israel was located...

I proceeded with my walk, gradually savoring the sweet sopapilla. What was in this dough that drew me to it like a magnet? What made sopapilla so special that it inspired near veneration? I repeated the question to myself as I wiped off the sticky confection.

And then, suddenly, I remembered! I have known this Sopapilla since forever. It always took me back to that treat I loved as a child in Israel. Memories flood my mind, and here I was again, a six-year-old, a first-grade student, when I first encountered the vendor who walked the streets of my hometown, Beer Sheva, pushing a cart similar to Señor Lopez's, even moving at the same pace, with a loud voice calling out to the whole street, "Wonderful, wonderful, sweet and fresh, today only, wonderful, wonderful!"

I saw myself waiting for my mother to take ten cents from her smooth black purse, and I counted them with her, one by one, firmly clasping my small hands around them, so that not a single penny would fall out. I quickly descended two flights of stairs, passed the entrance of Mrs. Niti, the Indian lady, whose home always gave off the scent of curry, and continued down to the first floor, passing the door of the Menashe family, those with the herbs against the evil eye placed in an orange clay pot next to their scratched door (why don't they repair this ugly door?). And there I was at our entrance, seeing the "Wonderful-Wonderful" vendor with his white apron, which had already gotten soiled with oil and honey today, wrapping a "Wonder-ful-Wonderful" for Romi, Mrs. Niti's neighbor's son. In a fraction of a second, a thought crossed my mind, this was his last "Wonderful-Wonderful" for today? There was not one left for me? But there was! In the corner of my right eye, I saw two more Wonderful-Wonderfuls in the covered tray.

"Give me one Wonderful-Wonderful," I gasped, and stretched out my tightly squeezed hands. "Here's ten cents."

"Alright, sweetie, here you go, take a Wonderful-Wonderful, the freshest," he handed me the sticky treat wrapped in white parchment paper, and was already pushing the cart with its giant wheels to the next block's entrance. I jumped and enthusiastically raced up the stairs, again passing the door of the Menashe family, those with the herbs in the pot next to the scratched door, still hearing the vendor's cries from afar, proclaiming to the neighbors in the next entrance, "Wonderful-Wonderful, today only, fresh, fresh!"

I continued walking, and more childhood scenes came back to me. Although we had a small and meager apartment, my special mother managed to create a warm and loving home for us. Considering that she became a widow at the age of forty-five, left with ten children, with me being the youngest of ten, there was no doubt it was not easy for her, even though my two oldest sisters were already married... We grieved our father's loss. Our mother always ensured we had clean clothes and a refrigerator full of delicious food. She knew how to give us warmth, love, and a kind word. And how my conscience had tormented me for years afterward, that I did not live in Israel during the last months of my mother's courageous battle with illness. I flew five times to Israel to see her that year, and I remembered how I walked each day with a broken heart and the gnawing guilt that kept me awake, and tears that refused to cease flowing until my eyes became red and burning, even ordinary eye drops no longer helped.

I paused my brisk walk in the park to try to remove a piece of irritating dough that had stuck to my back molar from the sopapilla I had eaten minutes before.

While I was digging at my teeth with my sharpest fingernail, nearly injuring the gum area next to the troublesome tooth, Mr. Taylor, with his enormous Dane, stopped beside me to say hello.

"Good morning, Ralph," Mr. Taylor greeted me, "already enjoying the sopapilla this morning?"

"Oh, excuse me, Mr. Taylor, something is stuck in my tooth. I think it is a piece of sticky dough," I replied, somewhat embarrassed. "How are you and how is Baxi?" I asked, stroking the enormous dog whose mouth always dribbled white saliva, the last thing I wanted to see after my daily sopapilla indulgence.

"He's, as usual, as you see," Mr. Taylor replied. "The dog

dictates our lives at home. He is the boss, and this morning he simply could not contain himself from his daily walk. Do you believe I have not even finished my first cup of coffee yet? He was already by the door waiting for us to go outside. What do you say, Baxi? Tell Mr. Ralph," he said, stroking the enormous dog affectionately in the area he loved most, precisely between his two big ears.

"Yes," I nodded. "We never had a dog, but I think a dog is like another child in the house, right?"

"Couldn't agree with you more," Mr. Taylor replied, waving goodbye and hurrying after Baxi, who tugged forcefully on his black leash to continue walking.

After finishing my meal of Senior Lopez's sopapilla, I wiped my face with the sticky wrapping paper. And so, with a "song and verse" that lasted as long as I felt the sweetness in my mouth, I continued my walk to reach the public swimming pool building, on the north side of the park, where I could wash my face and hands in the public faucet near the tennis courts.

The water in the rough concrete faucet was icy-cold, but I had no choice. I wanted to get rid of the sopapilla sauce stickiness. If there was one negative thing about my daily feasting ritual, it was the stickiness of the honey that spread over me and took over my chin, cheeks, and, unbelievably, sometimes even my eyelashes. I was a grown-up/little boy, I said, right?

With clean but freezing hands from the icy water, and a cool but dry face, I continued walking along the park path. The cool breeze whipped my face, and I tucked my hands into the pockets of my warm flannel sweatshirt to warm my frozen fingertips.

Utah Park was a large park, and to circle it all required walking a mile and a half. It was not easy, but I did it every morning for my daily ritual. Four miles was my route, including walking to the park, a circuit of a mile and a half in the park itself, and walking back home. Then, when I got home, the espresso machine I turned on before leaving for my walk was already hot and ready to give me my first cup of coffee for the day, and make no mistake. Coffee was my second mantra every morning.

The sun shone brighter when I got home. My hands were starting to warm.

The thick sweatshirt I wore warmed my body thoroughly. After walking approximately four miles, I felt liberated and full of energy.

Upon entering the house, I inhaled the aroma emanating from the espresso machine. My wife, Rachel, was busy clearing the clean dishes from the dishwasher, with her phone, on speaker, placed before her on the counter. She was on an overseas call.

"Right, Michal, good idea," she said, sending a small, good morning smile on my way, "Here's Ralph back from his walk. It was worth waiting for him with coffee. You know he is an espresso expert?"

"Rachel, of course, there's nothing like top-notch coffee. How we enjoyed drinking this excellent Israeli coffee," Michal said.

"What can I tell you, we always say this, right? When it comes to food and fashion, there is no comparison between America and Israel," Rachel sighed lightly, "I'm giving the credit to the homeland. Anyway, you had a wonderful visit to the Holy Land, but it's good you're back. There's nothing you can do, right now, Colorado is home sweet home."

For a moment, there was silence, then Michal said, "But Rachel, it's hard for me..."

And suddenly we heard a sob. I had never heard Michal cry aloud, and even over the phone... It was a painful moment, and honestly, it was a familiar, painful moment for all of us who lived abroad.

Rachel looked at me, then reached for a kitchen towel from the drawer next to the dishwasher and wiped her eyes, which were also brimming with tears. With hand gestures, I signaled for her to end the call. I wanted to comfort her, but it angered her. In response, she made an impatient gesture for me to be quiet, again wiping her tears with the kitchen towel and searching for tissues to blow her nose.

"Michal, look, right, it's not easy," Rachel said gently. "Don't cry, I understand you. Nothing beats a close, loving, and pampering family. But longing is part of the price we pay for living on the other side of the world. You know, I always say that saying goodbye is hard, and coming back after a visit is even harder. Stop crying, you are doing your best. Maybe in the end, you will return to your homeland when Lidor finishes university, what do you think?"

"I hope... and I hope even more that he will agree to return with us," Michal sniffled. "I can only pray. He can look for a job in English, in the tech industry, where it's the prevailing language anyway. But Rachel, that is not the problem, the language. What if we want to return, but he wants to stay here and marry Stacy?" Her voice became hoarse, and it was clear she was about to cry again.

"Let's worry about that if and when," Rachel interrupted the sad conversation.

"Yes," Michal sniffled again. "In the meantime, enjoy the pastries we bought for you in Israel. I had to assure the customs officers, with a courteous demeanor, that the cookies were manufactured in a factory in order to secure permission for them to pass through customs. So, come on, tell your neighbors, Miss Louise and Miss Pat, to come for coffee and enjoy the pastries while they're fresh."

Rachel smiled. "We'll finish what's in the box soon. There is no way Ralph will not eat from it this morning with his espresso..."

Finally, Rachel hung up the phone. She looked at me with a look of "no comment about the crying," then said, "Hey Ralph, Michal and Uri returned from a visit to Israel last night, and Uri stopped by on the way to work and brought us this treat box from the 'Sababa' confectionery. Remember how much we loved their pastries? Especially fried doughnuts with sticky syrup... What are they called in Israel?"

I looked at the white cardboard box on the table, a white box with pink and yellow flowers, and the word "Sababa" printed large on each side. The corners of the box were crumpled, and all four sides were stained with oily spots, a reminder of the long and arduous journey from hot Beer Sheva to cold Denver. I tore off the yellow note that was stuck to the top of the lid and read:

"Hey Ralph,

We returned from our homeland last night. I stopped by this morning for two minutes on the way to work to bring you something sweet from the Holy Land, to make you feel a little taste of Israel.

Bye, talk to you tonight, Uri."

I opened the lid. The pleasant scent immediately evoked memories of my early childhood, specifically recalling first grade and life in neighborhood A in Beer Sheva during the 1960s. If the vendor of "Yofi-Yofi"—wonderful-wonderful were aware, he would know that he was a notable part of my recollections of Israel, which I regarded as significant in my personal history. If he only knew...

SEVENTEEN
SOMETIMES, "GIGI" IS ALL A PERSON HAS

DURING THE WEEK of International Holocaust Remembrance Day, we visited our daughter, Inbar, in Boston, Massachusetts. The next day, we left early in the morning for the bustling farmers' market, "Hay market" (the Straw Market), which earned its nickname from the large straw hats the vendors wore to protect themselves from the strong summer sun. The market, near the Italian neighborhood, bordered a small park that, believe it or not, was a memorial site for victims of the Holocaust. In the center of the small park stood two enormous glass walls, at least four meters high and stretching over ten meters long. The thick, transparent walls bore etched on them, in large English and Hebrew letters, the names of hundreds of thousands of Holocaust victims. A concrete pavement featured a narrow path between glass walls, where the word "Remember" was etched in Hebrew, and the names of extermination camps and ghettos were inscribed at one-meter intervals.

I walked along the narrow path, reading the names of the extermination camps with sorrow. Each name struck me with a painful memory of stories and recollections shared during "Remember and never Forget" evening gatherings we had attended in the past.

"A memorial site this amazing next to a bustling farmers' market?" Rafi, my husband, said, walking beside me.

"This is the last thing I expected to see here," I replied, shaking my head.

"I guess someone failed in the planning," I added, feeling a mix of sadness and anger. Where was the logic in building a unique memorial with such profound meaning for millions around the world, exactly next to a crowded, noisy market filled with vendors' cries, trucks' and lorries' rumbles, and the smells of food, fruits, and vegetables, not to mention the unpleasant picture of rotting vegetables piled beside the roads in the blazing sun?

We walked quietly around the special site. Many people gathered around the glass walls, talking amongst themselves and pointing at specific names, while others were taking pictures of the site from all angles. We moved closer to see, to photograph, and to briefly connect with the names on the walls. As we stopped to look more closely at some of the names, we encountered an elderly man sitting in an old wheelchair. A large blue and white Israeli flag was attached to the wheelchair's backrest, with the words "Remember and Never Forget" written on it. A spotted black and white cat with the most beautiful, clear blue eyes I had ever seen was resting on his lap, indifferent to the crowds.

Suddenly, the cat jumped off the old man's lap and began to move away from us quickly.

"Gigi," the old man grumbled in a raspy voice, "come back at once, or—" and he agitatedly steered the wheelchair toward the direction the cat had run.

I understood that he could not stand up and chase the quick animal, so I turned to Rafi for help. Rafi started chasing the cat, but Gigi, the cat, had other plans. He leaped and darted with ease between the many people standing near the glass walls, slipping between their legs and darting from one person to another until he bumped into a woman who dropped the bag she was carrying, and vanished.

Rafi did not give up and relentlessly chased the rebellious cat, while the tourists followed them with their eyes, not wanting to lose sight of the cat. Gigi continued to move away from the site, occasionally encountering more people. Two young boys also joined the chase, running from various parts of the small park, until, after several minutes, they managed to help Rafi close the circle around the playful Gigi. Rafi crouched down, caught him in his hand, and returned him to his owner. The tourists around us cheered joyfully and applauded the success of the "mission."

The old man smiled and, turning to Gigi, remonstrated, "How can you do this to me again, Gigi? I thought we agreed that you would not run away from me again. Now, thank this nice person."

"That was quite an operation," a tourist said to Rafi with a smile. "If our cats understood how important they are to our lives, they wouldn't behave like this. Right?"

Rafi continued chattering with the tourists, and I looked at the cat, contentedly back on the old man's lap.

"I'm sorry," the old man said to me, noticing my gaze. "He knows he's not supposed to run away, but he's playful. He thinks it is a game. He wants me to chase him, just like we used to play in the past, but unfortunately, those days of being able to chase him and tickle him when I finally caught him are over now. I am ninety years old. I don't have the strength I once had."

I nodded in understanding and smiled. "Here, see what Gigi did to me the last time he ran away," the old man added. "But I still love him. He's still my Gigi."

The old man pushed back his sleeve and showed me a deep scratch that left a long, thin scar along his left elbow, precisely over a faded blue tattoo of a number: 270145.

I felt as if someone had shaken me violently, trembling my body and soul. Not because of the scar, but because of its location!

The old man noticed my shock, and I quickly composed myself. "Don't worry..."

"I'm happy to help," I smiled at him, trying to hide the storm raging within me, how terrified and trembling I was to see where the cat chose to claw at him.

He nodded, and I continued, "May I ask you about the flag?"

"Certainly," he replied cheerfully, "I'm proud of my Jewish flag." He smiled a pleasant smile, and his bright-blue eyes smiled as well. "It's the flag of my homeland, even though I've lived in Israel for only two years."

"Oh, I'm glad to hear that. We are Israelis," I added with a smile. "And I'm happy to meet you. My name is Yaffa," I said, and offered him my hand.

"What a lovely thing," the elder exclaimed, and a wide smile spread across his face. "My name is Albrecht, and this is my Gigi."

I nodded in understanding. Deep down, I hoped he would continue speaking and tell me more, and to my joy, he did.

"I will never forget what a girl said to me in school in Poland," Albrecht continued. "When the disturbances of the Jews first began. I was in the ninth grade, I think. We were sitting during lunch break, and each student took out the lunch they brought from home. Next to me sat a Jewish girl named Gilda, and when Gilda opened her lunch bag, she discovered that her mother had forgotten to include a spoon. She asked if I had an extra spoon to give her, and I answered that I only had one and that I needed it for my soup. A Polish girl sitting behind us turned to Gilda, laughed, and said, 'It is okay, you can use Albrecht's spoon, after all, both of you are Jews and you have the same Jewish germs. You do not have germs like ours, the Christians. You certainly will not get my spoon.'

"And that was just the beginning. Oh," he sighed from the depths of his heart. "It's hard to remember these things, but it's etched in my heart, and I need to tell future generations so they will know and understand what we went through just because we are Jews. They need to know and never forget, ever."

Albrecht paused for a moment. I felt an urge to hold his hand, tell him that everything was all right, tell him how Israel had developed and grown and was now a small powerhouse, with some of the best tech companies in the world. I wanted to ask many more questions, but I was afraid that my questions would lead him to remember things that would hurt him even more, that would scar him with another new and fresh wound, adding to the mountain of pain that was accumulating in his heart and choking his throat as he spoke.

But he was absolutely right about what he said—we are obliged to remember and not forget, and these memories should be a beacon of light for every Jew, wherever they were, and declare to the world that we had a country of our own, the Jewish state. Whether we lived in it or not, and each for his reasons, we must remember the history, the disturbances, the hardships, and the persecutions that the Jews suffered simply because they were Jews, and in our memory, we must do everything possible to ensure that these hardships never return.

These thoughts reminded me of what Yigal Allon, a minister in the past government in Israel, said in a speech many years ago, which was still etched in my mind, "People who do not know their past have a poor present, and their future is shrouded in fog."

Albrecht's raspy voice interrupted my thoughts.

Albrecht still had a Polish accent. What a kind old man, but after about seventy years of speaking English, it was clear that this was the language he lived and spoke in. He clutched Gigi, the cat, so tightly that I feared it would upset him and that he would lash out and scratch.

"Do you live close by?" I asked, trying to change the subject.

"Not far," he smiled again, "about a quarter of an hour's walk. But do not worry, I get around well with my wheelchair. I get tired quickly when walking, so I no longer take the risk of coming here on foot."

"And do you come here often?" I found myself looking for more questions.

"It depends on the weather. As you know, in Boston, the heat hits us relentlessly in the short summer season, and we sweat all day, and winter is tough, the damp cold and the freezing winds that come from the sea and nearby Canada penetrate our bones.

"Sometimes the cold is so intense that even with gloves on, my hands freeze solidly. So, yes, I try to go out whenever possible. At home, it is just me and Gigi. When I am outside, I see the world, greet people I know, and observe what's happening around me, and I know I'm not alone. Do you understand what I mean?"

"I understand perfectly," I smiled.

"Don't get me wrong," he stroked the cat on his lap, "Gigi is a good cat, a loyal friend. He eats dinner with me every day, and we manage with what we have, even on days when there isn't much."

Albrecht gently adjusted his cap to allow a woman with a dog to pass and asked me, "Do you live here? Or are you just visiting?"

I told him we had come to Boston to meet our daughter Aviv, who's arriving from New York, and together we will visit our daughter Inbar, who is doing research at Harvard. For the visit, we rented an apartment for a week, near here. "Albrecht," I continued to ask, "Do you speak Hebrew a little?"

Albrecht smiled and replied with a laugh, "I lived in Israel for barely two years, then I lived in an immigrant center for Holocaust survivors. We all spoke Yiddish, Polish, or German, so I did not have enough time to properly learn Hebrew. I did learn to read and write, but since I hardly used what I had learned, I quickly forgot a bit. Since we came here to America, and unfortunately, not even once have I visited Israel. We could not afford trips to Israel, and the years went by. With dreamy eyes fixed on the glass walls, he smiled and said quietly, "At least I met some Israelis here—and so many Jews."

"I was young then," he said, "and when the cursed war ended, I joined a group of young people, and together we left for the Holy Land. There, in the welcoming camp, I met Vera, the one who became my beloved wife. We married, and we had a son, a lovely baby. Sadly, as a young child, he fell ill with a serious autoimmune disease. The doctors in Israel at that time could not treat him; there was no knowledge or suitable medication, and they suggested that we fly to Boston. Here, at that time, advanced research studies were being conducted in universities on autoimmune diseases, and there were advanced hospitals and doctors among the best in the world. It was clear to us that we would do everything for our child. We moved here, even though it was a difficult and painful decision, accompanied by deep disappointment for us—after all, the dream of everyone who was with us in the ghetto or who escaped from the camps was to come to the Land of Israel, the Promised Land, where we could live in peace and security, in the land of the Jews, what everyone calls 'the land of our fathers and mothers,' our ancestors, right?"

I nodded, and Albrecht continued speaking. "With mixed feelings and a heavy heart, we arrived in Boston. And I remember my wife, Vera, crying throughout the flight. Both from fear and worry for our son, and also because the doctors had prepared us for the fact that this would be a long period, and it was not known when we could return to Israel."

He paused for a moment, as if remembering the past, and continued his story. "A short time after we arrived here, we were granted the status of war refugees, and the government helped us to settle in. I looked for work and received an offer to help the American government with anything related to war refugees who suffered from serious diseases and arrived in Boston for treatment. My job was to help with translation into English—I knew Polish and German, and enough English to accompany the patients to their treatments and appointments with the relevant offices. I also helped at the community center that was established specifically for the holocaust survivors, where they tried to locate family members.

"Vera didn't work, of course. She stayed home with our son, because he needed close care, and he also needed to be hospitalized from time to time for this or that treatment."

"And did the treatments help?" I asked with a slight smile, hoping for good news.

"A little," Albrecht fixed his gaze on the commemorative wall. "Initially. There was a time when one of the experimental treatments seemed promising, but unfortunately, it was only short-lived. After a few weeks, all the symptoms returned, and Nathaniel, our son, had difficulty breathing; we had to return to the hospital."

I remained silent, only nodding sympathetically.

"The years passed," Albrecht continued, "and Nathaniel suffered greatly and passed away shortly after the age of fifteen. But the Giver of Life above blessed us with a gift," he looked at me and tried to smile. "Even fifteen years with a son were a gift, right?"

Warm emotions flooded me. All I wanted at that moment was to embrace this gentleman warmly, encourage him, and tell him kind words. I surveyed his old, worn-out wheelchair, which had seen better days—it was scratched in many places, and the Boston seawater, which corrodes all good metal, had gnawed at its bottom in several spots. Albrecht was wearing light clothing that kept him cool in the humid Boston air; indeed, it was hot that day. It was only ten o'clock in the morning, but we already felt how the air was still, and the humidity from the nearby ocean was already dampening Albrecht's shirt collar and the large, gray, mesh hat he wore. From time to time, he would reach out and straighten it on his head because it was too big.

I did not want to directly ask if all his family members perished in the Holocaust, fearing to tread on a painful sore, and thus I chose a more cautious approach.

"Albrecht, do you have family or relatives in Israel? Or here in Boston?" I asked gently.

"No..." He shook his head sadly and lowered his face for a moment. "They perished. Of all the close family, only I survived. For a long time, I tried in many ways to locate someone... every relative— in Poland, I had two sisters, a brother, parents, uncles—but without success. I understood that all of them were murdered in Auschwitz. But shortly after we arrived in Boston, we received a notification from the Ministry of Aliyah in Israel that Vera's sister, Lena, arrived on a ship to Haifa. Vera was so excited and wanted us to return to Israel, but how could we with the sick child? We felt so divided—the body here and the heart there, and we were devastated by the thought that our dream of raising a family in the Land of Israel was crumbling before our eyes. And again, as in the ghetto, she prayed for the day she could be in the Land of Israel, and Vera lived with the hope that one day she would be able to realize her longed-for dream, with which she went to sleep every night and with which she woke up every morning. I understood her and identified with her desire, but I was the less emotional one of us, and every day I reminded her that we are here for Nathaniel, and who knows, perhaps he will be cured, and our story will have another happy ending in the Land of Israel."

I could not find words to comfort him, but as often happened, he, with all his difficulty, was the one who said encouraging words to me.

"You know," Albrecht continued, "I read somewhere that giving is more blessed to be the recipient, and precisely when we are going through a crisis and are in difficult situations, giving helps us feel better. One doctor who treated Nathaniel told me that when we donate, give, or help someone, our brains release a hormone called dopamine, and this causes us a good, pleasant, and fulfilling feeling. So, when Nathaniel passed away, we felt like our world had collapsed, yet our giving and helping others helped us feel better and soothed some of the longing for the brief time we lived in the Land of Israel."

"After Nathaniel passed away," I said gently, "actually, could you have returned to Israel?" I tried to understand the story.

"When Lena heard that Nathaniel had passed away, she came to Boston to be with us and to help Vera cope with the great loss. Soon, she joined our effort to help and rebuild the Boston Holocaust survivors' community, and because she was so enthusiastic about the idea and felt that she was doing holy work, she postponed her return to Israel every time the subject came up. Vera, too, found it difficult to think about leaving because our Nathaniel is buried here in Boston, and she could not part with him. She used to go to his grave every Friday morning, and together with her sister, they established a small flower garden around the grave. Vera felt so torn and divided that we even discussed the idea of bringing Nathaniel's bones to the Land of Israel, but we couldn't afford such an expense."

I thought, What a tragic story.

"I never showed Vera how hard it is for me here," Albrecht sighed slightly. "I never complained or said how much I hope to make my old dream and return to Israel, to learn Hebrew well, to speak the holy language—Hebrew! I wanted us to have Israeli friends, to celebrate holidays together, to get to know our beautiful country through our feet, on trips, to breathe the fresh air of Jerusalem, as in the beautiful song, to be free and proud in our country, the Land of Israel. I wanted... to live in a place where no one could tell me, 'Go away, you don't look like us, you're not one of us.'"

"Yes..." I agreed with him. "That's a very important thing for a person, a sense of non-Jews come to this site to remember the terrible Holocaust. There are those who shake my hand, and some who want to talk to me because they read what I wrote on my flag, but I prefer not to speak with them." He waved his hand dismissively, and his face clouded. "Too many memories, too much pain, too much etched into my flesh. Too much.

"So, as you see, I stayed in Boston. We did not bring any more children into the world, but we set ourselves the goal of helping everyone we could—refugees, patients who came here from Germany, Poland, Hungary, and more. We felt that this was an important goal, and that we too were taking part in the worldwide effort to heal their bodies and minds and comfort their broken hearts, and yes, even our own, by engaging ourselves in the community center for Holocaust survivors, and our whole lives revolved around our small community. Five years ago, my Vera passed away, and a year later, her sister, Lena, passed away. She had already been very ill."

The sun beat down on his face, and he pulled a crumpled paper handkerchief from his pocket and wiped the sweat from his brow. I looked at him and Gigi, nestled comfortably on his lap, and my heart ached for both.

"Albrecht, will you be able to come to our Shabbat dinner next Friday?" I offered. "We'd be happy if you joined us for Shabbat dinner; our daughter and her husband will also come. Please, join us?"

Albrecht raised his blue eyes to me. "Really? That is so kind of you. Are you sure? Can Gigi come with me?" he asked enthusiastically.

"Yes, certainly," I replied with a smile. "Gigi is welcome, too." We exchanged details and agreed on Friday at 6:00 PM.

I warmly said goodbye to him, found Rafi standing a short distance away talking to an English couple, and we headed to the flea market to buy what we needed for our extended stay in Boston. An hour later, light rain began to fall, and we started walking back to the rented apartment. I thought again about Albrecht, the kind old man, and turned to Rafi.

"I'm asking myself, if this kind old man doesn't have many sources of income, why does he keep a cat? It is not cheap to keep a pet; there are many expenses, like a vet, and the special food he buys for the cat, when he himself is a disabled person who needs help…"

"Yes," Rafi agreed, "it's true, but I'm not surprised. There are people for whom something like Gigi is all they have, and they find comfort in it, which encourages and strengthens them."

"Right," I replied, "and you were so busy talking to that tourist, I didn't want to interrupt you and show you how much it shook me to see the location of the scratch."

"What do you mean? What scratch?" Rafi slowed his pace and looked at me.

"The cat scratched Albrecht right on his elbow, on the numbers, on the tattoo they branded on his arm in the Ghetto extermination camp!"

"Wow," my Rafi said, "how symbolic, and how powerful."

"I interpret it as if Gigi the cat is feeling Albrecht's pain, and as if he wanted to erase the tattooed number. He was trying to obliterate any visual reminder of Albrecht's horrific past as a young boy, to help him erase the past and soften the memories. By scratching a line precisely over the tattooed numbers, it was as if he was saying to him, 'Never again.'"

"Wow," my partner said, "how symbolic, and how powerful."

We continued walking in silence. I was happy that Albrecht agreed to come to our Shabbat dinner, and I had already begun planning what to cook and how to treat him. I thought to myself that if he lived near us, I would adopt him, as I know myself and my weaknesses. In my heart, I thanked him for what I learned from him today, that despite everything that happened, the horrors of the Holocaust, the grief of a parent who lost his only son and then his wife, who was the love of his life, who suffered from pain and longing to return to live in Israel, in his simple wisdom, he found the little good he had in his later years and appreciated the little good he had with his Gigi.

EIGHTEEN
EVERYONE HAS A DREAM

NIRIT, my friend, proudly presented her signature cake, a chocolate cake with layers of delicate mascarpone cream and playful, fresh raspberries peeking from each layer, and placed generous slices on delicate white porcelain plates. Then she moved among the guests, distributing a delightful portion of the delicious dessert to each.

I sat on the comfortable sofa in the elegant, decorated living room and observed the other guests standing on the far side of the spacious room, chatting. I knew all the guests beforehand, and others I met for the first time at Nirit's festive evening gathering.

Suddenly, Leviah, a young Israeli woman who had come to Denver for a family wedding and was staying with her aunt, my close friend Nili, turned to me.

"So, tell me, are you planning to stay and grow old here, or will you return to Israel someday?"

Slowly, I turned my gaze to her.

"Our dream, or rather, my dream, is to live abroad," Leviah continued without waiting for my response. "I dream of becoming a successful makeup artist in Los Angeles and having a huge swimming pool in my backyard. What was your dream? Why are you here? Do you love life outside of Israel?"

She sat close to me on the sofa, and now I could scrutinize her more closely—long, wavy auburn hair, large brown eyes tastefully made up, enormous, artificial eyelashes, and the reddest possible lipstick. Her appearance reminded me of a beautiful doll. Two curly children, three and four years old, played with colorful magnets near her feet, occasionally turning to her for help.

I remained silent for a moment. As we ate, I noticed that Leviah had tracked the conversation and understood that out of all the guests who had come to the Shabbat dinner, we represented the "mature group," or as some call us, the "older ones"; those who had lived abroad for many years. I assumed that this was the reason she chose me to answer her questions.

Did I love life abroad? I quietly repeated the question to myself. How did you answer such a complex question? Could my answer tilt the balance in favor of or against Leviah's and her husband's decision? Would my words influence their decision to take a life-altering step? If so, I needed to consider my response carefully.

Morally, I felt it was important to give her the truest and most honest answer I could.

As I tried to decide how to respond, she continued speaking. "We came here for ten days, for my cousin's wedding," she explained, "but it was important for us to take an extra two weeks to travel and explore the area. And frankly, I will be honest with you, for at least a year, we've been considering leaving Israel and trying to live in America, and today we pushed back our return date to Israel by two weeks. During this time, it's important for me to hear from people like you who have made the move and to know if you're happy with your decision."

From our earlier conversation, I remembered her telling me about her professional makeup training, that she worked from home in Kiryat Ono, and that she had a stable clientele.

Her business was growing, and their life in Israel was good, but she had a long-held dream.

"Since I was a child, I've dreamt of moving to Los Angeles," Leviah continued. "I want to live there, develop and build a career, and of course, earn money. My goal is to do makeup for famous people, movie stars, and celebrities. I want to gain recognition, and have my name mentioned alongside those of other famous people..."

I nodded. She leaned down and touched the younger child's head. "As you see, our children are young, and I know that this is the perfect time to move, as long as they haven't started school. So, what do you say? Can you share with me your experience with the move? What did you like best about moving here...?"

My expression stiffened as I looked at her again. Seriously? "What did you like?" Is that what she wants to know? What did we like? What about all the things we did not like? What about the challenging aspects of leaving one's homeland and immigrating to a foreign place?

Initially, I really considered telling her about the things we "liked," the things that were tempting, alluring, dazzling—the businesses we established, the significant successes, the amazing trips we took in America and the world, the enormous house we could only dream of in Israel, with a swimming pool, a fountain, and two brand-new cars in the garage. I could describe our high standard of living, the fact that we own eighteen rental properties, ensuring a comfortable lifestyle like the sun rising each morning, how our children attended camps that cost $4,000 a week—it was no problem when money flowed in from all directions.

But if that was what I "sold" her, she would want to move tomorrow, the thought crossed my mind, assuming that was what she was hoping for. Everyone I knew envisioned a similar dream, a fantasy that I just described.

But what about the rest? What about all the things we did not like? The tears we shed, the lost connections... The good and warm times we had with family and friends that we missed so much, which quickly faded after we left, until some connections were completely severed. Should I tell her how heartbroken we were when loved ones passed away in Israel and we couldn't attend the funeral or shiva, and conversely, how many important events, such as weddings, bar mitz-vahs, and births, we missed because we were far away and couldn't be there due to commitments we had here?

And what about the Israeli friends we met here who betrayed us (yes, there were jealous ones), or other things that made us regret leaving the homeland? Why didn't she ask me, "What didn't you like about moving to America?" Was she uninterested in learning about the difficulties that were part of immigration? And to be more precise, the challenges of leaving the homeland and one's family, friends, mindset, tasty food, and feeling of belonging, regardless of whether one moved for work, family reunification, or simply to pursue a dream? Why didn't she inquire about the frustration of changes in lifestyle, a new language and manner of expression, a different and foreign mindset? People from diverse backgrounds? Change of priori-ties? Why didn't she ask me about antisemitism? About the dangers of life in a "host country"? And what about personal development, which may be halted in certain cases? And the choice of education system for the children? Would she be able to afford a Jewish private school (USD 25,000-45,000 per year), or would they have to compro-mise on a neighborhood school, where her children would also learn about Christmas and Christianity and the history of America, so different from their Jewish-Israeli history? And what about the influ-ence of the environment on her children? She would have to deal with social pressure and exposure to things her children would not have been exposed to in Israel, and social pressure that caused children to behave and think differently than they would if they lived in Israel.

Her innocent question reminded me of an episode from a movie —a customer in a pastry shop savoring his chocolate croissant, and suddenly someone enters and asks him, in the utmost innocence, "What do you like about the pastry?" hoping the answer would be,

"Delicious, heavenly!" And because the customer confirmed that the croissant was delicious, the questioner ordered the same. But what the customer didn't tell the visitor was that the croissant was also a little dry, not extremely sweet, and contained a minimal amount of chocolate?

Regarding her question, it encompassed the entire world. I was tormented within, because even if I spoke about leaving the country endlessly, I still would not be able to mention everything that needed to be discussed when a person decided to completely change their world overnight.

I tried to muster all my honesty to be as straightforward as possible. It was important to me that she understood the full meaning of their decision as a family, not as individuals—after all, she was not planning to immigrate alone; she was married and had two young children who needed to be raised while transitioning to a different world.

I wanted to tell her that this decision would affect every aspect of her life, her husband's life, and her children's lives, both individually and as a family. Things would change for the better, and others—not for the better, even for the worse. There would be more experiences than could be mentioned, moments of enjoyment and hardship, joy and regret, fear and apprehension, moments of satisfaction and disappointment, and many more. Of course, I did not rule out the possibility that she would succeed and achieve the goals she hoped for, in her career, financially, and so on, but would she live in peace with the price it might expect from her? Would she withstand the crises when they came? And they would come, who better than I knew that. Would she compromise when necessary? And what? And at what cost?

Would she manage to build a new social circle for herself? Very quickly, one learned that being alone was a real thing abroad, and one must work hard and strive not to be alone.

And how would she cope with the longing for family? Especially if family members did not visit her frequently, a disconnect would begin to form.

Would she be able to afford frequent trips to Israel? Expensive flights, lost workdays... And if there wasn't money, would they not see family members for years? And how would she feel during holidays, when the family she was used to was not celebrating with her, and all that remained was to celebrate with friends who weren't necessarily close to her in the homeland?

There were so many issues to consider before making such a far-reaching decision, literally and figuratively.

I thought to myself that, naturally, I was optimistic and didn't foresee negativity, and that many good things could certainly happen with immigration to a new place, but that didn't prevent us from facing everything life threw at us, just as in any other place in the world. We would still have to face various challenges, only these would be struggles on the other side of the world, and perhaps in the country, we would receive a little more support, because there the feeling of being alone is "cushioned" by everyone who surrounded us in our daily lives—family, friends, acquaintances, and the environment we were used to. Even if it was just a psychological sense of security, we knew that someone was close to us whom we could approach and receive a hug, a kind word, and friendly advice. On the other hand, when we were on the other side of the world, far from everything and everyone we were connected to in our homeland, being alone could make you feel much lonelier.

A wave of memories and images from our first two years in Colorado flooded me as I recalled the challenges, the difficulties we faced in adaptation, and the self-assessments and tests that I had not anticipated having to endure. Things like the surgery my daughter had to undergo at the age of four, how I sat there alone in the hospital waiting room, without any family member beside me, waiting to hear from the surgeon. I felt so alone, the loneliest I could ever feel, and it was painful and difficult. However, I also remembered the excitement we experienced when visiting unfamiliar places and the feeling of joy we had whenever we succeeded and adopted something we loved in the new lives we chose.

"When we decided to leave Israel, we went straight ahead, like when horses had coverings over their eyes to prevent them from looking to the sides, so they would focus only on what they saw in front of them. We were not thinking about anything except that we were moving to America," a friend confessed to me during a tough time, and I thought I should tell Leviah the opposite. Please, look to the sides, for there awaits all the things you might not have considered needing to face when you were on the other side of the world, alone.

I paused in my reminiscing, took a deep breath. I felt inundated by a film reel of joy and sorrow, sleepless days, and mixed emotions, successes, and failures.

"Back then," I began, answering her, "there wasn't anyone to tell me all the things I'm telling you now. It is important for me to detail to you not only the advantages—what we loved—but especially the drawbacks. Perhaps, after learning about the disadvantages of leaving Israel and moving to another country, you will think differently."

"Of course, there are disadvantages, I understand perfectly," Leviah said, shaking her head impatiently. "But see, we all look at challenges differently and deal with them differently. Some people are stronger, some are weaker, and will react more intensely to crises."

"Exactly," I replied. "The true test comes when the crisis arrives, because you are not always prepared and able to cope the way you expected. Perhaps just hearing what I am saying will make you realize that if this is a crisis you can avoid, you will do everything to prevent it, right?"

"Yes, I agree with you, but still," Leviah insisted. "Who's to say it will be hard for me? I am one of those who know how to manage everything well in any place."

"If you have strong willpower and a lot of motivation, that will certainly help you," I answered.

"Look, it's easiest to talk about 'if,' but try to imagine how you will feel when the crisis hits, and you realize you are unable to cope with it the way you thought you would, and you are far from everyone who could help you, all alone facing it? That's the question, and I can give you my example.

"Fate intervened," I continued, "and I went through difficult crises I hadn't imagined in my worst dreams. Though I overcame them, and I can testify that I emerged stronger, places that were broken have healed; the wounds have healed. But today I know and understand clearly that if, years ago, someone had asked me if I was willing to consider crises of the kind I experienced, and had detailed some of them, I might have decided differently."

"To the point of not immigrating?" Leviah asked, perplexed.

"To that extent," I replied honestly.

I could sense Leviah's enthusiasm for our conversation waning, and the eyes that had sparkled at me earlier were now somewhat dimmed. I had not provided her with the answers she expected, but I was determined that if I ever had to share both the good and bad aspects of immigration, I would always show both sides to the questioner. And if I helped someone think twice before taking this significant step, I would have done my job.

"Leviah, they say every beginning is hard, right? And I wish you the smoothest transition, if that is what you choose to do," I said softly. "But what I'm saying is that immigration brings us challenges that are specifically crises related to the act of immigration itself. Thinking you are strong when you already know yourself is not enough. The question is whether and how you will face a completely different kind of crisis, when it arises."

Leviah looked at me seriously with her big eyes. Then she said, "I appreciate everything you're telling me, and thank you for being honest with me, but you don't know me at all. I am strong, and my husband manages everything easily, so I don't see us crashing and breaking down against challenges. What could be so awful about moving to Los Angeles? Maximum, if it's so awful, we'll return to the homeland."

"Of course, of course," I placed a light hand on her arm. "I am the last person who wants to burst your beautiful dream bubble, and I'm sure you are a determined and serious woman. I once knew someone like you," I smiled. "When I had a large kindergarten with 21 staff members, I once interviewed someone for a job, and knew that she had no chance of getting a job at another kindergarten due to her past background, but I saw the potential, the desire, and the determination, and it was enough for me to say, 'I will help you realize your dream of becoming a certified kindergarten teacher. The path is not easy, but I understand that this is your dream.' For a long time, I went on, explaining the challenges that she would face, and she was not intimidated, worked hard, and succeeded in overcoming significant challenges to realize her dream—getting a certified kindergarten teacher's certificate. Nine years later, after we sold the large kindergarten preschool, I heard she became the preschool director!"

Leviah smiled, and I continued. "Everyone has a dream, and I'm happy for you that you have a wonderful, ambitious dream, and I hope you achieve it. It is equally important for me to mention the obstacles that might stand in your way. I suggest you take what I have told you and give yourself time to think about everything. People immigrated to America and succeeded in realizing their dream, and some failed. And it is fair and important to say that one cannot judge a person who has a dream and takes a step to realize it. You are no different from any of us. And I completely agree that it's individual, and that everyone looks at a challenge differently and copes differently, and there are things you can only say about yourself after experiencing them, but at least I can give you another perspective from our experience."

I saw her resistance diminish, and that she was ready to listen, but I still pondered internally how to present the picture to her as clearly as possible. And then I remembered an article I wrote for the Israeli magazine *The Good Life*, in which I described life in a divided world, because that is what we, those who left Israel, are, divided within ourselves.

I sipped my coffee, which had begun to cool, and said, "In the divided world, as I call it, on the one hand, there will always be a warm and loving place in our hearts for the Land of Israel, for family, for friends, for childhood memories, for military service, and so on. On the other hand, we have created a second world for ourselves, new, different, and exciting lives. I live between these two worlds in so many aspects of my life.

"Thus, when I walk each morning along the green paths by my house, these are not my childhood paths, but my children's childhood paths.

"I greet everyone I encounter with a good morning or hello, but not in Hebrew, the language of my first world, but in the second language I adopted when I came here, with which I connect with and relate to my new friends and neighbors, who over the years have become part of my second history.

"But in this divided world, they are only half of my history, because the previous good neighbors and friends from childhood, my navy service, and family members, are an integral part of it.

"In this divided world, I've adopted the local slang to be better understood, and it's frustrating when I'm corrected in the new language. I do not want to sound foreign, too different. A person naturally wants to feel part of the whole and the environment in which one lives. Today, even when I speak with other Israelis, every sentence is composed of words from both languages. To make sure that I feel secure that they understand me, or because speaking in two languages has become a habit and is more convenient.

"As a result of not using my first language and using the language I've adopted for many years, I've forgotten much of my vocabulary, and one could say that today I have 75% of the Hebrew language and 75% of the English language.

"In this divided world, I often remember the landscapes and people I left behind and can't find here, in my second world, and I miss them very much. And in moments when I miss them, part of me thinks about the half I am not in right now, the half that is so missed. Because of this, I have taught myself to live with longing—one cannot travel to the other side of the world every couple of days for a visit, and I dedicate most of the money I've set aside for myself for vacations to buying plane tickets to Israel to visit everyone and everything that's important to me in the country I left.

"In a divided world, every year in November we celebrate Thanksgiving, and I've adopted the custom of preparing a traditional turkey, and at the dinner where our American friends participate, I explain to my new Israeli friends that it's not a religious holiday, and that I'm going along with the local tradition in my new world.

"When Israelis celebrate the Jewish holidays I grew up with, I also set a festive table, invite friends for a joyous meal and fine wine, and explain to all the children at the table the customs and rituals— the apple in honey or the head of the fish on Rosh Hashanah, the afikomen and matzah on Passover, and I try not to be too upset or disappointed when my daughter recites a Passover Haggadah passage in English instead of Hebrew.

"On October 31st, Halloween, when I walk with my daughter in costume, as is customary in America, going from door to door, showing off their costumes and receiving candies, I see how excited my daughter is, and I'm excited myself because it reminds me of how I used to get excited about dressing up for Purim. The difference is that I knew why I was dressing up and celebrating the holiday, but my daughter did not know why she was celebrating and dressing up— she dressed up because of social pressure and because she was happy to receive treats. It didn't please her when I told her that Halloween has some history of witches involved in it from the past.

"When I raise a toast, I always remember the names of the people we miss, Mom with a broken heart and Dad, who is struggling because he doesn't see his grandchildren enough, who live far away from him, on the other side of the world.

"In the divided world, when I planted fruit trees in our garden, I wanted them to give me beauty and fruit, but also to fill the void of missing the beauty and fruit I left behind in my childhood garden. I justified this by claiming that there would also be beauty and fruit for children in future generations, but what are the chances that my children will grow up in the first half where I grew up and enjoy what I planted there? History shows—very slim chances.

"So, yes, I live in a world where my ship has two anchors, one in the Land of Israel and the other in the country to which I immigrated. In this current half, I find myself seeking closeness to everything connected to my previous half, because by nature, I want to live my first language, and I miss the culture. I am no longer up to date on new plays, new songs, Israeli films, successful TV series, and interesting books.

"I read English literature and have a subscription to the Country Dinner Playhouse for English plays, and I watch English-language films and performances by American artists, simply because it is accessible and easier here.

"In the divided world, we sing the American national anthem and salute the Stars and Stripes, because we don't want to offend our neighbors and friends or the audience standing next to us. And when our children choose to enlist in the army, they salute a different flag, not the blue and white flag with the Magen David.

"In Israel, they call us 'those who descended,' and indeed, that is the truth and the reality we chose to live in when we decided to immigrate, 'to descend' to another country. Like me, you too will feel within you that you have indeed 'descended' from the whole you once were, to a half."

Leviah's face stiffened, her eyes wandered somewhere in the horizon of thoughts, and I could feel the hesitations and doubts that my words had instilled in her.

I looked at her kindly. "Leviah, are you still considering moving to live in the divided hearts world?"

ABOUT THE AUTHOR

Yaffa Turgeman was born in Israel and immigrated to Colorado 36 years ago, she teaches Hebrew and Judaism in the Jewish community of Denver Colorado, owner of a YouTube channel- Timeless Stories By Yaffa Turgeman

** For all her other books check out her author page here- https://amazon.com/author/yaffaturgeman

** Join her Facebook page- Timeless Stories By Yaffa Turgeman

** Visit her website- www.yaffaturgeman.com.com

Her first book is an authentic cookbook on Sephardic and Middle Eastern cooking, published in English.

Her true enjoyment is writing children's books and baking cookies with her three granddaughters- Lyla, Noa, and baby Orli.

Reviews are always appreciated:

https://amazon.com/author/yaffaturgeman